THE NUCLEAR BAN TREATY

The contributors to this book describe, discuss and evaluate the normative reframing brought about by the Treaty on the Prohibition of Nuclear Weapons (the Ban Treaty), taking you on a journey through its genesis and negotiation history to the shape of the emerging global nuclear order.

Adopted by the United Nations on 7 July 2017, the Ban Treaty came into effect on 22 January 2021. For advocates and supporters, weapons that were always immoral are now also illegal. To critics, it represents a profound threat to the stability of the existing global nuclear order with the Nuclear Non-proliferation Treaty as the normative anchor. As the most significant leap in nuclear disarmament in 50 years and a rare case study of successful state-civil society partnership in multilateral diplomacy, the Ban Treaty challenges the established order. The book's contributors are leading experts on the Ban Treaty, including senior scholars, policymakers and civil society activists.

This book is a vital guide to the Ban Treaty for students of nuclear disarmament, arms control and diplomacy, as well as for policymakers in those fields.

Ramesh Thakur is Emeritus Professor at the Crawford School of Public Policy, The Australian National University (ANU); Senior Research Fellow, Toda Peace Institute; and a Fellow of the Australian Institute of International Affairs. His last post was Director of the Centre for Nuclear Non-Proliferation and Disarmament at the ANU. He was formerly Senior Vice-Rector of the United Nations University (and Assistant Secretary-General of the United Nations). Educated in India and Canada, he has held fulltime academic appointments in Fiji, New Zealand, Canada and Australia and been a consultant to the Australian, New Zealand and Norwegian governments on arms control, disarmament and international security issues. He was a Commissioner and one of the principal authors of *The Responsibility to Protect* and Principal Writer of Secretary-General Kofi Annan's second reform report; and Co-Convenor of the Asia–Pacific Leadership Network for Nuclear Non-Proliferation and Disarmament. His books include *Nuclear Weapons: The State of Play 2015* (CNND); *Nuclear Weapons and International Security: Selected Essays* (Routledge); and *The United Nations, Peace and Security: From Collective Security to the Responsibility to Protect*, 2nd Ed. (Cambridge University Press).

THE NUCLEAR BAN TREATY

A Transformational Reframing of the Global Nuclear Order

Edited by Ramesh Thakur

Routledge
Taylor & Francis Group
LONDON AND NEW YORK

First published 2022
by Routledge
2 Park Square, Milton Park, Abingdon, Oxon OX14 4RN

and by Routledge
605 Third Avenue, New York, NY 10158

Routledge is an imprint of the Taylor & Francis Group, an Informa business

British Library Cataloguing-in-Publication Data
A catalogue record for this book is available from the British Library

Library of Congress Cataloging-in-Publication Data
A catalog record has been requested for this book

ISBN: 978-1-032-13071-2 (hbk)
ISBN: 978-1-032-13070-5 (pbk)
ISBN: 978-1-003-22750-2 (ebk)

DOI: 10.4324/9781003227502

Typeset in Bembo
by Taylor & Francis Books

CONTENTS

ILLUSTRATIONS

Figures

Tables

Box

CONTRIBUTORS

Ramesh Thakur is Emeritus Professor at the Crawford School of Public Policy, The Australian National University (ANU); Senior Research Fellow, Toda Peace Institute; and a Fellow of the Australian Institute of International Affairs. His last post was Director of the Centre for Nuclear Non-Proliferation and Disarmament at the ANU. He was formerly Senior Vice-Rector of the United Nations University (and Assistant Secretary-General of the United Nations). Educated in India and Canada, he has held fulltime academic appointments in Fiji, New Zealand, Canada and Australia and been a consultant to the Australian, New Zealand and Norwegian governments on arms control, disarmament and international security issues. He was a Commissioner and one of the principal authors of The Responsibility to Protect and Principal Writer of Secretary-General Kofi Annan's second reform report; and Co-Convenor of the Asia–Pacific Leadership Network for Nuclear Non-Proliferation and Disarmament. His books include *Nuclear Weapons: The State of Play 2015* (CNND); *Nuclear Weapons and International Security: Selected Essays* (Routledge); and *The United Nations, Peace and Security: From Collective Security to the Responsibility to Protect*, 2nd Ed. (Cambridge University Press).

Professor Vladimir Baranovsky is a Board Member of the Moscow-based think tank, Primakov National Research Institute of World Economy and International Relations, Russian Academy of Sciences. He is also Professor at Moscow State Institute of International Relations and a member of the Toda International Research Advisory Council.

Joseph Camilleri is Emeritus Professor at La Trobe University, where he held the Chair in International Relations (1994–2012). He was founding Director of the Centre for Dialogue in 2006–12. He is a Fellow of the Australian Academy of Social Sciences. He has authored or edited some 30 major books and written over

100 book chapters and journal articles, including *The 2017 Nuclear Ban Treaty: A New Path to Nuclear Disarmament* (co-edited with Michael Hamel-Green, 2019).

John Carlson AM is Counsellor to the Nuclear Threat Initiative, Washington, DC, and Non-resident Senior Fellow at the Vienna Center for Disarmament and Non-Proliferation. He was previously Director-General of the Australian Safeguards and Non-Proliferation Office (1989–2010), Chairman of the International Atomic Energy Agency's Standing Advisory Group on Safeguards Implementation (2001–06) and founding Chair of the Asia–Pacific Safeguards Network (2009–12).

Jorge Hersschens is currently a member of the peace movement Pax Christi Vlaanderen's working group, International Security and Disarmament. He has a master's degree in English Language and Literature from St Andrews University (Scotland) and in Political Science from Antwerp University (Belgium) and intends to start a PhD in political science at the University of Antwerp on the topic of European disintegration.

Jan Hoekema is the Chair of Pugwash Netherlands and a former Ambassador, Mayor and Member of Parliament (Netherlands).

David Holloway is the Raymond A. Spruance Professor in International History, Professor of Political Science, and Senior Fellow at the Freeman-Spogli Institute for International Studies Emeritus at Stanford University. After teaching at the universities of Lancaster and Edinburgh, he joined the Stanford faculty in 1986, where he has been co-director of the Center for International Security and Cooperation (1991–97) and director of the Freeman Spogli Institute for International Studies (1998–2003). He is the author of *The Soviet Union and the Arms Race* (Yale University Press, 1983) and *Stalin and the Bomb: the Soviet Union and Atomic Energy 1939–1956* (Yale University Press, 1994), among other works.

Cesar Jaramillo is Executive Director of Project Ploughshares, based in Canada. In addition to work on conventional weapons control, including Canada's arms sales, his work has focused on such programme areas as nuclear disarmament and outer space security.

Angela Kane is the former UN High Representative for Disarmament Affairs. She is the Vice-President of the International Institute for Peace and a Senior Fellow at the Vienna Center for Disarmament and Non-Proliferation, in addition to serving on several non-profit boards in Europe and the USA. She had a 35-year career at the United Nations, including in political affairs, peacekeeping and management.

Alexander Kmentt is an Austrian career diplomat and Director of Disarmament, Arms Control and Non-Proliferation in the Austrian Foreign Ministry. He has worked extensively on disarmament and non-proliferation issues, is one of the architects of the initiative on the humanitarian impact of nuclear weapons and the TPNW, and the author of *The Treaty on the Prohibition of Nuclear Weapons: How it was achieved and why it matters* (Routledge, 2021).

Moritz Kütt is a Senior Researcher at the Institute for Peace Research and Security Policy, Hamburg.

Sverre Lodgaard is senior research fellow and former director (1997–2007) of the Norwegian Institute of International Affairs (NUPI). He is also a senior research fellow of the Toda Peace Institute in Tokyo. Before joining NUPI he directed the United Nations Institute for Disarmament Research (1992–96). His most recent books are *External Powers and The Arab Spring* (Scandinavian Academic Press, 2016) and *Stable Nuclear Zero* (Routledge, 2017).

Noah Mayhew is a Research Associate at the Vienna Center for Disarmament and Non-Proliferation. Prior to this, he completed an internship with the International Atomic Energy Agency's Office of Public Information and Communication. He has a master's degree programme in non-proliferation studies from the Middlebury Institute of International Studies at Monterey and the Moscow State Institute of International Relations.

Paul Meyer is a former Canadian Ambassador for Disarmament and currently is Adjunct Professor of International Studies and Fellow in International Security at Simon Fraser University, Vancouver. He is the current Chair of the Canadian Pugwash Group, as well as a Senior Adviser to ICT4Peace and a founding member of the Outer Space Institute.

Hugh Miall is Emeritus Professor of International Relations at the University of Kent and Chair of the Conflict Research Society, the main professional association for peace and conflict researchers in the UK. He has been Director of the Conflict Analysis Research Centre and Head of the School of Politics and International Relations at the University of Kent and a Research Fellow in the European Programme at Chatham House.

Dr Tanya Ogilvie-White is Research Adviser to the Asia-Pacific Leadership Network, director of the New Zealand Centre for Global Studies and senior fellow at the Strategic and Defence Studies Centre, Australian National University. Previously, she was research director of the Centre for Nuclear Non-Proliferation and Disarmament and senior analyst at the Australian Strategic Policy Institute. Her most recent publication is *The Logic of Nuclear Deterrence: Assessments, Assumptions, Uncertainties and Failure Modes* (UNIDIR, 2020).

George Perkovich is the Ken Olivier and Angela Nomellini Chair and Vice-President for Studies at the Carnegie Endowment for International Peace in Washington,

DC. He is the co-editor of *Abolishing Nuclear Weapons: A Debate (2009)* and most recently of *Toward Accountable Nuclear Deterrents: How Much is Too Much?*

Joelien Pretorius teaches International Relations at the University of the Western Cape in South Africa. She is a member of South African branch of the Pugwash Conferences on Science and World Affairs that was awarded the Nobel Peace Prize in 1995 for its work on nuclear non-proliferation and disarmament.

Tariq Rauf is former Head of Verification and Security Policy (2002–11) at the International Atomic Energy Agency (IAEA) and Alternate Head of IAEA Delegation to Non-Proliferation Treaty (NPT) Review Conferences (2002–10). He was a member of Japan's Group of Eminent Persons for Substantive Advancement of Nuclear Disarmament (2017–20), served as Senior Advisor to the Chair of Main Committee I (nuclear disarmament) at the 2015 NPT Review Conference and has attended all NPT meetings as an official delegate since 1987.

Douglas Roche is a former Canadian Senator and ambassador for disarmament.

Gem Romuld is the Director of the International Campaign to Abolish Nuclear Weapons, Australia. She has worked with Australians for War Powers Reform and 3CR Radio. She has degrees in communications and law and is based in Sydney/Wollongong.

Tilman Ruff AO is a physician, co-founder and the founding international and Australian chair of the International Campaign to Abolish Nuclear Weapons (ICAN), Co-President of International Physicians for the Prevention of Nuclear War (IPPNW, Nobel Peace Prize 1985), and Honorary Principal Fellow in the School of Population and Global Health, University of Melbourne; and is a past president of the Medical Association for Prevention of War (Australia) which IPPNW established ICAN.

Tom Sauer is a Professor in international politics at the Universiteit Antwerpen in Belgium. A former fellow at the John F. Kennedy School of Government, Harvard University, Sauer received the 2019 Rotary International Alumni Global Service Award.

Manpreet Sethi is Distinguished Fellow, Centre for Air Power Studies, New Delhi, where she heads the project on nuclear security. Over the past 20 years Dr Sethi has been researching and writing on nuclear energy, strategy, non-proliferation, disarmament, arms and export controls and ballistic missile defence and has published eight books and over 100 papers in several reputed journals.

Thomas E. Shea, PhD, is currently an Adjunct Senior Fellow at the Federation of American Scientists. Shea served in the Safeguards Department at the International

Atomic Energy Agency (IAEA) for 24 years and headed IAEA efforts under the six-year Trilateral Initiative, which explored the feasibility of IAEA verification of classified forms of fissile material released from Russian and US nuclear weapon programmes.

Rakesh Sood is a Distinguished Fellow at the Observer Research Foundation, New Delhi. He served in India's Foreign Service and was India's Ambassador to Nepal, Afghanistan and France and the country's first Ambassador in charge of Disarmament in Geneva. He was Prime Minister Manmohan Singh's Special Envoy for Disarmament and Non-Proliferation (2013–14) before retirement. He was Joint Secretary Disarmament and International Security Affairs – a division that he set up and led from 1992 until 2000.

Herbert Wulf is a Professor of International Relations and former Director of the Bonn International Center for Conversion (BICC). He is presently a Senior Fellow at BICC, an Adjunct Senior Researcher at the Institute for Development and Peace, University of Duisburg/Essen, Germany, and a Research Affiliate at the National Centre for Peace and Conflict Studies, University of Otago, New Zealand. He serves on the Scientific Councils of SIPRI and the Centre for Conflict Studies of the University of Marburg, Germany.

ACKNOWLEDGEMENTS

I would like to express my warmest appreciation to Simon Bates, Shubhayan Chakrabarti and their team at Routledge. Their help, assistance and encouragement throughout, from conception to completion, was exemplary in their professionalism and it has been a pleasure working with them.

An equally warm note of appreciation and gratitude is due to the Toda Peace Institute for their generous support of the idea of bringing together this collection, to the Institute's Director Professor Kevin Clements for his hands-on engagement with the project and to the Institute's Editor Rosemary McBryde for working closely with me in bringing together all the chapters from the Policy Briefs and *Global Outlook* articles on the Institute's website.

On behalf of the Toda Peace Institute, I would also like to record my thanks to the first publishers of the following chapters for granting us permission to reprint their articles under the Toda imprimatur, first as Policy Briefs or *Global Outlook* articles, and then again as chapters in this collection:

Chapter 6: Tom Sauer and Ramesh Thakur, "How many intensive care beds will a nuclear weapon explosion require," *Bulletin of the Atomic Scientists*

Chapter 10: Ramesh Thakur, "Sovereignty as responsibility and the Ban Treaty," *Bulletin of the Atomic Scientists*

Chapter 13: Tom Sauer, "NATO allies, don't dismiss the TPNW," *European Leadership Network*

Chapter 14: Manpreet Sethi, "Disarming the unarmed: Current reality of the nuclear Ban Treaty," *Sunday Guardian*

Chapter 19: Moritz Kütt, Jan Hoekama and Tom Sauer, "Banning nuclear weapons: A role for Germany, the Netherlands and Belgium?" De *Volkskrant, Le Soir, De Morgen* and *Spiegel Online*

Chapter 20: Douglas Roche, "In subtle diplomatic move, Canada ceases its opposition to the Nuclear Weapons Prohibition Treaty," *The Hill Times*

Chapter 27: Ramesh Thakur, "Mobilising the world behind the nuclear weapons Ban Treaty," *The Japan Times*

Chapter 31: Angela Kane and Noah Mayhew "The future of nuclear arms control: Time for an update," Development and Peace Foundation

Chapter 32: Sverre Lodgaard, "Arms control and world order," *Journal for Peace and Nuclear Disarmament*

INTRODUCTION

Completing the nuclear disarmament agenda: From the Non-proliferation Treaty to the Ban Treaty

Ramesh Thakur

Barack Obama became the first American president – and so far the only one – to visit Hiroshima or Nagasaki while still in office. In his emotionally-charged address at the Hiroshima Peace Memorial on 27 May 2016, demonstrating his usual flair for pitch-perfect language and cadence, referencing 6 August 1945, he said: "on a bright, cloudless morning, death fell from the sky and the world was changed. A flash of light and a wall of fire destroyed a city and demonstrated that mankind possessed the means to destroy itself."[1] Characteristically, however, the rhetoric was undercut by the furious lobbying by his officials in the same final year of his presidency against the negotiations then underway for a nuclear ban treaty under the auspices of the United Nations. The survivors of the unfathomable horrors that rained down on Hiroshima and Nagasaki on 6 and 9 August 1945, respectively, are known as *hibakusha*. Among their dwindling number is Setsuko Thurlow who lives in Canada. Her prominent face as a potent symbol of the cause and her active advocacy for the cause of nuclear abolition were recognised by including her in the delegation of the International Campaign to Abolish Nuclear Weapons for receiving the Nobel Peace Prize in Oslo on 10 December 2017. Speaking at the United Nations in New York on 7 July 2017 after the historic vote by 122 states to adopt the Treaty on the Prohibition of Nuclear Weapons (TPNW, commonly known as the Ban Treaty), she celebrated that nuclear weapons, always "immoral," were now "also illegal."[2] Her remarks were slightly premature but did become a reality on 22 January 2021 when the treaty entered into force.

What is curious to an analyst is how the distance from immoral to illegal is so short conceptually, yet has proven to be inordinately long chronologically. There are moral, legal and existential imperatives to reduce and eventually eliminate nuclear weapons. The Nuclear Non-Proliferation Treaty (NPT) was signed in 1968 and came into force in 1970. Article 6 commits each state party "to pursue negotiations in good faith on effective measures relating to cessation of the nuclear

DOI: 10.4324/9781003227502-1

arms race at an early date and to nuclear disarmament." In a 1996 Advisory Opinion, the World Court strengthened this: "There exists an obligation to pursue in good faith *and bring to a conclusion* negotiations leading to nuclear disarmament in all its aspects" (emphasis added).[3] The Ban Treaty builds on the World Court's advice. Of the NPT's current 188 states parties,[4] five are recognised as nuclear weapon states (NWS) because they conducted a nuclear test before 1 January 1967: China, France, Russia, the UK and the USA. On 16 March 2021, 73 years after the treaty was negotiated, the UK announced the decision to increase nuclear warheads to 260 by mid-decade because of the "evolving security environment."[5] It gave no explanation of how this is consistent with NPT Article 6 and the Ban Treaty less than two months after its entry into force.

This epitomises the biggest challenge for the NPT. We are in an exceptionally dangerous period in the atomic age with about 13,100 nuclear warheads still held by nine countries.[6] For half a century, nuclear peace has rested on the normative pillars of the NPT. In the six years since the last failed NPT Review Conference (RevCon), geopolitical tensions have spiked in Europe, the Middle East, the Himalayas and East Asia. Russia and the USA, as the two nuclear superpowers, with over 90 percent of global nuclear stockpiles, have reinvested heavily in modernising, upgrading and expanding their nuclear arsenals. The existing nuclear arms control architecture is fraying, with no negotiations being held currently or scheduled to reduce global nuclear stockpiles. A hostile international security environment, proliferation of nuclear weapons and emergence of new space, cyber and AI technologies have increased the risk of accidental or deliberate use of nuclear weapons. The growing risks and uncertainty in turn have fuelled a vicious cycle of renewed interest in the nuclear deterrent among US allies as a hedge against receding US primacy and reliability. Against this generally gloomy strategic landscape, the two over-the-horizon glimmers of hope are the renewal of New START for five years by US President Joe Biden among his first decisions on taking office, and the opportunity to undertake a major review of the entire nuclear policy agenda at the postponed 50th anniversary NPT RevCon sometime soon.

Redesigning the envelope of nuclear prohibitions

The fatal conceit in relation to nuclear energy is that its immense power can be harnessed for the benefit of humankind while keeping its destructive capacity permanently in check. After the Second World War states were both attracted to its developmental potential and fearful of the Armageddon it could unleash. The hard divisions of the Cold War fed the fears of the bomb and the 1962 Cuban Missile Crisis concentrated minds on the need to reduce nuclear risks. The first tangible products of that were the Treaty of Tlatelolco creating the Latin American nuclear-weapon-free zone in 1967 (followed since the 1980s by several other regional zones) and the NPT a year later. The NPT embeds a triangular bargain. The non-NWS gave up their sovereign right to acquire nuclear weapons in return for the promise from countries with nuclear materials and expertise to share the benefits of nuclear energy, and from countries with the bomb that they would pursue nuclear disarmament.

Interest in nuclear energy rose for several decades and the advanced countries did share their knowledge and resources with non-NWS NPT parties, subject to states complying with the evolving safeguards requirements of the International Atomic Energy Agency (IAEA). Especially after the nuclear accident in Fukushima, Japan in 2011 caused by a massive tsunami, however, interest in nuclear power waned significantly, albeit not universally.

The IAEA is the UN's nuclear watchdog to establish rigorous standards for nuclear safety, security and safeguards and to monitor nuclear activities to assure their non-military uses. Other instruments developed to address issues not comprehended by the NPT include the Nuclear Suppliers Group that controls traded nuclear items and the Missile Technology Control Regime. Several treaties restricting nuclear testing are also part of the broader NPT regime, the most important of which is the Comprehensive Nuclear-Test-Ban Treaty (CTBT). Unfortunately, owing to a flawed and excessively rigid entry-into-force provision, the CTBT is in the unique situation of being fully operational without actually having entered into force and unlikely to do so in the foreseeable future.

The NPT entered into force when the three depositary states of the UK, the USA and the USSR, together with 40 other states, ratified it in 1970. It was extended indefinitely in 1995 and operates as the centrepiece of the global nuclear order. Its membership has steadily expanded and, with the exception of South Sudan that has yet to conclude the process, all non-possessor states are NPT parties. Therefore the second, non-proliferation pillar of the NPT is also completed. The importance of this should never be under-estimated and the gains need to be protected and preserved. On 13 October 1960 President John F. Kennedy warned that up to 20 countries could possess the bomb by the end of 1964.[7] He subsequently extended the estimate to 25 countries in the 1970s, saying: "I regard that as the greatest possible danger and hazard."[8] The fact that there are only nine possessor countries is thus a remarkable achievement, but one that is fragile.

Holding the line on non-proliferation is a continuing challenge, but not the only one. The NPT is unusual among multilateral agreements for its manifold institutional deficits,[9] including no secretariat or implementing organisation. States parties can adopt reports, make decisions and approve recommendations for further action only at quinquennial RevCons. Consequently the NPT suffers from a debilitating lack of institutional machinery to monitor and provide regular oversight of treaty implementation and challenges. The RevCons have alternated between being able to and failing to adopt a final document that summarises the forward-looking program of work and action points. The 2005 and 2015 RevCons could not agree on an outcome document. The "decisions" taken at RevCons are recommendations with no binding effect, a shortcoming that is only made worse by the absence of any meaningful reporting requirement, monitoring mechanism and compliance authority.

Not surprisingly, therefore, a performance assessment of compliance with the decisions of the 2010 RevCon – the last one with an agreed final document – found the results to be very patchy and especially poor with respect to progress on nuclear disarmament.[10] The nine nuclear-armed states[11] pay lip-service to it but on the evidence of the size of their weapons arsenals, fissile material stocks, force modernisation plans, stated doctrine and known deployment practices, all nine possessor states foresee indefinite retention of nuclear weapons in their security policies. Yet for most non-NWS, the problem is not proliferation but the weapons themselves. Non-proliferation was a necessary but clearly not a sufficient condition for disarmament. Conversely, no disarmament is a sufficient condition of proliferation. Nuclear weapons could not proliferate if they did not exist. Because they do exist, they will proliferate. The best guarantee of nuclear non-proliferation, therefore, is nuclear disarmament. The focus on the former to the neglect of the latter ensures that we get neither. The de facto transformation of the NPT into solely a non-proliferation regime established a global nuclear order built on apartheid: a vast majority of non-NWS; a tiny group of legal and legitimate NWS; and a group of supposedly illicit nuclear-armed states outside the NPT.

The Ban Treaty's compliance pull

The TPNW establishes a new normative settling point on the ethics, legality and legitimacy of the bomb.[12] The NPT and the TPNW embed the geopolitical and normative balance of power, respectively, 49 years apart in time. The vague language of Article 6 in comparison to the precise non-proliferation obligations of the NPT reflects the disproportionate influence of the two powerful states that drove the negotiations, namely the USA and the Soviet Union, around the middle of the 20th century. By contrast, the prohibition treaty reflects the preferences of the majority of states in a polycentric 21st century. Against the twin backdrop of the receding nuclear arms control and disarmament tide and elevated nuclear threat levels, many countries concluded that fresh 'out of the box' efforts were needed. The normative prop for the new initiative was humanitarian principles which permit advocates to transcend national and international security arguments.

On 22 October 2012 a 34-country statement emphasised that the catastrophic humanitarian consequences of nuclear weapons are the concern of the community of states as a whole. They must never be used again, under any circumstances. "The only way to guarantee this is the total, irreversible and verifiable elimination of nuclear weapons."[13] This was repeated in 2013 and 2014, with supporting countries increasing to 155. Three conferences were held in 2013–14 on the humanitarian impacts of nuclear weapons in Norway, Mexico and Vienna. At the conclusion of the last, on 9 December 2014, Austria pledged to work with like-minded states to "fill the legal gap for the prohibition and elimination of nuclear weapons"[14], and 127 countries agreed "to stigmatise, prohibit and eliminate nuclear weapons."[15] A year later the UN General Assembly established an open-ended working group on the issue that decided to operate under General Assembly rules that permit decisions by vote, instead of the decision-blocking consensus rule of the Conference on Disarmament. Its report in August 2016 urged the commencement of UN negotiations for a legal instrument to prohibit nuclear weapons, leading to their eventual elimination. On 23 December the General Assembly duly authorised this.[16]

Meanwhile, in an unclassified North Atlantic Treaty Organization (NATO) document of 17 October 2016, Washington urged allies to vote against a call to hold the negotiations and secondly, not to take part in any negotiations that were convened because "efforts to negotiate an immediate ban on nuclear weapons or to delegitimise nuclear deterrence are fundamentally at odds with NATO's basic policies on deterrence and our shared security interests." The "wide-ranging" potential effects of a ban treaty included making nuclear planning more challenging.[17] The NWS and US allies duly refused to attend the UN conference, describing it as impractical, ineffective and unrealistic. Prima facie, non-participation placed them in non-compliance with the Article 6 obligation of every NPT state party.

In the event the conference, held over two sessions in March–July 2017, did succeed in negotiating a new universal, non-discriminatory treaty with a comprehensive set of prohibitions of nuclear activities, giving it historic significance as the first to ban the bomb without any "ifs" and "buts." It prohibits the possession of nuclear weapons; bans the use and threat of use of nuclear weapons, thereby delegitimising the doctrine and practice of nuclear deterrence; prohibits nuclear testing; and bans the hosting of nuclear weapons (Article 1). This would affect NATO allies Belgium, Germany, Italy, Netherlands and Turkey, but not any of the three Pacific allies Australia, Japan and South Korea, although it would preclude the reintroduction of US tactical weapons into South Korea. States that host nuclear weapons controlled by possessor states can join on condition of verifiably removing them promptly (Article 4.4). The treaty requires assistance to the victims of, and for environmental remediation of areas contaminated by, the use or testing of nuclear weapons (Article 6). It offsets some of the NPT's institutional deficits by scheduling biennial assemblies of states parties. Extraordinary meetings can be convened as necessary (Article 8). Although the treaty is of indefinite duration and not subject to any reservations, a party may withdraw from it on 12 months' notice if "extraordinary events … have jeopardized [its] supreme interests" (Article 17).

A second historic significance of the Ban Treaty is that it both reflects and deepens the democratisation of the process of international policymaking. The non-Western and small states of international society forced through an instrument of international humanitarian law against the will of most Western countries and all major powers. The states that created the laws of war for the first time in history find themselves the objects of that law as ownership is taken over by the rest. The NPT recognised the major powers' right to possess nuclear weapons as part of their special managerial responsibilities for world order; the leaders and peoples of the NWS continue to assert that right; but in the TPNW, international society as such has derecognised that right. As Brazil's Foreign Minister Aloysio Nunes Ferreira put it: The treaty "reflects the historical aspiration from the large majority of the international community to ban the existence of such weapons" and as such is "an important complement" to Article 6 of the NPT.[18]

The NWS and their allies, however, argue that the TPNW is impractical and ineffective and they are among the world's most honourable states. While legal norms impose binding legal obligations, political norms create moral obligations that can nonetheless be encased in a wider legal context and have legal effects. In regulating state conduct, both laws and norms serve enabling (licence) and restraining (leash) functions. The history of human rights movements (suffrage, anti-slavery, anti-apartheid) shows that while the social movements are motivated to enact moral norms into law, the moral authority of the norms by themselves exert a powerful "compliance pull."[19] In general, legal norms are more effective in regulating state behaviour. But in specific instances, a particular law may be breached while a political norm shapes a decision – on an act of commission or omission – through a calculation of reputational costs.

On mass atrocity crimes, for example, the 1948 Genocide Convention imposes legal obligations on states to act. By contrast, the Responsibility to Protect (R2P) principle is a global political norm that creates a moral responsibility but no legal duty on outside states to prevent and halt atrocities. However, even R2P has to be interpreted and applied in the broader context of binding obligations on states under national and international, humanitarian and human rights laws. For great powers in particular, R2P makes it more costly, on the one hand, to resort to self-interested unilateral interventions, including so-called "humanitarian interventions"; and on the other hand, it also makes it more costly to block disinterested UN-authorised calls to collective action to save strangers from mass atrocities.

The TPNW is legally binding, but only for signatories. The Preamble notes it is based on the "principles and rules of international humanitarian law" including distinction between civilians and combatants, proportionality, and the prevention of unnecessary suffering. It is not relevant to *jus ad bellum* – the law of going to war – but it aims to apply to *jus in bello*, how a war is conducted. The TPNW may not impose binding legal obligations on non-parties such as the nuclear-armed states and their allies, as per the Vienna Convention on the Law of Treaties (1969), but it does have legal *implications* for them. International law comprises both treaty law and customary international law. The latter has two roots, state practice and *opinio juris* which at its simplest means that the practice of states is based in a sense of legal obligation.[20] To reach the threshold of law, the practice must be both widespread and consistent. This is the basis on which North Korea's program of nuclear testing can be condemned and sanctioned, even though it is not a CTBT party. Given the explicit rejection of the Ban Treaty by a substantial number of states, however, and the identity of the rejectionist states – in particular the five permanent members of the UN Security Council (P5) – the Ban Treaty cannot credibly be claimed to impose any legal obligation on non-signatories. But it does substantially qualify, even for non-signatories, the legitimacy of possessing nuclear weapons and relying on the threat of using them for national security.

The nuclear discourse of the NWS had moved disingenuously from the position that the NPT permits them to possess and deploy nuclear weapons, "to the language of entitlement, legal rights and enduring legitimacy."[21] They were able to claim NPT-sourced legitimacy because it allegedly gave legal cover to their possession of nuclear weapons – and to no one else – until such time as they themselves negotiate the elimination of their stockpiles. But non-NWS are the majority shareholders in the NPT society of states and by acting together they have taken back that legitimacy. By changing the prevailing normative structure, the TPNW shifts the balance of costs and benefits of possession, deterrence doctrines and deployment practices, and will create a deepening crisis of legitimacy. It removes the NPT-rooted fig leaf of international legitimacy that the NWS have used to cloak their nuclear weapons, while insisting that the pursuit of nuclear weapons by anyone else is both illegal (a violation of the international law of treaties) and illegitimate (a violation of the global norm).

The TPNW reaffirms the global nuclear norms of non-proliferation, disarmament, security and non-use, and thereby devalues the currency of nuclear weapons. Its legal effect will lie in strengthening the *disarmament norm* under Article 6 of the NPT itself for NPT parties, and removing the NPT-sourced legal and legitimising plank for continued possession, deployment and doctrines of use by the NWS. Since adoption in 2017 the TPNW has been deployed by supporter states and civil society advocates as evidence of a new global political norm *against possession*. Its normative impact will expand once the number of states parties crosses the psychological threshold of 100 and will gain further weight if some of the key NATO and Pacific allies defect from the rejectionist camp and join the ban treaty under civil society pressure whose advocacy explicitly references the TPNW. Meanwhile, the *non-use norm* (or, in a weaker variant, the nuclear restraint norm) does satisfy the threshold of consistent and widespread state practice and is arguably a mandatory norm, *jus cogens*: a peremptory norm framed in the language of prohibition from which no state can opt out unilaterally. The normative taboo against use is so strong that on several occasions the NWS accepted defeat in places like Vietnam and Afghanistan rather than use the bomb to destroy their enemies.[22]

Technological developments have blurred the dividing line between conventional precision munitions and nuclear weapons. The TPNW will harden the normative boundary between conventional and nuclear weapons. Another critical legal gap that has been closed is the *threat of use* of nuclear weapons. Arguably, such a prohibition is already covered under the general prohibition on the use or threat of use of force in Article 2(4) of the UN Charter. The political reality, however, is that threats to use force are a regular staple of world affairs ("All options are on the table") and, given the existing state of nuclear politics, the inclusion of an explicit prohibition on the threat of use of nuclear weapons fills a legal gap. In this way too, the treaty has legal effects on non-signatory state actions.

Short of abolition, stigmatisation implies illegitimacy of a practice based on the collective moral revulsion of a community. The *foreseeable effects* of any future use make the doctrine of deterrence and the possession of nuclear weapons *morally unacceptable* today to the community at large. The TPNW negotiating conference was mandated by the UN General Assembly in December 2016 explicitly to negotiate a prohibition treaty *leading to the eventual elimination* of nuclear weapons. Since the experience of the Chemical Weapons Convention demonstrated that it could take one or two decades, at least, to eliminate an entire category of weapons of mass destruction, the thought was that the safe, secure and verified decommissioning, dismantlement and destruction or conversion of all bombs following a nuclear weapons convention, if and when one is negotiated in the future, could take a similar, lengthy period of time.

The Ban Treaty has created a fresh challenge for the NPT. The possessor states reject it as impractical virtue-signalling and instead extoll the decades-long efforts at step-by-step measures to advance the cause of nuclear disarmament that had seen global stockpiles plummet by 80 percent from their Cold War peak. Against this, advocates insist that rather than damaging the NPT, the Ban Treaty supports it. It outlines one possible pathway to elimination consistent with the NPT. The two instruments should be seen as reinforcing each other: doctrinally they are compatible and in practical terms it makes no sense either to insist on non-proliferation while sidestepping disarmament, or to allow proliferation while working for disarmament. Thus a focus on putative 'gaps' between the two treaties is an unhelpful false premise.

Far from damaging the NPT, the Ban Treaty might have rescued it from a deepening crisis of legitimacy and the threat of mass exit. Anger and frustration at the failure to implement Article 6 over half a century was leading to calls for states parties to exit from the NPT as a sham treaty that merely legitimises the continued monopolistic possessor status of the five NWS.[23] The agenda of the legally binding prohibition of all three classes of weapons of mass destruction, with biological and chemical weapons having been banned by universal conventions in 1972 and 1993, respectively, is now complete. The nuclear-armed states and their allies insist that under current circumstances of an unfavourable international security environment, nuclear deterrence remains essential. If the two treaties are to coexist, therefore, the deterrence-disarmament relationship needs to be explored and any tension between them has to be resolved. They can converge in a framework approach that minimises nuclear threats in the near term, for example through postures of no first use of nuclear weapons and taking them off high alert status; reduces the number of nuclear weapons in the medium term; and aspires to the complete, verifiable and irreversible elimination of nuclear weapons in the long term. Meanwhile the TPNW has reinforced the normative boundary between conventional and nuclear weapons, strengthened the norm of non-use of nuclear weapons and reaffirmed both the non-proliferation and disarmament norms. For all these reasons, it can be a useful building block for the eventual nuclear weapons convention.

Another challenge for the NPT has a particular resonance for Asia. Four of the nine possessor countries are not NPT parties and it cannot therefore function as the normative framework for regulating their nuclear behaviour. Now that the five

NPT-licit NWS are themselves in violation of the TPNW standard of nuclear legitimacy, they can no longer tell the non-NPT possessor states to abide by the NPT as the affirmation of universally applicable norms.

This could have one other unintended but significant consequence. Once the international community has successfully stigmatised *all* nuclear-weapon possessors, how can the P5-controlled Security Council continue to function as the enforcement authority on nuclear issues? What will fill the enforcement gap with regards to nuclear threats to international peace and security?

The fraying normative consensus around the NPT as the embodiment of the global nuclear order as well as the framework for setting global nuclear policy directions has been in effect broken. The nine nuclear-armed states will undoubtedly ignore the TPNW to double down on their investment in nuclear weapons, delivery systems, doctrines and deployments. They and those of their allies who shelter under the nuclear umbrella of the NWS will also continue to affirm faith and confidence in the credibility of nuclear deterrence doctrine and practices. But the NPT's five NWS will no longer be able to claim the mantle of international legality and legitimacy that the NPT had conferred on their possessor status. They might not like the result, but their constant refrain that the nuclear genie cannot be put back in the bottle can now be turned against them: neither can the Ban Treaty.

The NPT regime is at a crossroads. If the NWS continue to disrespect the mandated multilateral process and negotiated treaty, the divide between the two camps could harden. Such a destabilising outcome would not be in anyone's interest. The polarisation and divisions have resulted from the decision of the nuclear-armed states and their allies to part company with the dominant sentiment and policy preferences of the international community. It is time for them to rejoin the global mainstream on nuclear policy and work collectively to implement practical and credible measures towards nuclear risk reduction and disarmament, while holding fast to non-proliferation.

Outline of the book

The essays collected in this book describe, discuss and evaluate the transformational normative reframing from the NPT to the Ban Treaty, taking readers on a journey through the genesis and negotiation history of the treaty and the humanitarian initiative behind it, to the possible trajectories and shape of the emerging normative architecture of the global nuclear order. The book brings together a collection of medium-length articles published as Policy Briefs by the Toda Peace Institute, and a selection of opinion length articles published in the *Global Outlook* blog by the Toda Peace Institute. None was an unsolicited article. All were specially commissioned within a coherent framework of complementary and reinforcing themes, with an effort to match authors to topics. All manuscripts were read by two in-house experts and comments, questions and suggestions – including expanding an op-ed into a policy brief or vice versa – were sent back to the authors and were mostly incorporated into the revised versions that were then published by Toda.

They are published here essentially in their original versions, with two minor sets of changes to reflect a consistency of style, format, spelling, etc; and to rephrase references to events that were still in the future when the chapter was first written. Almost all the authors will be familiar experts to the scholars and students of nuclear arms control and disarmament. They range from senior scholars, policy-makers and early career researchers to engaged civil society advocates and activists. The chapters are organised in three parts. The first traces the origins and describes the content and potential impact of the Ban Treaty. The second part provides a range of national perspectives from the points of view of selected nuclear armed states, their allies and some non-nuclear armed and non-nuclear-dependent countries. The third and final part situates the debate on the Ban Treaty in the wider context of arms control, disarmament and the global order.

Notes

1 "Remarks by President Obama and Prime Minister Abe of Japan at Hiroshima Peace Memorial," White House, Office of the Press Secretary, 27 May 2016, https://obamawhitehouse.archives.gov/the-press-office/2016/05/27/remarks-president-obama-and-prime-minister-abe-japan-hiroshima-peace.
2 Transcript, "Setsuko Thurlow Gives Final Remarks at Ban Treaty Adoption," Hibakusha Stories, https://hibakushastories.org/setsuko-thurlow-gives-final-remarks-at-ban-treaty-adoption.
3 *Legality of the Threat or Use of Nuclear Weapons: Advisory Opinion*. The Hague: International Court of Justice, 8 July 1996, www.un.org/law/icjsum/9623.htm.
4 The United Nations says the NPT has 191 states parties (www.un.org/disarmament/wmd/nuclear/npt). However, the "official" list includes the Democratic People's Republic of Korea (DPRK), which withdrew from the NPT in 2003; and also the Holy See and the State of Palestine. In reality, the non-parties are the DPRK, India, Israel and Pakistan, all four of which possess nuclear weapons outside the NPT; and the relatively new state of South Sudan, thus giving us 188 states as NPT parties.
5 BBC, "Integrated review: UK to lift cap on nuclear stockpile," 17 March 2021, www.bbc.com/news/uk-56413920.
6 Hans M. Kristensen and Matt Korda, "Status of World Nuclear Forces," Federation of American Scientists, March 2021, https://fas.org/issues/nuclear-weapons/status-world-nuclear-forces.
7 "JFK on Nuclear Weapons and Non-proliferation," Carnegie Endowment for International Peace, 17 November 2003, https://carnegieendowment.org/2003/11/17/jfk-on-nuclear-weapons-and-non-proliferation-pub-14652.
8 Robert G. Gard, "JFK's Nuclear Proliferation Warnings: Up to 25 Countries With Nuclear Weapons," Council for a Livable World, 11 May 2012, https://livableworld.org/jfks-nuclear-proliferation-warnings-up-to-25-countries-with-nuclear-weapons.
9 Paul Meyer, "Overcoming the NPT's 'institutional deficit': A Canadian saga," *International Journal*, 75:1 (2020): 49–64.
10 Gareth Evans, Tanya Ogilvie-White and Ramesh Thakur, *Nuclear Weapons: The State of Play 2015* (Canberra: Centre for Nuclear Non-Proliferation and Disarmament, 2015), https://cnnd.crawford.anu.edu.au/publication/cnnd/5328/nuclear-weapons-state-play-2015.
11 The NPT's arbitrary chronological definition of a NWS restricts that status to countries that conducted nuclear tests before 1 January 1967: China, France, Russia, the UK and the US. This book works around the legal restriction by describing any country that

possesses nuclear weapons as a nuclear-armed state and restricts the designation NWS for the five NPT-recognised possessor states.

12 Ramesh Thakur, "The Nuclear Ban Treaty: Recasting a Normative Framework for Disarmament," *The Washington Quarterly*, 40:4 (2018): 71–95.

13 Joint Statement on the humanitarian dimension of nuclear disarmament, 22 October 2012, www.eda.admin.ch/dam/eda/en/documents/aktuell/un-speeches_2/22102012-statement-nuclear-disarmament_EN.pdf.

14 "Pledge presented at the Vienna Conference on the Humanitarian Impact of Nuclear Weapons by Austrian Deputy Foreign Minister Michael Linhart," 9 December 2014. https://www.bmeia.gv.at/fileadmin/user_upload/Zentrale/Aussenpolitik/Abruestung/HINW14/HINW14_Austrian_Pledge.pdf.

15 "Humanitarian Pledge," Vienna Conference on the Humanitarian Impact of Nuclear Weapons, 8–9 December 2014, www.bmeia.gv.at/fileadmin/user_upload/Zentrale/Aussenpolitik/Abruestung/HINW14/HINW14vienna_Pledge_Document.pdf.

16 A/RES/71/258, UN General Assembly, 23 December 2016, www.icanw.org/wp-content/uploads/2017/01/N1646669.pdf.

17 NATO, "United States Non-Paper: Defense Impacts of Potential United Nations General Assembly Nuclear Weapons Ban Treaty," 17 October 2016, www.icanw.org/wp-content/uploads/2016/10/NATO_OCT2016.pdf.

18 "Towards a World Free of Nuclear Weapons," *Folha de S. Paulo*, 17 July 2017, www.itamaraty.gov.br/en/speeches-articles-and-interviews/minister-of-foreign-affairs-articles/16886-rumo-a-um-mundo-sem-armas-nucleares-folha-de-s-paulo-17-7-2018.

19 Thomas M. Franck, *The Power of Legitimacy Among Nations* (Oxford: Oxford University Press, 1990).

20 Anthony J. Colangelo, "The Duty to Disobey Illegal Nuclear Strike Orders," NAPSNet Policy Forum (9 October 2017), 14, https://nautilus.org/napsnet/napsnet-policy-forum/the-duty-to-disobey-illegal-nuclear-strike-orders.

21 Nick Ritchie, "Nuclear Disarmament and a Nuclear Weapons Ban Treaty," in *The NPT and the Prohibition Negotiation: Scope for Bridge-building* (Geneva: UNIDIR, May 2017), 13, www.unidir.org/files/publications/pdfs/the-npt-and-the-prohibition-negotiation-en-682.pdf.

22 Nina Tannenwald, *The Nuclear Taboo: The United States and the Non-Use of Nuclear Weapons Since 1945* (Cambridge: Cambridge University Press, 2007).

23 Thomas E. Doyle, "The moral implications of the subversion of the Nonproliferation Treaty regime," *Ethics and Global Politics* 2:2 (2009): 131–53; Joelien Pretorius and Tom Sauer, "Is it Time to Ditch the NPT?" *Bulletin of the Atomic Scientists*, 6 September 2019, https://thebulletin.org/2019/09/is-it-time-to-ditch-the-npt.

PART I

Origins, nature, impact

1

THE HUMANITARIAN INITIATIVE AND THE TPNW[1]

Alexander Kmentt

At the 2010 Non-Proliferation Treaty (NPT) Review Conference, states parties agreed by consensus to express their "deep concern at the catastrophic humanitarian consequences of any use of nuclear weapons."[2] In the following years, non-nuclear weapons state' (non-NWS) and civil society representatives focused increasingly on the humanitarian impact and the risks associated with nuclear weapons. This focus of activities – later referred to as the Humanitarian Initiative – was done primarily through several international conferences where new research on the humanitarian consequences and nuclear risks aspects was presented, as well as joint cross-regional statements highlighting the concern about these aspects. The latest iteration of the initiative's joint statement in 2015 has been subscribed to by 159 states. The Treaty on the Prohibition of Nuclear Weapons (TPNW) builds on the Humanitarian Initiative. It was adopted by 122 states in 2017 and entered into legal force on 22 January 2021. This chapter outlines the rationale of the Humanitarian Initiative which underpins the TPNW and responds to the counter-narratives and critiques against the TPNW presented by NWS and nuclear-umbrella states.

The humanitarian TPNW rationale

The Humanitarian Initiative and the resulting TPNW challenge the parameters of the nuclear weapons discourse. Reframing this discourse around the humanitarian consequences and risks of nuclear weapons was effective because it countered the NWS narrative on the security, responsibility and legitimacy of the nuclear status quo. This reframing formed the basis of the Humanitarian Initiative, the Humanitarian Pledge, underpinned the TPNW negotiations and is reiterated in the TPNW's preamble.

The perspective on the global humanitarian consequences, across a wide range of sectors, and the lack of response capability to the human suffering, placed the

DOI: 10.4324/9781003227502-3

nuclear weapons issue firmly in a *human security* context. The Humanitarian Initiative promoted a globalist and comprehensive view of security, in juxtaposition to the "state-centred" security arguments of NWS, who stress that nuclear weapons are essential for their and their allies' security. It asserted that states relying on nuclear deterrence defend a narrower and self-serving, but ultimately short-sighted, perspective of security, which comes at the expense of the security of all.

From the human security perspective ensues the question of responsibility. Can the threat of not only mutually assured destruction between adversaries but also the risk of inflicting global catastrophic humanitarian consequences, possibly threatening all humankind, be considered a responsible policy? Conversely, if nuclear-armed states are apparently trapped in a vicious circle, justifying their own need to have nuclear weapons with the possession of nuclear weapons by other nuclear-armed states, what is then the *responsibility* of non-NWS? The human security arguments about humanitarian consequences and risks of nuclear weapons thus lead to an appeal to the sense of responsibility of all states and to a call for action to strengthen the normative framework of the nuclear disarmament and non-proliferation regime.

The focus on the humanitarian consequences and risks of nuclear weapons questions the "normalisation" of nuclear deterrence in the security policy discourse of NWS. It demands a reassessment of what constitutes responsible behaviour. This focus raises pertinent questions on the legitimacy of the existing nuclear disarmament and non-proliferation regime. The humanitarian arguments reinforced the reasoning that it is the responsibility and in the legitimate security interest of non-NWS to take matters into their own hands, given the unwillingness or inability of NWS to take more credible steps towards nuclear disarmament. Rather than continue to merely demand disarmament progress from NWS, a prohibition of nuclear weapons emerged as the one concrete action that non-NWS were able to effect themselves.

The counter-narrative

In relation to the TPNW, a number of counter-narratives have been and continue to be presented by NWS and nuclear-umbrella states. Closer analysis shows that the broad range of procedural and substantive criticisms of the TPNW are relatively easy to counter, do not stand up to scrutiny and/or cannot be substantiated. Rather, they are the expressions of a politically motivated counter-narrative from those states who object to the Humanitarian Initiative and the TPNW, because of the challenge they present to the nuclear status quo and a particular interpretation of what the NPT represents in terms of obligations and commitments.

Deflection

The NWS have shown very limited engagement on the actual issue of humanitarian consequences of nuclear weapons, at no stage going further than a general acknowledgement that these consequences exist and to affirm their resolve to prevent them from materialising. The NWS have not provided answers or commented in any detail on the key Humanitarian Initiative conclusions, arguably owing to a lack of valid counterarguments. Such a conversation would inevitably entail admitting that the impact of nuclear weapons explosions affects not only one's own and the adversary's populations, but also the populations of innocent bystander states. It would reveal a willingness to accept these effects on third states and, indeed, on all of humanity, as a "necessary collateral" to maintaining a nuclear deterrence-based notion of security and stability. Whenever the humanitarian consequences and risks were raised, the response of the NWS – and of the nuclear-umbrella states – was to deflect and criticise a possible ban treaty instead.

Distraction and division

> At best [the TPNW] is a distraction (…). At worst, it will deepen political divisions.[3]

Given the severity of the humanitarian consequences and risks of nuclear weapons for the entire planet, the "distraction" argument is, per se, highly problematic. Moreover, it is hard to argue that the TPNW distracts from the implementation of other disarmament steps because such steps are not being taken by the NWS. The TPNW is supposed to instil more urgency into the currently non-existent nuclear disarmament and facilitate a focus on precisely those necessary steps not implemented.

"Divisions" on this issue have existed since 1945 but today's divisions exist *because* of the loss of credibility in the implementation of NPT Article 6 and not because of initiatives to help remedy this, such as the TPNW. Moreover, the NWS boycotted the humanitarian conferences, the open-ended working group and the treaty negotiations. When NWS do not agree and choose not to engage with a discussion and a process, then – by definition – the discussions and processes, rather than the refusal to engage with them, must be divisive. Moreover, NWS do not like the TPNW because it is divisive, but it is only divisive because they do not like it. The redundancy of this argument is striking.

Inefficacy

> (…) it is not realistic to expect that 'effective' nuclear disarmament can advance without engaging those States that possess nuclear weapons.[4]

The "inefficacy" counterargument is made by states that possess or rely on nuclear weapons, as a reason for not joining the TPNW. In terms of logic, this connection of cause and effect is circular: states with nuclear weapons are not willing to join the TPNW because, in their view, it will not eliminate a single nuclear weapon. Of course, the TPNW cannot eliminate a single weapon in itself, as long as NWS are not joining. But apart from this point of logic, this argument misses the point that a legally binding non-discriminatory prohibition of nuclear weapons creates the legal basis for their elimination and a practical measure towards this objective. This was the case with the Biological and Chemical Weapons Conventions. The pressure and momentum created by the TPNW for progress on nuclear disarmament as well as on non-proliferation, is intended to facilitate reductions of nuclear weapons and establish potential pathways to abandon them, once countries possessing these weapons are ready.

Challenging the legality and the legitimacy of nuclear weapons and nuclear deterrence might not in itself eliminate nuclear weapons, but has the potential to impact current nuclear weapons-related practices and nuclear deterrence. From the point of view of the Humanitarian Initiative, this is exactly why the TPNW is valid.

The TPNW supporters are also implicitly accused of inadvertently playing into the hands of autocracies at the expense of democratic states because the latter will face more civil society pressure. The TPNW is directed against nuclear weapons as such and not against any states or alliances currently relying on them. Certainly, the public discourse in an open society is, by definition, more vibrant, and sometimes very contested. But this argument has nothing to do with the issue of nuclear weapons or the TPNW; it is a natural function of democratic political systems. It is to be expected, and must indeed be hoped for, that democratic systems will have open societal discussions on the issue of nuclear weapons, including the humanitarian consequences and risks associated with them. Democratic states also have more intense discussions on issues such as human rights and climate change. Progress and change on these and other issues are expected to spring more from democratic debates and decision-making processes, than from closed and autocratic political systems.

The TPNW does not take the "security environment" into account

The threat perceptions of non-NWS, stemming from the concern about the humanitarian consequences and risks of nuclear weapons are not merely a humanitarian perspective but based on equally valid and pertinent security considerations. Contrary to the dominant NWS' nuclear deterrence views, the non-NWS security perspectives regarding nuclear weapons have been expressed for decades but have not been taken into account adequately, rather than the other way around. While opponents of the TPNW are perfectly entitled to their views on security, they neither own the exclusive right to interpret the NPT nor are they the sole arbiter of whose security perspectives are more valid than others.

Proponents of the TPNW have never disputed the difficult security challenges facing the international community today or argued that nuclear disarmament should be seen in isolation from the global security environment. Nor have they advocated the ban as a panacea for achieving a world without nuclear weapons. All disarmament, arms control and non-proliferation efforts, including the eventual elimination of nuclear weapons must inevitably proceed in the face of ongoing security challenges, during times of international crises and some form or another of geopolitical competition. From the perspective of the TPNW, the challenging international security environment, coupled with the continued reliance on nuclear weapons by possessor states, make nuclear disarmament efforts, if anything, even more urgent. The argument that one must wait for a future security environment in which nuclear deterrence is no longer needed as a precondition for nuclear disarmament is disingenuous. There will always be real or perceived security imbalances between states, which, if one follows this line of argument, will provide excuses in perpetuity for not altering the nuclear status quo.

In addition, nuclear disarmament measures, including deep cuts in nuclear arsenals and disarmament verification, are easier and indeed might be possible only when they are based on a strong and comprehensive prohibition of nuclear weapons. States are more likely to eliminate a weapon if this weapon is morally unacceptable and legally prohibited, than in a situation where the alleged "virtues" of these weapons continue to be highlighted at every opportunity. For TPNW supporting states, this logic is compelling and firmly based on security considerations.

Finally, NWS and nuclear-umbrella states do not tire of highlighting that nuclear weapons are necessary for their security and have done so in particular to express their opposition to the TPNW. There are, however, many non-NWS who could justifiably claim that their security environment is at least as challenging as the security environment of states "relying" on nuclear weapons. By underscoring the challenging security environment and the necessity to keep relying on nuclear weapons because of it, NWS and nuclear-umbrella states only highlight a striking double standard as regards the concept of security.

The TPNW undermines the NPT

Firstly, the states at the forefront of this process have been among the strongest supporters of the NPT and enjoy an unblemished record of implementation. They are all longstanding promoters of various initiatives in support of nuclear disarmament and non-proliferation. For example, to accuse Ireland, which is considered to have invented the NPT, or South Africa, which actually disarmed its nuclear weapons and joined the NPT as a non-NWS of undermining the NPT must be considered grossly confrontational. This is exacerbated by the fact that these accusations come primarily from those states whose own lacklustre NPT implementation records were the reason why the Humanitarian Initiative and the TPNW process were initiated in the first place. In fact, the negotiations of the TPNW were marked by the utmost care to make the TPNW a new legal instrument in line with the existing disarmament and non-proliferation regime. The treaty explicitly and structurally fits into the framework created by the NPT and constitutes a necessary measure for the implementation of its Article 6. This is a disingenuous accusation.

Secondly, as stated above, NWS assert the need to keep nuclear weapons for their security. Promoting the value and utility of nuclear weapons encourages proliferation. One can even argue that such promotion is, in fact, an act of proliferation. It might not be proliferation in its literal sense, but it is nevertheless the proliferation of the *concept* of nuclear weapons as a desirable "guarantee" of security. At a minimum, this runs counter to the spirit of the NPT.

How can the proliferation of nuclear weapons be countered effectively in the long run, while simultaneously stressing their necessity and desirability? Without strong counterarguments, the view that nuclear weapons are necessary will only gain in attractiveness. The TPNW provides an unequivocal counterargument, which the NPT is unable to do, given its discriminatory nature and in-built double standard. By legally prohibiting these weapons and declaring them morally indefensible and detrimental to the undiminished security for all, the TPNW creates a real taboo against both the possession of nuclear weapons and the practice of nuclear deterrence, thus, providing a crucial contribution to achieving the objective of a world without nuclear weapons to which all NPT states have committed themselves.

At a time when security challenges are on the rise and without credible leadership on nuclear disarmament by states that rely on these weapons, the TPNW provides much needed normative reinforcement of nuclear non-proliferation efforts. It is the double-standard in the NPT and the lacklustre implementation of its Article 6 that weakens it, not the TPNW with its new normative standard to redress exactly those weaknesses and strengthen the NPT.

"Safeguards"

The critique against the TPNW safeguards provisions is disingenuous. The TPNW ensures that states maintain, as a minimum, their existing International Atomic Energy Agency (IAEA) safeguards obligations. The majority of states have IAEA Additional Protocols in place. Consequently, the TPNW legally secures the Additional Protocol as the current verification, which is a higher standard than the one stipulated by the NPT. For states that currently do not have an Additional Protocol, the TPNW sets the IAEA Comprehensive Safeguards Agreement as the minimum requirement, the same as in the NPT. The TPNW also explicitly refers to the possibility of strengthening these obligations in the future. Importantly, and omitted by the critiques, the TPNW also goes beyond the NPT in relation to nuclear-armed states. When joining the TPNW, they are obliged to negotiate, conclude, and maintain an adequate safeguards agreement. Thus, the TPNW provides a partially higher safeguards standard than the NPT, and partially hews as closely as possible to the NPT approach, precisely to avoid diverging from this standard.

TPNW impact: What does the TPNW represent?

Democracy

The human security focus provided non-NWS with additional arguments with which to oppose nuclear weapons. The possession of these weapons by nine nuclear-armed states and the lack of progress on nuclear disarmament pose legitimate security concerns and perceptions of threat also in non-NWS. The reframing of the nuclear weapons discourse in a humanitarian direction made this issue more accessible, for more states, and for a broader set of stakeholders than the usual restricted circle of security policy experts. Given that nuclear weapons are an existential threat to the survival of all humankind, they should not be dealt with as a national security prerogative of a select few states.

Thus, the Humanitarian Initiative and the TPNW represent a democratic shift in the nuclear weapons debate. Also, non-NWS were prepared to pursue their interests through the UN General Assembly, the central democratic body of the United Nations, and seek a mandate for the TPNW negotiations and conclude this treaty. Moreover, the unequivocal TPNW prohibition of nuclear weapons, containing no exceptions for any actor, are a further manifestation of the demand for a more egalitarian approach to nuclear weapons.

The rationale for nuclear disarmament

How can nuclear disarmament be an urgent priority when nuclear-armed states deem their nuclear weapons essential for international peace and security? As long as this is the case, it is difficult to see these states wanting to take transformative steps to move away from relying on these weapons. Hence nuclear disarmament is mired in an unsolvable contradiction, managed conceptually only by viewing nuclear disarmament as an aspirational goal, achievable in an as yet wholly undefined international security environment in a distant future.

The reasons why a norm-setting approach to prohibiting nuclear weapons emerged as a viable route forward for a majority of states are twofold. Firstly, it was the only potentially transformational step achievable without the engagement of the nuclear-armed states. Secondly, it emerged precisely because NWS were themselves unable or unwilling to demonstrate a sense of urgency or leadership for nuclear disarmament, let alone formulate any vision of how a world without nuclear weapons could be achieved.

The adoption of the TPNW is, thus, a legally binding clarification on the part of the non-NWS that nuclear disarmament is an urgent priority and that the implementation of NPT disarmament obligations and commitments by the NWS has been far from satisfactory or credible. Obfuscation of this fact and the issuing of aspirational affirmations regarding nuclear disarmament will no longer be satisfactory.

Challenging nuclear deterrence

The TPNW is a particular legal response to the evidence on the humanitarian consequences and risks of nuclear weapons. One can agree or disagree with the legal dimension of the TPNW. However, as the findings on the consequences of nuclear explosions and nuclear risks are based on empirically demonstrable facts, they should be considered seriously in any cost-benefit analysis underpinning prevailing assumptions on nuclear deterrence. The breadth of consequences and the risks of nuclear weapons should be weighed against the posited security benefit of nuclear weapons. What is the balance of probability between the belief that nuclear weapons deter and prevent large-scale wars and the knowledge that deterrence, including nuclear deterrence, can fail causing measurable humanitarian and other consequences? A focus on humanitarian consequences and risks of nuclear weapons challenges the assumptions that underpin nuclear deterrence.

If the short, medium and long term consequences of nuclear weapon explosions and the interrelationship of these consequences are not only grave, but graver than previously realised and not yet fully understood, does this impact the nuclear deterrence cost-benefit analysis? What is the impact of these graver humanitarian consequences on the credibility of nuclear deterrence? At what stage and at which level of impact on the economy, public health, migratory movements, and food security, or an aggregate combination of such consequences, would the deterrence equation start to change? What in terms of humanitarian consequences is acceptable and for whom? Are there objective criteria to gauge this and can they be assessed? How exactly do the nuclear-armed states integrate the humanitarian consequences on their own population, the presumptive opponent's population and on the rest of the world, innocent bystanders to this conflict, into their nuclear deterrence calculations?

Moreover, how exactly do nuclear planners weigh a military target against collateral damage and what are the parameters for this, for example in the case of a major city? Given the probable transboundary consequences of nuclear weapons use, how are the International Humanitarian Law principles of distinction and proportionality applied vis-à-vis populations, including in third countries that are not party to the conflict? What about the responsibility and the ability to clean up after an accident or use of nuclear weapons and to provide compensation? To what extent is this responsibility included in the decision-making process and in nuclear doctrines in nuclear-armed states? Once these issues are discussed in concrete terms – here the humanitarian consequences and the question of the legality of nuclear weapons use naturally converge – the rationalisation of nuclear deterrence and the balance of arguments could shift significantly.

One of the key contributions of the Humanitarian Initiative is the increased focus on risks associated with the possession of nuclear weapons and the practice of nuclear deterrence *per se,* rather than from the actions of individual states. This provides an aggregated view of the nuclear weapons practices of all nuclear-armed states and the resulting risk for all of humanity. This defines the perspective of non-NWS regarding nuclear risks today.

For non-NWS, the grave humanitarian consequences that would result from nuclear explosions *are* the risks to which they are exposed, against their will and outside their control. These risks stem from the fact that nine states in the world possess nuclear weapons and have based their security policies on nuclear deterrence. The risks could be realised through deliberate use of nuclear weapons, a miscalculation leading to a nuclear conflict, or indeed any form of accident.

From this perspective, nuclear deterrence is not only seen as a high-risk practice, owing to the grave consequences of nuclear weapons but also because it is practiced by humans and relies on machines and processes designed by humans. The risks are inherent in possessing and maintaining nuclear weapons. The actions and the behaviour of one state or one leader in a nuclear-armed state can be assessed to be more risk prone than that of another. However, from the TPNW perspective, these differences are not the central issue. The collective nuclear weapons policies and actions of all nuclear-armed states and their allies create an aggregated and interconnected set of global nuclear risks.

Consequently, non-NWS want to reduce the likelihood of any nuclear weapons explosions whether intentional, inadvertent, unintentional or from accidents owing to human or technical reasons. In addition to progress on nuclear disarmament and the elimination of nuclear weapons – evidently the risk reduction gold-standard – they request measures to take nuclear weapons as far away from use or accidents as possible. These include de-alerting, taking weapons out of operational service, more transparency about postures and actual use scenarios, further reductions of stockpiles, confidence building measures and political and legal steps aimed at strengthening the nuclear disarmament and non-proliferation regime.

This is different to the risk reduction approach which NWS want to pursue. The focus is on "strategic risk reduction," that is, countering risks that could undermine nuclear deterrence relationships. Risk reduction measures are geared towards avoiding or managing crisis situations and to achieving a better understanding of the policies and intentions between adversaries, so as to maintain stable and less risky deterrence relationships. In short, the focus of this form of risk reduction is to make nuclear deterrence work better, rather than consider the risks of the practice of nuclear deterrence itself.

Risk reduction measures are considered only insofar as they do not impact the nuclear deterrence calculus. Here one sees the inherent contradiction and conundrum posed by the necessity to maintain nuclear weapons in a manner that demonstrates readiness and resolve to always use them, as required for the credibility of nuclear deterrence, and a more comprehensive approach to risk reduction measures aimed at ensuring that they will never be used, intentionally or unintentionally, or through human or technical error.

Conclusion

The TPNW is thus underpinned by an assessment of the humanitarian and other consequences of nuclear weapons explosions and the legality of nuclear weapons use scenarios in a concrete, rather than abstract, manner. Nuclear risks are considered from the perspective of the aggregate risks stemming from the possession of these weapons and the practice of nuclear deterrence by all nuclear-armed states. Scrutiny of the consequences, legality, and risks associated with nuclear weapons, leads to the legal, ethical and rational conclusions contained in the TPNW. These reject arguments that posit the security value of nuclear weapons and/or find wisdom in maintaining the practice of nuclear deterrence.

Notes

1 The points made in this chapter are developed in Alexander Kmentt, *The treaty prohibiting nuclear weapons – How it was achieved and why it matters* (London: Routledge, 2021). The views expressed in the chapter are those of the author and do not necessarily reflect the positions of the Austrian Foreign Ministry.
2 Extracted from 2010 Review Conference of the Parties to the Treaty on the Non-Proliferation of Nuclear Weapons, Final Document, document NPT/CONF.2010/50 (Vol. I), 2010.
3 Press Statement, US Department of State on 7 July 2017, available at https://2017-2021.state.gov/conclusion-of-un-negotiations-on-a-treaty-to-ban-nuclear-weapons/index.html.
4 Statement by German Government on 22 February 2016, available at www.unog.ch/__80256ee600585943.nsf/(httpPages)/5ee5df8a4a4bfd97c1257fb60054c6ce?OpenDocument&ExpandSection=3%2C2#_Section3.

2

CO-OPERATION OR CONFLICT? WALKING THE TIGHTROPE OF NPT AND BAN TREATY SUPPORTERS

Angela Kane

The Treaty on the Prohibition of Nuclear Weapons (TPNW) has changed the paradigm of the Nuclear Non-Proliferation Treaty (NPT). The two preparatory meetings preceding the next NPT Review Conference showed in stark relief the differences and the convergence between the nuclear allies and the Ban Treaty supporters. The paper looks at the emergence of the frustrations of the non-nuclear-weapon states that led to the Ban Treaty and its adoption by almost two-thirds of the United Nations (UN) member states. It outlines the arguments against the Ban Treaty put forward by the nuclear allies and the hardening of positions in light of their cavalier dismissal of the Ban Treaty. The paper addresses these criticisms, discusses the positions put forward by the Ban Treaty supporters, and examines the possible repercussions for the debate on nuclear issues and security. The paper argues that the nuclear possessors should accept the Ban Treaty as a reality and focus on the way forward: renewed dialogue and cooperation with the non-nuclear-weapon states. Suggestions for constructive engagement are addressed to both nuclear allies and Ban Treaty supporters, arguing that vision and leadership is needed from both sides in order to avoid a further disintegration of the nuclear architecture.

Much has been made of the fact that the 2010 NPT Review Conference included a statement of "concern at the catastrophic humanitarian consequences of any use of nuclear weapons and reaffirms the need for all states at all times to comply with applicable international law, including international humanitarian law."[1] This laid the foundation for what was subsequently labelled the humanitarian initiative. Under this banner three conferences were organised in 2013 and 2014 (in Oslo, Nayarit and Vienna) and resulted, finally, in the negotiations to conclude the treaty that was adopted on 7 July 2017 in New York.

We sometimes forget how quickly the international political climate can change. The 2010 NPT Review Conference took place only months after former President

DOI: 10.4324/9781003227502-4

Barack Obama made his famous "Prague speech," raising hopes for substantial progress in nuclear disarmament between the USA and Russia. Had this been followed up and progress been made on nuclear agreements, the TPNW might possibly have been avoided.

Yet today, more than seven years after Obama's Prague speech, the security landscape is dramatically worse: a US President with a pro-military agenda is in power, bilateral US–Russian relations are at their nadir, the nuclear progress and sabre-rattling of the Democratic People's Republic of Korea (DPRK or North Korea) has alarmed the international community and agreements like the Joint Comprehensive Plan of Action, which halted the possible military dimensions of Iran's nuclear programme, are under attack in the USA. In early 2021 the Doomsday Clock was advanced to two minutes to midnight – it was only once before so close to midnight, in 1953, following the US decision to pursue the hydrogen bomb.[2]

In today's security environment, how will the relationship between the TPNW – also called the "Ban Treaty" – and the NPT evolve? Will it conflict? Will it be cooperative? Will it develop in parallel? These are the questions that are foremost in the minds of experts,[3] considering how close we are to the next NPT Review Conference: the historic milestone of a fiftieth commemoration of the entry into force of the NPT.

The supporters of the TPNW have all the moral arguments on their side, all the ethical considerations, as well as the long history of disarmament efforts, begun in 1946 at the United Nations with the very first General Assembly resolution which called for the elimination of nuclear weapons and all other weapons "adaptable to mass destruction."[4] And yes, almost two-thirds (63 percent) of the entire UN membership – 122 states – voted to adopt the Treaty. Fifty-six states signed it since its opening for signature on 20 September last year, five have ratified as of 28 February 2018. The bar to entry into force was set deliberately low, at 50 ratifications.

I will skip over the details of the negotiations and the criticisms that have been levied by the nuclear-weapon states (NWS) and their allies against the treaty. It is true that the negotiations brought together states that were likeminded and that were united in their goal of achieving a consensus text within the short time allotted to the negotiations. They were mindful of the efforts by the USA in 2016 – ultimately unsuccessful – to stymie the process by not allocating the necessary funds to the General Assembly to hold two negotiating sessions in 2017 and they were fearful that a longer negotiating timetable could unravel the delicate consensus that had held them together.

The negotiations were accompanied by a very large number of disarmament activists who – with generous funding from some governments – were able to be present at the various meetings, working groups and the actual negotiations in New York. They kept up the pressure on governments. The International Campaign to Abolish Nuclear Weapons (ICAN) – an umbrella organisation of several hundred NGOs which was founded just ten years ago – was recognised last year by the Nobel Committee for their effective advocacy efforts and awarded the Peace Prize – a prize that Hiroshima survivor Setsuko Thurlow accepted together with ICAN.

Alleged detrimental effects of the treaty

Widened gap between NWS and allies and ban proponents

Having witnessed for a number of years the discussions in the NPT context, I find this view extremely misleading. The gap was already there and got worse each year that disarmament efforts were not pursued, especially after the 2010 NPT Review Conference and the abandonment of the commitment to hold a conference on a weapons of mass destruction (WMD)-free zone in the Middle East in 2012. The gap – I would rather call it the chasm – was evident in the NPT deliberations, in the Conference on Disarmament, in the UN General Assembly and its First Committee.

None of these fora has had any concrete achievements on its record for years. The non-possessors of nuclear weapons consider that all obligations are on their side, while the obligation of Article 6 ("to undertake to pursue negotiations in good faith on effective measures relating to the cessation of the nuclear arms race"[5]) was not being implemented.

In their view, Article 6 should have obliged the NWS to engage in the preparatory process for the TPNW and the negotiations leading up to its adoption – even if they had not signed on in the end. Instead, the five NWS, who are also the permanent members of the UN Security Council (P5), and the states under their nuclear umbrella largely stayed away from the preparatory process and did not participate in the negotiations. The only exception was the Netherlands – but their motivation was not in line with the supporters of the treaty: owing to strong public support, they were mandated by their Parliament to participate in the negotiations, and in the end voted against the treaty, spoiling, together with Singapore's abstention, what would otherwise have been a consensus adoption.

On the day the TPNW was adopted, France, the UK and the USA issued a joint press statement which inflamed passions further, stating that they "do not intend to sign, ratify or ever become part of it."[6] They noted that "importantly, other states possessing nuclear weapons and almost all other states relying on nuclear deterrence have also not taken part in the negotiations," and that "accession to the Ban Treaty is incompatible with the policy of nuclear deterrence, which has been essential to keeping the peace in Europe and North Asia for over 70 years." They added that "a ban treaty … risks undermining the existing international security architecture which contributes to the maintenance of international peace and security."

The TPNW thus shone a spotlight on the entrenched positions of both sides. It also brought into focus the position of the nuclear umbrella states which receive nuclear guarantees from the NWS. These states have a long history of domestically advocating nuclear disarmament, but of not openly acknowledging the benefits they derive from the umbrella relationship. They may well have to contend from now on with domestic audiences for whom the Ban Treaty is a victory and the culmination of many years of disarmament advocacy. Sweden, which voted for the treaty, is currently conducting an inquiry into the consequences of a possible Swedish accession to the treaty. Parliamentary inquiries are also being conducted in Italy and Norway, though neither country participated in the treaty negotiations. The domestic pressures from constituents will have to be managed as – and when – the Ban Treaty comes into force.

Another interesting effect is seen in the four states that possess nuclear weapons but are outside the NPT. India and Pakistan had claimed to be in favour of nuclear disarmament yet maintained that the NPT was not the proper instrument because of its distinction between the nuclear haves and the have-nots. So now that there is the TPNW, they clearly do not consider it the right vehicle for achieving nuclear disarmament either.

And finally, the fallout from the TPNW was already evidenced at the General Assembly's First Committee in October 2020, as there were clear indications from the nuclear-armed states that they are more committed than ever to retaining their nuclear arms.[7] In 2020 a total of 30 of the 58 resolutions and decisions were approved by recorded vote. Of these, 16 resolutions and two decisions related to nuclear weapons. Many of the texts usually reiterate language from year to year, yet several of the draft resolutions in 2017 deviated from the texts of versions that had been tabled previously. These texts were objected to on the basis of undermining consensus documents, of omitting language that had been agreed to in prior years, or that the text fell short of expectations and obligations related to the TPNW.[8] By contrast, in 2016 the First Committee approved 26 texts, only seven of them with a recorded vote.[9]

A threat to the NPT regime

Let me be clear: the NPT has already been suffering a crisis of confidence, and the TPNW is likely adding another divisive issue to the Review Process. It has been suggested – and not only by the three Western members of the P5 quoted above – that the TPNW is creating divisions in the international community regarding the pace and the manner in which nuclear disarmament should occur.

We all know that the only nuclear disarmament that has ever taken place has been unilateral, or bilateral between the USA and the Russian Federation. No nuclear disarmament discussions have occurred in the context of Article 6 of the NPT – and that is precisely the reason for the long-standing dissatisfaction and frustration on the part of the overwhelming majority of the NPT members. It therefore follows that the TPNW is not the cause of the division but rather a symptom of the division between the nuclear haves and the nuclear have-nots.

And why would the treaty be a threat to the NPT if the treaties on nuclear-weapon-free zones are not? In 2017 the oldest, the Treaty of Tlatelolco, which preceded the NPT by a year, commemorated its 50th year since establishment, and the various regional arrangements which establish nuclear-weapon-free zones are seen as complementary to – even supportive of – the NPT, not detracting from it.

Damage prospects for nuclear disarmament

I fail to see how this could be. Clearly, the aim of the treaty is to delegitimise nuclear weapons and to make it more difficult for states to continue stressing their reliance on nuclear weapons as part of their military and security strategies. Why would anyone believe that the treaty would slow down or prevent implementation of New START and a follow-on treaty? Or to make progress on the entry into force of the Comprehensive Nuclear-Test-Ban Treaty (CTBT)?

We have heard dire statements about the current global instability and the strategy touted by the P5 of the "step-by-step" approach, yet no steps have been identified that could constitute building blocks towards a world with fewer – or no – nuclear weapons. Even smaller steps, like the implementation of the 2010 NPT Action Plan, were not taken by the NWS, despite the adoption by consensus of this Plan.

In fact, the TPNW has been criticised for not outlining concrete steps which would result in a reduction of nuclear weapons. Yet how could this be achieved by the negotiators of the treaty, absent the nuclear weapons possessors? Nothing in the treaty would obstruct or impede reductions in the number of nuclear weapons – in fact, any movement in that direction would be wildly cheered by the non-nuclear possessors.

Encourage "forum shopping"

It is unclear why this would be controversial: the TPNW closely mirrors the NPT language, in its inclusion of a withdrawal clause as well as in the treatment of safeguards. In a speech before the First Committee in New York in October 2017, Ambassador Dell Higgie of New Zealand explained:

> The treaty has been designed to ensure that no State can evade the basic safeguards underpinning the NPT. The new Treaty parallels the NPT's legal obligation to have a Comprehensive Safeguards Agreement (CSA) and establishes this as a minimum baseline. It goes further than the NPT by requiring – as a legal obligation under the terms of the Prohibition Treaty itself – those of its States Parties who have an Additional Protocol to retain this in place as their minimum baseline. The allegation that the new treaty does not strengthen the NPT has overlooked the fact that successive Review Conferences have not been able to require NPT States Parties to go beyond the CSA as the safeguards baseline.[10]

Positive Aspects of the Ban Treaty

Having discussed the negative aspects of the TPNW, let me now turn to what could be considered the positive ones, though this view depends of course on one's perspective on the TPNW.

Strengthening humanitarian and environmental norms against nuclear weapons

The strongest argument in favour of the TPNW is its contribution to the strengthening of the norm which holds that nuclear weapons are inhumane and against international humanitarian law, have detrimental effects on the environment and pose an existential threat to humanity. This was first enshrined in the NPT Preamble,[11] affirmed in later documents – such as the 2010 NPT Review Conference – and on which proponents base their demand to outlaw them.

Two of the three weapons of mass destruction, biological and chemical weapons are already outlawed. Their conventions were signed and ratified by a majority of states. The arguments that these weapons were essential to guarantee security and for deterrence were not advanced at the time the treaties were negotiated nor when they opened for signature. In fact, most states strongly condemn the use of chemical weapons and demand compliance with the Chemical Weapons Convention, yet they find it polarising or divisive for the vast majority of states to demand compliance with NPT obligations.

Equally, there is a strong norm against nuclear testing which took many years to take hold. It first manifested itself in the Partial Test-Ban Treaty of 1963, to be succeeded by the CTBT in 1997, following the disastrous effects of years of nuclear testing on humans and the environment that are still with us.

North Korea is being widely condemned for its nuclear tests (the only country having tested in this century). It is interesting to note that North Korea, not a party to the CTBT, is being condemned by the international community for violating the norm against nuclear testing, not because it is violating a treaty.

Yet the establishment of a norm against nuclear weapons is precisely what the NWS wish to avoid. In the disarmament deliberations in the General Assembly last year, they vocally objected to all explicit or implicit references to the TPNW in almost a dozen First Committee resolutions. France, the UK and the USA called the treaty "dangerous," Russia described it as a "mistake," and Pakistan said it was not inclusive.[12] The US opposed references to the TPNW, because it is "counterproductive, divisive, and only serves to divert attention from actual effective measures," according to US Ambassador Robert Wood, who also posited that the treaty "will not result in the elimination of a single nuclear warhead or improve the security of any state."[13]

Strengthening the NPT

In the view of the treaty supporters, the TPNW will strengthen the NPT, as it will constitute an important step in the implementation of its Article 6 obligation to pursue negotiations in good faith on effective measures relating to nuclear disarmament. It will not disturb any legal obligations arising from the NPT, as there are well-established rules to manage overlapping provisions arising from successive treaties, and the inclusion of key prohibitions (such as testing, possession, use, transfer and stationing) in fact strengthen current NPT provisions.

Establishing a legal framework for nuclear disarmament

The treaty also articulates and establishes a legal framework for what was previously seen as a mere aspiration. It is now possible to envisage a treaty format through which nuclear disarmament can be achieved. It is a concrete result that challenges those who disagree with it: how would they devise an alternative or engage with the treaty's proponents?

Moral high ground

The TPNW supporters are occupying the moral high ground. This has been amplified by Pope Francis who added his powerful voice to the discussions on nuclear weapons: "The threat of their use as well as their possession is to be firmly condemned," he said, adding that the policy of nuclear deterrence could be morally acceptable "as long as real work was underway on a complete ban of the weapons."[14]

The award of the Nobel Peace Prize to ICAN has added strong support to the issue and at the same time elevated the profile of advocacy organisations to promote nuclear disarmament. The ensuing press coverage certainly will help disarmament advocates to lobby their governments, but whether it will be sufficient to sway governments to change their policies is unclear – even doubtful. The case of Japan is proving the resilience of the nuclear weapon argument: despite being the only country having suffered the effects of two atomic bombs and a very strong and vocal disarmament movement, Japan continues to enjoy the advantages of the US nuclear umbrella and did not participate in the TPNW process.

Re-examination of nuclear deterrence

The debate is also leading to a re-examination of the concept of deterrence. Wars are still being fought, but it cannot be demonstrated that any were averted, owing to the threat of using nuclear weapons. A thoughtful analysis published in *The Guardian* shows that until 1945, the purpose of military forces had been to win wars, yet afterwards the chief purpose was to avoid wars.[15] Thus deterrence became not only a strategy, but the very grounds on which governments justified nuclear weapons themselves. Every nuclear-possessor state now claims that they deter attacks by their threat of catastrophic retaliation,[16] yet an examination of post-World War II history shows that this theory simply does not hold. And the value of nuclear deterrence is only upheld by the possessors of nuclear weapons: non-possessors do not share this assessment.

Next steps

So, the question before us is the following: what comes next?

It is clear from the above account that none of the nuclear possessor states will sign the TPNW. They acquired nuclear weapons for reasons of national security, of prestige, threat perceptions or other internal political rationales that will not be swayed by the mere existence of a framework or treaty for giving them up.

An additional factor of contention is the decision by the NWS to upgrade their nuclear arsenals over the next decades. This decision predated the TPNW itself yet was taken while the humanitarian consequences of a nuclear explosion were debated at length. The USA will spend $1.2 trillion over 30 years to modernise and maintain nuclear weapons – a signal that they intend to keep them as an entitlement rather than downsizing or given them up. And recently, the US Nuclear Posture Review has upended the discussion on nuclear deterrence by adding scenarios of use in cases such as "significant non-nuclear strategic attacks," to include attacks on "civilian population of infrastructure," as well as calling for the development of new, less powerful warheads which critics fear will make them more usable, with potentially catastrophic consequences.[17]

These developments have further heightened the concerns of the Ban Treaty supporters. What, then, can be done to change the situation? First of all, can a head-on collision at the NPT Review Conference be avoided?

Some thoughts on remedial action

For the NWS, it is most important that instead of an outright rejection of discussion about nuclear disarmament, an honest dialogue is started with the non-NWS. It is no longer business as usual, where the demands by the non-NWS were simply brushed aside or even ignored. I would suggest that the NWS:

1. Accept the reality of the TPNW: it exists and was voted with a two-thirds majority of member states;
2. Accept that the TPNW proponents are not against the NPT and nor are they trying to undermine it;
3. Abandon the dismissive and offensive language against the TPNW supporters;
4. Include the non-NPT nuclear possessors in the discussion;
5. Identify the role of nuclear weapons in their national strategy;
6. Similar to rules of engagement in conventional war, can such rules be considered for nuclear war?

7. Consider more transparency regarding possession, numbers and deployment of nuclear weapons;
8. Determine if there is a lowest number of nuclear weapons at which nuclear deterrence is still valid;
9. Assess what would be the level of stability or security to be reached before nuclear disarmament can be considered; could such a scenario be defined or outlined?
10. Determine what are some of the steps towards nuclear disarmament that can be envisaged;
11. Consider what progress can be made on negative security assurances, a long-standing demand of the Non-Aligned Group;
12. Make a risk assessment to ensure that nuclear weapons are not at danger of terrorism, theft, accidents or cyber attack;
13. In advance of the 2020 NPT Review Conference, determine whether language can be negotiated for the Final Document that is acceptable to TPNW supporters.

And finally, Russia, the UK and the USA need to address the question of the WMD-free zone in the Middle East. It is still a festering problem and has the potential to again disrupt the NPT deliberations. The three guarantors need to make efforts to engage with the states in the region, to respond to the Arab states' pressure to comply with the commitments made.

For the nuclear disarmers, there are also questions to be considered:

1. How do you address security concerns not only of one nation but of an alliance like NATO which has adopted a doctrine of nuclear deterrence?
2. How do you convince the military establishment to give up – or reduce the role of – nuclear weapons in their defence strategy?
3. How do you convince the military industrial complex – with its reliance on the financial benefits deriving from the existence and modernisation of nuclear weapons – to support nuclear disarmament?
4. How do you engage public opinion to demand from their government a reduction in nuclear weapons or in leaving the nuclear umbrella altogether?
5. How do you explain why nuclear weapons are so resistant to ostracism, in contrast to chemical and biological weapons? Is there more that can be done to "name and shame"?
6. How would you handle inspection and monitoring in a non-nuclear world? Would this continue to be handled by the International Atomic Energy Agency? And how would you prevent possible break-outs or rogue actors?[18]
7. In advance of the 2020 NPT Review Conference, determine whether language can be negotiated for the Final Document that is acceptable to NWS.

For all states, here are more suggestions:

1. Demonstrate more ownership of the NPT – in statements but also by making some concrete and practical suggestions. These could be reports, bridge-building proposals or something akin to the "gift baskets" that had been a successful feature of the Nuclear Security Summits.
2. Do not only focus on the outcome of the Review Conference but also on the review process. How could this process be made more effective?
3. Try to identify "bridge-builders" who could help both sides arrive at a discussion that is free of hostility and emotion.

These questions and suggestions are not only highly relevant, but they also show that engagement from both sides is needed in order to prevent a train-wreck at the 2020 NPT Review Conference. The blame game from the NWS is already in full swing; what is needed is vision and leadership from the P5: rather than focusing on what they consider "the negative" – that is, the TPNW – they should shift their attention to the origin of this effort – the humanitarian consequences – and show cooperation and positive steps. The probability of using the TPNW as a political tool to sow heightened distrust and dissension is high.

The rise of DPRK's nuclear status has further disturbed the status quo and is used to deny any progress on nuclear disarmament. Demands are made on North Korea to give up their nuclear weapons before engagement can take place. Yet North Korea withdrew from the NPT in 2003 – even if this withdrawal is not considered effective (it is still listed as a State Party on the official UN website). It is hard not to draw parallels with the situation of the three other nuclear possessors outside the NPT, and that brings the question: what other states aspire to acquiring nuclear weapons?

In South Korea, public opinion polls show the majority of the population favours the acquisition of nuclear weapons – 60 percent. In Japan, mindful of the Hiroshima-Nagasaki experience, only 10 percent of the public is in favour of nuclear weapons, but this could quickly change with increasing threats coming from North Korea – and dire utterances from the USA to retaliate. Both countries have access to sensitive nuclear materials, have mastered the technology and could rapidly advance to becoming a nuclear power.

The desire of Saudi Arabia to enter the nuclear power business and erect as many as 16 nuclear reactors for electricity generation has raised fears that they may build these as a hedge against their arch-rival, Iran. The current discussions with the United States centre on bilateral civil nuclear agreements that require adherence to strict non-proliferation criteria – the so-called "gold standard" for civil nuclear cooperation – which Saudi Arabia is resisting. This could leave them free to repurpose the technology for nuclear weapons. If the sale is agreed to, it would show yet again a double standard by one of the NWS, just like the ongoing pressure by the USA to admit India into the Nuclear Suppliers Group (NSG) and dispense with the requirement that any NSG member must have acceded to the NPT.

These examples again show the divisiveness and the lack of trust between the nuclear haves and the have-nots.

The TPNW presents a watershed. The consensus around the NPT has in effect been put on hold, with two-thirds of states having endorsed a nuclear-free world as a norm. The five NWS can no longer claim that their possession of nuclear weapons has international approval and legitimacy – and will continue unchanged into the future.

Surely, now is the time to pull together rather than engage in verbal sparring and disparagement. Let us hope that wisdom and cool heads will prevail – and that constructive engagement will win the day and a relatively positive atmosphere at the NPT Preparatory Commissions and the Review Conference in 2020. Yet words will not suffice, concrete steps must be discussed and offered. If not, it is difficult to see how a hardening of positions and a negative outcome – which is in no one's interest – can be avoided.

Notes

1 Final Document of the 2010 NPT Review Conference (NPT/CONF.2010/50, Vol. I).
2 By contrast, in early 2010, the clock stood at six minutes to midnight, and the assessment was: "we are poised to bend the arc of history toward a world free of nuclear weapons." See www.thebulletin.org/timeline.
3 Several conferences were held recently at which papers on the TPNW were presented. I would like to mention the prepared remarks by Trevor Findlay at the 27th United Nations Conference on Disarmament Issues, Hiroshima, 29–30 November 2017, as a useful contribution to the debate.
4 Resolution 1 (1) adopted on 24 January 1946, entitled "Establishment of a Commission to Deal with the Problem Raised by the Discovery of Atomic Energy."
5 UNODA, Treaty on the Non-Proliferation of Nuclear Weapons (NPT), www.un.org/disarmament/wmd/nuclear/npt/text.
6 US Mission to the UN, "Joint Press Statement from the Permanent Representatives to the United Nations of the United States, United Kingdom and France Following the Adoption," 7 July 2017. https://usun.usmission.gov/joint-press-statement-from-the-permanent-representatives-to-the-united-nations-of-the-united-states-united-kingdom-and-france-following-the-adoption.
7 Reaching Critical Will, "First Committee concludes; views diverge over what progress on disarmament really means," www.reachingcriticalwill.org/news/latestnews/12249-first-committee-concludes-views-divergeover-what-progress-on-disarmament-really-means.
8 For a fuller account see "Approving 18 Drafts on Disarmament Measure, First Committee Urges General Assembly Call for States to Sign Nuclear-Weapon-Ban Treaty," GA/DIS/3590 of 27 October 2017.
9 "Addressing Arms Proliferation Risks, First Committee Approves 26 Texts, Including Draft Promoting Nuclear weapon-free Middle East," GA/DIS/3566 of 1 November 2016.
10 Dell Higgie, Nuclear Weapons Statement by New Zealand, 13 October 2017, www.converge.org.nz/pma/nz-1c13oct17.pdf
11 "Considering the devastation that would be visited upon all mankind by a nuclear war and the consequent need to make every effort to avert the danger of such a war and to take measures to safeguard the security of peoples."
12 Alicia Sanders-Zakre, "US Signals Shift at UN First Committee," *Arms Control Today*, 1 December 2017, www.armscontrol.org/act/2017-12/news/us-signals-shift-un-first-committee.
13 Ibid.

14 Catholic News Service, 11 November 2017. https://catholicherald.co.uk/pope-francis-the-possession-of-nuclear-weapons-should-be-firmly-condemned.
15 David P. Barash, "Nuclear deterrence is a myth. And a lethal one at that," *The Guardian*, 14 January 2018. https://theguardian.com/world/2018/jan/14/nuclear-deterrence-myth-lethal-david-barash.
16 Bernard Brodie, "The Development of Nuclear Strategy," *International Security*, 2:4 (1978): 65–83.
17 US Department of Defense, Nuclear Posture Review, February 2018, https://media.defense.gov/2018/Feb/02/2001872886/-1/-1/1/2018-NUCLEAR-POSTURE-REVIEW-FINAL-REPORT.PDF.
18 John Carlson, "Verifying the elimination of nuclear weapons and providing assurance against breakout," Chapter 28 of this volume.

3

TOWARDS A NUCLEAR RESTRAINT REGIME

From a normative Ban Treaty to a substantive agenda

Manpreet Sethi

Many strategic analysts fear that the Treaty on the Prohibition of Nuclear Weapons (TPNW) could widen the rift between the nuclear-weapon states (NWS) and the non-NWS by stigmatising the nuclear-weapon possessors rather than the weapons. The pertinent questions are therefore how to translate the normative pressure that the treaty poses into something more substantive? Can some measures be identified for the NWS to take, and for the non-NWS to encourage them into taking, to promote its objectives? Can bridges be built between the positions of NWS and non-NWS; and between adversarial nuclear rivals? Can pursuit of the cause of disarmament become inclusive? This chapter argues that the pathway to elimination is as important as the process of elimination itself. It suggests a nuclear restraint regime that addresses many dimensions of nuclear weapons deployment: their role, targets, force postures, types and numbers, and also the circumstances in which they are employed. Each restraint would circumscribe the role of nuclear weapons, and as the circle of their utility becomes smaller, eventual elimination will become possible.

Multilaterally negotiated treaties are never easy to conclude given conflicting interests of nations and the rifts that often exist among stakeholders. However, when they do come into being, they reflect the mood of the member states. The TPNW, popularly called the Ban Treaty, adopted at the United Nations (UN) General Assembly in July 2017 by 122 non-NWS, likewise serves as a barometer of the collective frustration of the latter on their inability to get the NWS to move towards nuclear disarmament.

Unfortunately, the non-NWS had lost any leverage they might have enjoyed in the Nuclear Non-Proliferation Treaty (NPT) to push the NWS in this direction when they agreed to grant the treaty an indefinite and unconditional extension in 1995. The treaty had always been skewed in favour of non-proliferation, which was certainly the primary objective of the USA and USSR when they joined hands

DOI: 10.4324/9781003227502-5

to realise it in the late 1960s. The non-NWS could have used the opportunity of the review and extension conference of the treaty when it turned 25 in 1995 to redress the non-proliferation-disarmament imbalance. But they did not, and the NPT became a permanent non-proliferation mechanism.

With little hope of the NPT ever being able to bring about nuclear disarmament, it is not difficult to understand why many non-NWS found the need to construct another instrument to mount pressure on the issue of disarmament. So, a multilaterally negotiated treaty that prohibits development, testing, production, manufacture, acquisition, transfer, possession, and stockpiling of nuclear weapons, as well as their use or threat of use, was concluded and opened for signature on 20 September 2017. Fifty countries, again all non-nuclear, signed it on the same day. The treaty entered into force 90 days after 50 countries ratified it. The NWS are nowhere on the scene.

The Ban Treaty supporters contend that the intention of the treaty is to exert normative pressure on nuclear-weapon possessors. There are few indications though that any of the nuclear-weapons-possessing states is feeling pressured into rethinking its commitment to nuclear deterrence. In fact, if anything, all of them are engaged in buttressing their nuclear capabilities. Consequently, the world seems to be caught between two camps – those wanting to make nuclear weapons somehow disappear and those asserting the salience of these weapons like never before since the end of the Cold War.

The postponed 2020 NPT Review Conference (RevCon), whenever it is held, could prove to be a clash of the titans when the NWS (entrenched in their nuclear deterrence strategies) and the great majority of the non-NWS (exhilarated by the successful negotiation of the Ban Treaty) come together. Many strategic analysts have expressed apprehension that by widening a rift between the NWS and the non-NWS, the Ban Treaty might have caused harm to the NPT. It could end up breaking the consensus on non-proliferation.[1]

Another way of looking at the Ban Treaty, however, could be to view it as scaffolding for the NPT – to bolster its pillar of disarmament, which seemed to have remained stunted even as the pillar of non-proliferation had shot up substantially, creating thereby a lop-sided structure. Considering the Ban Treaty from this perspective does not create a gap between the two treaties. Rather, it makes the Ban Treaty another additional measure of the non-proliferation and disarmament regime to strengthen an element which had not got the necessary attention within the NPT.

Certainly, in the years to come, the NPT-Ban Treaty dynamic will find its balance. The more critical issue, however, is whether the latter will be able to push the nuclear possessors towards disarmament? Will normative pressure work? This chapter argues that for all its seminal importance in terms of the objective it seeks, the Ban Treaty might end up being only an expression of exasperation of the non-NWS with the current state of nuclear disarmament. For now, it seems to have banned nuclear weapons only for the non-possessors. The major possessors, the USA and Russia, have expressed a rather rigid stand on never joining such a treaty.

In that case, the real intention of the Ban Treaty might never be obtained. If such an outcome is to be avoided, it becomes imperative to identify some measures that the NWS could be encouraged to take – individually, bilaterally or multilaterally – that could create the ground for future elimination of nuclear weapons.

Even though little seems possible in the near term given the contemporary strident positions of major nuclear powers, nevertheless the need for these is clear for two reasons. First, it is important to appreciate that the pathway to elimination is as important as the process of elimination itself. The Ban Treaty seems to have ignored this dimension. As one analyst puts it, the treaty supporters hope to "exploit their power of numbers to attach such a deep stigma to possessing the bomb that the nuclear powers will be shamed into stepping off the nuclear weapons path."[2] This might, however, be the problem. The treaty has ended up stigmatising the weapon possessors, not just the nuclear weapon. In the process, it has created a divide between the two sets of states that makes a conversation difficult.

The lesson to be learnt is that only by following the right measures that enhance security, rather than those that exacerbate insecurities and rifts, will universal nuclear disarmament ever be possible. While the goal of nuclear disarmament is worthy of pursuit, the manner in which it is obtained is even more important for it to become attainable and sustainable. Accordingly, this paper suggests an approach in which each small step that is taken one at a time reinforces the possibility of the next.

Second, history shows that nuclear situations are like shifting landscapes of sand. Apparently intransigent positions could change if, for instance, a leader or two of nuclear-weapons-possessing states were to act like statesmen and take steps to change belief systems on nuclear weapons; or if an untoward nuclear incident were to take place anywhere. In both cases, the global nuclear mood could change quickly. This impermanence of nuclear positions provides the impetus for ideas to be kept ready for sowing when the time appears right.

Elements of a nuclear restraint regime – Preparing the soil for nuclear disarmament

An attempt is made to identify and flesh out some possible elements of a nuclear restraint regime as a first steady step towards eventual nuclear disarmament. While a Nuclear Weapons Convention should be the ultimate goal to achieve verifiable, universal elimination of nuclear weapons, the journey towards it must touch certain milestones that create a set of interlocking mechanisms of better security – a pre-requisite for a nuclear-weapon-free world. All of these should collectively reduce the salience of nuclear weapons and help leach them of their utility in national security strategies.

Restraint on role of nuclear weapons – Narrowing nuclear doctrines

Instead of catering only to nuclear deterrence, or deterrence of the use of nuclear weapons by the adversary, nuclear weapons have acquired multi-role utility over the years. Countries have found them useful for different objectives: to offset conventional military inferiority (Russia and Pakistan); to deter cyber attacks (USA, Russia, France); to guard against regime change (Democratic People's Republic of Korea, DPRK, or North Korea); to retain prestige and status (UK and France); to bargain for economic and security assistance (Pakistan and DPRK); and to deter interference in the conduct of their foreign policy (Russia and China).[3] Success of such strategies has been perceived as enhancing the utility of nuclear weapons beyond their primary purpose of nuclear deterrence. This can only motivate others to reach out for them.

More recently, another dimension of the use of nuclear weapons has re-emerged into prominence. This pertains to the projection of the use of low-yield, even sub-kiloton, weapons to undertake selective targeting as a feasible proposition to inflict "limited" damage. It might be recalled that the USA and the USSR had accumulated large stockpiles of nuclear weapons of different yields with the objective of gaining the advantage in nuclear exchanges. However, many individually and jointly-conducted war games showed that the concept of limited nuclear war with "surgically precise accuracy" was pure folly.

After toying with the idea for nearly two decades, in the late 1980s both sides under the stewardship of Presidents Ronald Reagan and Mikhail Gorbachev accepted the conclusion that achieving success in a limited nuclear war by confining attacks to counterforce targets could only be illusory and downright dangerous since escalation would be difficult to stop. This had closed the chapter on limited nuclear war as a feasible proposition. But the idea has seen a revival in more recent times.

The most recent *Nuclear Posture Review*, brought out by the Trump administration in 2018, asserts "expanding flexible US nuclear options now, to include low yield options."[4] It seeks additional "diversity in platforms, range, and survivability, and a valuable hedge against future nuclear 'break-out' scenarios."[5] The USA argues that it is compelled to take this direction[6] to meet similar projections from Russia which too threatens a strategy of "escalate to de-escalate" in its military doctrine. That might be so. But, individually and collectively, such doctrines enhance the salience of nuclear weapons, making disarmament well-nigh impossible.

Therefore, as a first step towards elimination of nuclear weapons, it is necessary to undertake some redrafting of nuclear doctrines to reduce their role to nuclear deterrence alone given that their high destruction potential makes their "limited" use unthinkable for any rational political end. The more usable the weapon is made to appear, the greater the value that gets ascribed to it and the more attractive it appears. In such circumstances, vertical and horizontal proliferation cannot be stopped. The role of the nuclear weapon must be circumscribed to dealing with only extreme circumstances. Restricted to a very limited utility, over a period of time, it would be possible to remove it from national arsenals.

Restraint on threats to non-NWS – Extending negative security assurances

It was to reduce the attraction of nuclear weapons as a strategic equaliser and to dissuade non-NWS from acquiring these that the concept of negative security assurances (NSA) to the non-NWS parties to the NPT had first developed in the late 1970s. Under such an NSA, the NWS were to provide an assurance or a guarantee to non-NWS that they would not use or threaten to use nuclear weapons as instruments of pressure, intimidation or blackmail against them. However, none of the five NWS (as recognised by the NPT) has actually made these assurances available unconditionally without any qualification, or as part of a binding legal agreement. Nearly all, in fact, maintain the right to use nuclear weapons to respond to attacks by a non-NWS in alliance or in association with other NWS.

In an attempt to take the idea forward, the 2010 NPT RevCon called upon the Conference on Disarmament (CD) to "discuss substantively, without limitation, in order to elaborate recommendations, including an internationally legally binding instrument" for extending legally recognised negative security assurances to non-NWS. However, except for reaffirming a discussion on the subject as part of the agenda of the CD,[7] no real progress on this front has been achieved.

Meanwhile, positive security assurances, or the guarantee that other NWS would come to the assistance of a state under nuclear attack, have been held out on the basis of alliance systems. Extended nuclear deterrence was the assurance to the allies of protection under the nuclear umbrella of an NWS. This was again to dissuade them from building their own nuclear weapons. NSAs and extended deterrence were, therefore, tools of non-proliferation.

Both these two assurances, if extended by NWS through some form of legally binding agreement, could make this non-proliferation measure a helpful step towards disarmament since it would drastically reduce the attractiveness of nuclear weapons for non-NWS and also foster a greater sense of security. Therefore, negative security assurances could provide credible guarantees of non-use of nuclear weapons against non-NWS and prove to be a far more useful step towards eventual elimination of nuclear weapons. It would help restrict the number of targets against which nuclear weapons could be used, circumscribing thereby their area of influence.

Restraint on Threats to NWS – Accepting no first use of nuclear weapons

While security assurances to the non-NWS would significantly reduce the attraction of nuclear weapons, an acceptance of no first use (NFU) by nuclear-weapon possessors would further remove the possibility of nuclear exchange between NWS too.[8] In fact, adoption of NFU would be a crucial step towards the eventual elimination of nuclear weapons since it would involve an assurance from every country that it would not be the first to introduce nuclear weapons into a conflict. Since there will no first user, it would in effect mean no use of nuclear weapons and hence, a reduced dependence on the weapon in national security strategies over a period of time.

More comprehensively, an NFU approach brings many advantageous restraints on nuclear weapons. First of all, the arsenal requirements of a state with an NFU are drastically reduced. Naturally, a country that professes first use of nuclear weapons can only look credible if it has the requisite first strike capability – a large nuclear arsenal, accurate and MIRVed missiles, and an elaborate command and control structure, including a certain pre-delegation of authority to maintain a high level of readiness for first use. An NFU arsenal, on the other hand, must only be capable of assured retaliation to cause unacceptable damage. This can be well carried out even with relatively fewer accurate missiles. Neither does the command and control structure have to be elaborate enough to co-ordinate the logistics of a large first strike over many targets. The arsenal must only be survivable to be able to launch a counterstrike.

Secondly, with a no first use doctrine, the decision maker in charge of authorising nuclear use is freed of the psychological burden of having to make the momentous decision that would vaporise millions in minutes. Since every nuclear-armed state today has a secure second-strike capability that rules out the possibility of a decapitating or a disarming first strike, no country that uses nuclear weapons first can hope to escape nuclear retaliation. Once this happens, the first user cannot hope to come out looking better even after its first use of nuclear weapons. Rather, the first use might well turn out to be suicidal, besides imposing on it the stigma of breaking a taboo on non-use of nuclear weapons which has a fairly sacrosanct status today. In such a situation then, where the military and political utility of nuclear weapons appears doubtful, even negative, the only rational purpose of these weapons can be deterrence of nuclear use. And, an NFU doctrine performs the task of deterrence most effectively, and entails least risk.

Thirdly, NFU allows a restrained force posture. Doctrines that ascribe a war-fighting role to nuclear weapons envisage 'first use' to retain the military advantage and, therefore, adopt launch-on-warning or launch-under-attack postures. A pre-emption capability requires a large infrastructure in the form of command and control, early warning, etc. NFU, on the other hand, frees the nation of such requirements. It allows for greater response time for self and a more relaxed posture for the adversary since he is liberated from the 'use or lose' syndrome.

Another advantage of NFU is that it would allow the NWS to retain the notional sense of security that they derive from their nuclear arsenals. They would still be able to keep their nuclear weapons if abandoning them looks too big a leap to take. But pledging not to use them first would gradually lessen the desire to improve an unusable weapon, making it easier to give it up.

Overall then, NFU has the potential to lessen inter-state tensions, increase mutual confidence and thus reinforce a cycle of positives. It would enhance the inclination towards non-proliferation by sending a strong signal of the diminishing utility of nuclear weapons. It would also lessen the drive of each NWS for new and modernised nuclear arsenals and thus lower interstate insecurities. Therefore, this step would work towards enhancing the gradual irrelevance of the nuclear weapon, especially when reinforced by a ban on use or threat of use of the weapon, quite as on the pattern and experience of the 1925 Geneva Convention.

One question, however, needs examination when one considers the decision to accept no first use of nuclear weapons. Would a decision/treaty that bans the first use of nuclear weapons lead to an arms race in conventional armaments in order to bridge a perceived security deficit? While there are no empirical studies on the subject, it well might be the case that in the short term, countries divesting themselves of nuclear weapons might lean towards greater conventional acquisitions. However, this trend is unlikely to last if nuclear disarmament is either the result of or results in more co-operative and secure inter-state relations. Hence, the possible spurt in conventional modernisation could subside over a period of time. This trend could be further encouraged by a parallel process of conventional arms control akin to the Treaty on Conventional Armed Forces in Europe model.[9]

Parallel agreements that provide means to control a conventional arms race would ease the pathway to nuclear disarmament and especially help address the second, and far thornier, question of how one could get countries like North Korea or Pakistan that perceive their nuclear weapons as 'strategic equalisers' or potent bargaining chips to prescribe to NFU. Acceptance of NFU goes against the purpose of their national nuclear arsenals.

However, a case for convincing/compelling states to accept a universal NFU can be made on three grounds:

- First, an international consensus on and acceptance of NFU will put pressure on such countries and a united approach could provide the necessary firmness to the international community to deal with holdouts.
- Second, it is a well-known fact established on the basis of elaborate war gaming exercises that a weaker military power can never come out better after the first use of nuclear weapons against another nuclear state. Therefore, first use against a nuclear adversary that also happens to have superior conventional and substantive nuclear capability is nothing short of suicidal for the first user. The admittance of this reality would demonstrate the futility of retaining a first use posture.
- Third, when the NFU is accompanied with comprehensive security assurances, and conventional arms control, it should significantly lower threat perceptions of these nations.

Currently, China and India are the only countries with NFU doctrines. In order to kick-start a process towards the universalisation of NFU, a first step might be taken by the two to formalise their own commitment into a bilateral agreement and offer that as a template to others. While this appears difficult at the present juncture owing to China's reluctance to accept India's nuclear weapons status, this nevertheless is a reality that Beijing cannot shy away from. Given the strident language used in the US 2018 *Nuclear Posture Review* and the equally aggressive response of President Vladimir Putin in seeking an "invincible" nuclear arsenal, it looks clear that both these countries that had long provided the example and anchor on strategic stability are unlikely to shoulder this responsibility for some time.

In this moment then, China and India are the only two countries whose nuclear doctrines are premised on the sensible concepts of minimum deterrence and use of nuclear weapons for retaliation only. They would do themselves and the world a service if they could come together to formalise this commitment and set a worthy example on restraint of use of nuclear weapons against other NWS.

Restraint on force posture – Formalising low alert levels

Acceptance of NFU enables nations to keep their arsenals in a restrained force posture. This makes it possible for them to undertake de-alerting, de-mating and de-targeting, all three steps that are critical for reducing dangers that accompany nuclear weapons. These steps could significantly reduce the high risk of unintentional or accidental use of nuclear weapons. In fact, a de-alerted and de-mated nuclear arsenal provides for a 'graduated deterrence' response thereby allowing more time to resolve the crisis before nations move towards a state of full alert. This again could significantly transform the mood and optics of nuclear weapons and help reduce their salience.

Restraint on employment of nuclear weapons – Prohibiting their use or threat of use

As stated earlier, the Ban Treaty prohibits not only the development, testing, production, manufacture, acquisition, transfer, possession, and stockpiling of nuclear weapons, but also their use or threat of use. These prohibitions, however, are applicable only to the parties to the treaty. Since NWS have not shown any inclination to accept the treaty, ways still need to be found for the NWS to accept a prohibition on use or threat of nuclear weapons. This intention is encapsulated in a Resolution entitled "Convention on the Prohibition of the Use of Nuclear Weapons" that India has annually tabled at the UN General Assembly since 1982.[10] The resolution aims at prohibiting the use or threat of use of nuclear weapons under any circumstances, a step that can substantially reduce the prospect of nuclear use and contribute towards the creation of a climate for a subsequent agreement on the prohibition of nuclear weapons *in toto*.

In case all NWS were to commit under a legal instrument that nuclear weapons shall not be used and that any country using them or threatening to use them shall face commensurate retribution and a total boycott by all the countries of the world, it would make these weapons of mass destruction impotent and useless. None would want to acquire weapons that could not be used in war, and hence not as a deterrent either. Consequently, the unique status that nuclear weapons are deemed to provide would no longer seem worth aspiring for.

A convention banning nuclear use, in fact, would send an important signal to all concerned constituencies – it would devalue the weapon substantially as a currency of power and status; it would reduce the likelihood of a nuclear exchange between NWS; it would reassure the non-NWS and reduce their temptation to acquire these weapons for deterrence; it would reinforce the taboo against nuclear use and this would influence non-state actors too.

Recommendations

In 1988 India's Prime Minister Rajiv Gandhi had said:

> Humanity is at a crossroads. One road will take us like lemmings to our suicide. That is the path indicated by doctrines of nuclear deterrence, deriving from traditional concepts of the balance of power. The other road will give us another chance. That is the path signposted by the doctrine of peaceful coexistence, deriving from the imperative values of non-violence, tolerance and compassion.[11]

More than three decades after that statement, we seem to be poised at the same juncture. One could consider this as fortunate since we have not yet blown ourselves up in a nuclear holocaust. But it is unfortunate too that we continue to flirt with nuclear dangers, which have only grown in dimension and become more sinister since then.

Today we inhabit a world where far more numbers of states have nuclear weapons; where nuclear modernisation is taking place in times of strident nationalism; where nuclear possessors speak of nuclear "fire and fury" in a rather cavalier fashion; where the possibility of nonstate actors acquiring nuclear material or weapons for terrorism, either with or without state complicity have multiplied; and where interstate relations are mired in mutual mistrust.

In some sense, the Ban Treaty has responded to the need of the times. But its bane might be the manner in which it has outlawed nuclear weapons without preparing the necessary ground for inclusion of NWS. One can argue that the nuclear possessors were showing no propensity to do so. Indeed, that would be true. But to conclude a treaty without their participation cannot be of much use either. It might have driven the wedge between the two classes of states even deeper.

It is now contingent upon the right-thinking constituencies on both sides to build bridges. Engaging the NWS to conclude some of the steps identified in the paper could result in a start towards elimination of nuclear weapons. A nuclear-weapon-free world cannot appear overnight. Nuclear deterrence has taken deep roots over seven decades. It will need more than just a ban to get nations to give them up. It will need a change in belief systems behind their utility.

A nuclear restraint regime that restricts the role, circumstances of their use, and posture of deploying nuclear weapons can offer a viable pathway to their elimination. Steps will need to be taken one at a time – each reinforcing the other to build a sense of security, and encouraging further movement towards nuclear disarmament. Only thus can the idea of the normative, as exemplified by the Ban Treaty, be turned into a substantive method for realising the noble intention of the treaty.

Notes

1 See for instance, Paul Meyer, "The Nuclear Non-Proliferation Treaty: Fin de Regime?," *Arms Control Today*, April 2017, 16.
2 Ramesh Thakur, "The Nuclear Ban Treaty: Recasting a Normative Framework for Disarmament," *The Washington Quarterly*, 40:4 (2018), 81.
3 India does not fit into any of these since its doctrine describes nuclear weapons use only for nuclear deterrence while Israel looks at them to deal with existential threats. In the above cases I was looking at utilities other than just nuclear deterrence, which is why these two countries are not mentioned.
4 *Nuclear Posture Review* (Washington DC: Office of the Secretary of Defense, February 2018), xii.
5 Ibid.
6 It is rather interesting to recall that the US representative to the UN in 1956 had responded to an appeal for an agreement on cessation of nuclear testing by India's Defence Minister Krishna Menon by saying: "The simple fact is that in the absence of arms control and in the face of constant new developments, a wide variety of weapons is required to provide the versatility and flexibility essential to defend against aggression whenever, wherever and however it may occur." J. P. Morray, *From Yalta to Disarmament: Cold War Debate* (New York: MR Press, 1961), 267. The US perceives similar threats to its security 60 years later!
7 The topic of negative security assurances first entered the CD agenda in 1979. Nearly, four decades later that is still where it stays.
8 At present, only two countries – India and China – accept NFU. China's NFU, however, does not apply to its own territory or territories that it claims as its own. Hence, there is ambiguity regarding the possibility of Chinese nuclear weapons in a conflict over Taiwan, or Arunachal Pradesh, an Indian state to which China lays claim. Meanwhile, the Indian NFU which had been unconditional as spelt out in the draft nuclear doctrine presented to the government on 17 August 1999 by the first National Security Advisory Board has since been somewhat diluted by a Cabinet Committee on Security note on operationalisation of the doctrine put forth on 4 January 2003 and which does not rule out India's nuclear use against a chemical or biological weapon attack.
9 The author is grateful to late Air Commodore Jasjit Singh, Director, Centre for Air Power Studies, for bringing out this point in a private conversation. It might also be recalled that the Rajiv Gandhi Action Plan of 1988 too had catered for simultaneous reduction in conventional weaponry as a means of moving towards a nuclear-free and non-violent world order. The full text of the Action Plan for Ushering in a Nuclear Weapon Free and Non-violent World Order is available as Appendix 2 in *Towards a Nuclear Weapon Free World*, edited by Manpreet Sethi (New Delhi: Knowledge World, 2009): 151–56. Such a comprehensive approach was also envisaged in Article 6 of the NPT.
10 UN General Assembly Resolution 63/75 (L.15), 2 December 2008.
11 Rajiv Gandhi, "A World Free of Nuclear Weapons," Speech accompanying the submission of Action Plan for Ushering in a Nuclear Weapon Free and Non-violent World Order at the Third Special Session on Disarmament of UN General Assembly, 9 June 1988. For full text of speech, see *Towards a Nuclear Weapon Free World*, edited by Manpreet Sethi (New Delhi: Knowledge World, 2009): 141–49.

4

DOES THE TPNW CONTRADICT OR UNDERMINE THE NPT?

Tariq Rauf

The Treaty on the Prohibition of Nuclear Weapons (TPNW) unnecessarily has become a bitter bone of contention between the non-nuclear-weapon states (NNWS) supporting this treaty and most of the nuclear-armed states and US allies in defence arrangements underpinned by US nuclear weapons. The opponents of the TPNW have raised a number of concerns and shortcomings[1] relating to the TPNW. This short paper responds to eight of the most common of these.

First, some critics claim that the TPNW does not define a nuclear weapon. This is correct, it does not – but neither does the Nuclear Non-Proliferation Treaty (NPT). Nor do four of the five nuclear-weapon-free zone (NWFZ) treaties; only the Treaty of Tlateloloco covering Latin America has a definition (Article 5).

Second, others complain that the TPNW does not constitute an "effective measure" for nuclear disarmament under the NPT (Article 6). In reality, the TPNW is an effective measure as called for in NPT Article 6 on nuclear disarmament, in parallel with the 1996 Comprehensive Nuclear-Test-Ban Treaty (CTBT), the bilateral USSR/Russia–US treaties such as 2010 New START and the 1987 Intermediate-Range Nuclear Forces Treaty (INF) even though these were concluded for national security not NPT reasons; and the five NWFZ treaties operational in Latin America and the Caribbean, South Pacific, Southeast Asia, Africa and Central Asia. The NPT is not a self-implementing treaty, it requires enabling actions, for example, safeguards agreements by NNWS with the International Atomic Energy Agency (IAEA) to verify non-proliferation commitments under Articles II and III of the NPT. Similarly, NWFZ treaties are required to implement Article VII, while nuclear co-operation agreements are needed to implement Article IV of the NPT on peaceful uses of nuclear energy.

A third criticism is that the TPNW does not include the latest IAEA safeguards (Additional Protocol). To be precise, Article 3 of the TPNW stipulates that each NNWS party "shall, at a minimum, maintain its [IAEA] safeguards obligations in

DOI: 10.4324/9781003227502-6

force at the time of entry into force of this Treaty, without prejudice to any additional relevant instruments that it may adopt in the future." It is indeed unfortunate that the IAEA's Board of Governors has been unable to agree to make the 1997 Model Additional Protocol (AP)(INFCIRC/540) an essential component of the IAEA NPT comprehensive safeguards agreement (INFCIRC/153) for NNWS, and the IAEA General Conference in its annual safeguards resolution[2] has said that "it is the sovereign decision of any State to conclude an additional protocol." That notwithstanding, the TPNW does require adhering NNWS to maintain, as a minimum, their existing safeguards agreements and provides for further strengthened safeguards. Thus for the 80 percent of NNWS[3] with APs in force, the TPNW secures the current de facto standard of non-proliferation verification, which is higher than the one stipulated by the NPT.

Fourth, some critics claim that the TPNW does not include verification of nuclear disarmament. This is correct, but neither the NPT nor NWFZ treaties include the technical details of verification. This is left to the "Agency's [IAEA] safeguards system"[4] in reality. The IAEA collaboratively with its member states during 1970–71 drew up comprehensive safeguards (INFCIRC/153) after the entry into force in 1970 of the NPT; and the Additional Protocol (INFCIRC/540) during 1993–97. TPNW/IAEA states, at the first meeting of states parties to be convened in Vienna in March 2022, should invite the IAEA to set up a technical working group to develop verification approaches and to this end sponsor a resolution at the next IAEA General Conference. Unlike the 1972 Biological Weapons Convention that has acquired customary international law status and has no provisions for verification, the TPNW does in fact stipulate an approach to verification.

A fifth criticism is that the TPNW is inconsistent as it allows for states with nuclear weapons to adhere to it and it also allows states to join that had nuclear weapons but have disarmed. It is instructive to recall that the Chemical Weapons Convention (CWC) allows both declared chemical weapon possessor states as well as those that have previously destroyed their chemical weapons stocks to adhere to the CWC. The TPNW follows a similar logic. States with nuclear weapons can adhere to the TPNW and then proceed to verifiably destroy them under auspices of a competent international authority to be designated by states parties.

Another criticism is that the TPNW "demonstrates that there is no legal norm on non-possession of nuclear weapons." One of the purposes of the TPNW is to establish a legal norm against the possession of nuclear weapons,[5] much along the lines of the two existing conventions outlawing biological and chemical weapons.

Seventh, it is alleged that the TPNW will establish a "competitor regime to the NPT" and may entice "defections from the NPT."[6] The Treaty of Tlatelolco was the first to "prohibit" nuclear weapons in its zone of application, a year before the NPT was negotiated. The subsequent four NWFZ treaties renounce nuclear weapons, but none is regarded as a competitor or an alternative to the NPT. Rather, they are considered as complementary. Moreover, it is spectacularly illogical to suggest that a TPNW state party could "defect" from the NPT to "shirk"[7] its non-proliferation obligations because, as already noted above, the TPNW itself requires each state party to "at a minimum, maintain its International Atomic Energy Agency safeguards obligations in force at the time of entry into force of this Treaty, without prejudice to any additional relevant instruments that it may adopt in the future" (Article 3).

Finally, critics claim that the TPNW would "delegitimise extended deterrence alliance relationships" and thus incentivise alliance NNWS to develop indigenous nuclear weapon programs. Such a claim calls into question the integrity and commitment of alliance NNWS to the NPT and suggests that their non-proliferation credentials might be suspect, as their fealty to the NPT is only because of reliance on extended nuclear deterrence. This sounds suspiciously like a case of "having one's cake and eating it too." To benefit from nuclear weapons, including in cases where such weapons are stationed on their territory, without actual possession, and also to preach non-proliferation to other NNWS, in effect contributes to undermining trust in the-NPT.

To conclude, it is abundantly clear that the TPNW already has created a prohibition of nuclear weapons, under customary international law, when it entered into force on 22 January 2021 as 50 signatory states had ratified it. As such, it has established a *jus cogens* rule creating an *erga omnes* not only for all NPT states parties but for other nuclear-armed states as well.

Notes

1 Tariq Rauf, "Nuclear-armed States Panic as Nuclear Weapons Prohibition Treaty becomes International Law," *Atomic Reporters*, 26 October 2020, www.atomicreporters.com/2020/10/nuclear-armed-states-panic-as-nuclear-weapons-prohibition-treaty-becomes-international-law.
2 IAEA, "Strengthening the Effectiveness and Improving the Efficiency of Agency Safeguards," GC(64) RES/13, September 2020, www.iaea.org/sites/default/files/gc/gc64-res13.pdf.
3 Adem Mutluer, IAEA Safeguards Now Applied in 183 States Worldwide – Safeguards Statement 2019, IAEA, 26 June 2020, www.iaea.org/newscenter/news/iaea-safeguards-now-applied-in-183-states-worldwide-safeguards-statement-2019.
4 Pierre Goldschmidt, "The IAEA Safeguards System Moves into the 21st Century," Supplement to the *IAEA Bulletin*, 41:4 (2019), www.iaea.org/sites/default/files/41403450122su.pdf.
5 Gro Nystuen, Kjolv Egeland and Torbjørn Graff Hugo, "The TPNW: Setting the Record Straight," Norwegian Academy of International Law, October 2018. http://intlaw.no/wp-content/uploads/2018/10/TPNW-Setting-the-record-straight-Oct-2018-WEB.pdf.
6 Christopher A. Ford, "Responding to the 'Ban'", Remarks to the Carnegie Endowment for International Peace, 22 August 2017, https://carnegieendowment.org/files/Ford_CEIP%20Ban%20Treaty%20Remarks%208-22-17.pdf.
7 Ibid.

5

HARMONISING THE NPT AND BAN TREATY IN NUCLEAR RISK REDUCTION MEASURES

Rakesh Sood

The international community has sought to address the challenges of nuclear risks that have existed since the beginning of the nuclear age by expressing abhorrence at the thought of nuclear weapons being used again. These efforts have ensured that the nuclear taboo has held and despite conflicts involving nuclear weapon states or their allies, nuclear weapons have not been used. With the return of inter-state strategic competition among major powers, technological developments and the shift of the geopolitical centre of gravity to the Indo-Pacific, the world is witnessing an age of nuclear asymmetry and a shift towards more usable nuclear weapons. Bilateral arms control no longer seems possible and among the multilateral instruments, the nuclear Non-Proliferation Treaty (NPT) has exhausted its normative potential while the Treaty on the Prohibition of Nuclear Weapons (TPNW) is yet to gain the desired political legitimacy and authority. Today's challenge is to ensure that both co-exist, without one weakening the other while incremental steps are taken to maintain the nuclear taboo until such time as nuclear threats are indeed eliminated by all possessor states, including those not party to the NPT.

In January 2018 the Doomsday Clock was moved forward by thirty seconds to two minutes to midnight, the point symbolising nuclear annihilation. This decision was announced by the Science and Security Board of the *Bulletin of the Atomic Scientists* on 25 January, citing a range of growing nuclear threats.[1] The last time it had been as close to midnight was in 1953, during the Cold War when both the USA and USSR had demonstrated thermonuclear capability. More revealing is the fact that in 2010, the Doomsday Clock stood at six minutes to midnight but during the past eight years, has inexorably inched closer.

The Board highlighted that the resetting of the Doomsday Clock should be seen as an urgent warning that the world leaders need to address the growing nuclear danger (as well as the existential threat posed by climate change) because the risk

DOI: 10.4324/9781003227502-7

that nuclear weapons might be used, either intentionally or on account of miscalculation, has risen during 2017. The *Bulletin*'s Science and Stability Board is not alone in raising concerns about growing nuclear risks.

Before venturing any further, it is necessary to restate one fundamental truth that has been evident since the nuclear age dawned in 1945. Nuclear weapons are immensely destructive and any use would be catastrophic; as long as some countries retain these weapons, other countries will have a justification to acquire them for their security; as long as nuclear weapons exist, it is likely they will be used again; and, therefore, the only lasting guarantee against their use is global elimination.[2]

Since this axiom is not universally accepted, the international community is obliged to grapple with the second-best option, namely, reducing the risk of use of nuclear weapons. This chapter is divided into three parts – assessing the growing risks; previous experience of managing them; and finally, examining possible measures in the contemporary nuclear age.

Growing nuclear risks

If the Cold War defined the first nuclear age, today we are living in a new nuclear age in which a range of both old and new threats co-exist. A nuclear exchange between the USA and the USSR escalating into mutual annihilation was the dominant threat during the first nuclear age. This receded during the second nuclear age but has made a comeback. Global terrorism and proliferation were the primary risks during the second nuclear age. These have not diminished. In addition, however, new technological developments are blurring the dividing line between conventional and nuclear weapons and nuclear frontiers have expanded to outer space and cyberspace.

Nuclear risks today can be divided into four categories:

1. Geopolitical rivalries have returned, raising the risk of premeditated nuclear exchange.
2. Lack of communications between different nuclear rival states has raised the risks of escalation. In the absence of clear red lines, the firebreak between conventional and nuclear weapons is being eroded.
3. The risk of miscalculation existed even during the first nuclear age and has been well documented.[3] Today, with compressed timelines and dependence on space-based and cyber assets, which can be tampered with, the risks of a system malfunction, rogue launch and miscalculation are much higher.
4. The risk of a global terrorist group acquiring a nuclear device has been partially addressed with improvements in nuclear security practices but it has not disappeared.

The USA came out with a National Security Strategy in December 2017, followed by a National Defense Strategy and in February 2018, the *Nuclear Posture Review* (NPR). These documents highlight a return to inter-state strategic competition, identify Russia and China as revisionist rivals and also broaden the role of nuclear weapons in US national security strategy. Had the 2018 NPR been released earlier, it is possible that the Science and Security Board of the *Bulletin* might even have been compelled to move the Doomsday Clock closer than two minutes to midnight. The new NPR adds to concerns because it reverses a number of key principles from the previous NPRs commissioned by Presidents Bill Clinton (1994), George W. Bush (2002) and Barack Obama (2010).

The most significant is a reversal of the assessment that since the end of the Cold War, the USA no longer faced the threat of extinction from Soviet nuclear weapons and was therefore able to reduce the role of nuclear weapons in its security calculus. The 2018 NPR declares that global threat conditions have worsened, "including increasingly explicit threats from potential adversaries."[4] Another development has been President Donald Trump's decision that the USA be ready to conduct a nuclear test at short notice, within six months of a decision.[5] Consequently, a 30-year modernisation plan has been announced with a price tag of $1.2 trillion that could rise to as much as $1.7 trillion.

The USA is not the only one thinking of modernisation though details of programs of other states that have nuclear weapons are less explicit. After the 1999 Kosovo war, Russia began to reconsider its approach to nuclear weapons because of technological asymmetry vis-à-vis US conventional capabilities. This led to the evolution of "escalate to de-escalate" doctrine,[6] indicating an increased reliance on nuclear weapons (escalation) with a view to bringing about a resolution of the dispute (de-escalation) on terms favourable to Russia. Subsequently, Russia began to modernise its nuclear arsenal while also undertaking improvements in its conventional capabilities. In a speech to the Russian parliament on 1 March 2018 President Vladimir Putin talked of five new weapons systems that can evade US interception capabilities.[7]

China too is undertaking a nuclear modernisation but geared more to ensuring mobility and survivability for its land-based forces, stealth capability for its bomber aircraft, quieter submarines and replacing liquid fuelled missiles by solid fuelled engines. China claims that its modernisation is intended to ensure its second-strike capabilities.

India is making steady progress towards operationalising its triad of land, sea and air-based platforms. In graduating to "full spectrum deterrence" with the introduction of tactical nuclear weapons, Pakistan has the fastest growing nuclear weapons program. Another source of growing risk is the increasingly shrill rhetoric between the leaders of the USA and the Democratic People's Republic of Korea (DPRK or North Korea). Trump has also put the nuclear deal with Iran – the Joint Comprehensive Plan of Action – on notice, unless it is tightened to cover other activity such as missile testing and regional behaviour.

Experience of managing risks

The international community has sought to manage nuclear risks since 1945. Though disarmament was the stated objective of many of the initiatives taken, it has not eliminated nuclear weapons. Nevertheless, the nuclear taboo has stood since 1945, whether because of human wisdom or sheer good luck, or a combination of both.

One key element of nuclear management has been arms control. The USA and USSR (now Russia) have traditionally accounted for over 90 percent of global nuclear stockpiles which peaked in the 1980s at some 65,000. Today, global stockpiles have come down to nearly 15,000 warheads, of which the USA and Russia account for about 13,800. The UK, France and China have between 200 and 300 each, India and Pakistan 100 and 130 each, Israel fewer than 100 and the DPRK could possess between 10 and 60 devices. So, while the number of states possessing nuclear weapons has gone up to nine, the global stockpile has come down to a fourth from the peak in 1980s. The bilateral arms control process, responsible for the dramatic reduction in 'global' stockpiles, has however ground to a halt.

Complementing the bilateral arms control track were multilateral negotiations with the stated aim of nuclear disarmament. The United Nations (UN) was created in 1945 and the very first resolution[8] adopted by the General Assembly on 24 January 1946 declared that atomic energy should be used only for peaceful purposes and atomic weapons should be eliminated. Though the UN has been unsuccessful in registering progress towards this objective, it remains the global platform for reminding the international community about the persisting challenge.

The NPT, negotiated in the mid-1960s and opened for signature on 1 July 1968 is the most widely adhered to arms control treaty with 190 states parties. India, Pakistan and Israel never joined it while the DPRK withdrew from the NPT in 2003. The four are nuclear-armed states, unlikely to disarm unilaterally to join the NPT that acknowledges only five countries [9] as nuclear weapon states (NWS) as they exploded a nuclear explosive device before 1 January 1967. In other words, the definition of an NWS is chronological – when the first test was conducted – and not empirical – possession of the bomb. This has created a strategic disjuncture between legal fiction and 'facts on the ground'. The other remaining non-party, South Sudan, has recently emerged as an independent state and might well accede to the NPT in due course.

Article 6 of the NPT obliges all parties to pursue negotiations "in good faith on effective measures relating to cessation of the nuclear arms race at an early date and to nuclear disarmament, and on a treaty on general and complete disarmament under strict and effective international control." These negotiations never happened and even some of the most die-hard loyalists of the NPT must acknowledge that these are unlikely. Article 6 is therefore destined to remain an unfulfilled obligation.

During discussions at the five-yearly NPT review conferences, the USA and Russia point to the reductions in their nuclear arsenals undertaken bilaterally as proof of their good intentions while the other three NWS parties to the NPT (the UK, France and China) reaffirm their commitment to join the process once the US and Russian arsenals come down to levels comparable to theirs.

The NPT had a 25-year life, after which the NPT parties were to decide "whether the Treaty shall continue in force indefinitely, or shall be extended for an additional fixed period or periods." At the 1995 conference, the NPT was extended indefinitely and unconditionally. Complementing this were other decisions relating to future treaties banning nuclear tests (Comprehensive Nuclear-Test-Ban Treaty – CTBT), production of fissile materials (Fissile Material Cut-off Treaty – FMCT), strengthening of the NPT review process and establishing a zone free of nuclear and other weapons of mass destruction (WMD) and their delivery systems in the Middle East.

A CTBT was negotiated and in 1996, opened for signature but has yet to enter into force. To do so it needs 44 countries (specified in the Annex 2 of the Treaty) to sign and ratify it, but eight out of the 44 countries have not done so. Of these, five are signatories (China, Egypt, Iran, Israel and the US) and the other three (the DPRK, India and Pakistan) have not signed it. Given the Trump administration's decision to increase readiness levels to be able to resume testing at Nevada, continued testing by the DPRK, and growing tensions in the Middle East, it is highly unlikely that the CTBT will ever enter into force with the existing provisions of Article 14 relating to Entry into Force. The other elements (the FMCT, a strengthened NPT review process and a WMD-free zone in the Middle East) have met the same fate as the Article 6 obligation pertaining to nuclear disarmament in the NPT.

Reducing nuclear risks by establishing nuclear-weapon-free zones (NWFZs) has been tried where agreements among the states of the region were feasible. This enables the geographical delimitation of the zone within which developing, testing, stationing, storing, and use of nuclear weapons are prohibited. The N5 – the NPT-recognised five NWS – undertake to respect the decision by signing a protocol. Currently, there are five such zones in existence covering Latin America and the Caribbean, South East Asia, Africa, the South Pacific and Central Asia. In addition, in 2000, Mongolia declared itself to be an NWFZ unilaterally. The NWFZ approach cannot go any further given that North America, Europe, North East Asia, South Asia and the Middle East are host to nuclear weapons.

Negative security assurances (NSAs) are a unilateral declaratory guarantee by an NWS that it will not use or threaten to use nuclear weapons against a state that does not have nuclear weapons. These are a complement to positive security assurances – that oblige a country to come to the assistance of its military allies. During the Cold War, NSAs were seen as an important assurance to nonaligned, non-NWS to encourage them to adhere to the NPT. Attempts to convert these into a negotiated legally binding treaty obligation in the Conference on Disarmament (CD) have failed.

The optimism that the end of the Cold War might lead to decisive steps towards nuclear disarmament soon evaporated and catalysed the humanitarian approach beginning with the reference to the International Court of Justice (ICJ) in 1990s. The 1996 ICJ opinion failed to impart any momentum and in 2012, there was a renewed push towards mobilising support for nuclear disarmament on the basis of a shared global concern arising out of the humanitarian consequences of nuclear weapons use. This led to negotiations last year in a multilateral conference convened under the aegis of the UN, resulting in the TPNW.

The TPNW was opened for signature on 20 September 2017, and, to date, 57 countries have signed and five have ratified it. [10]It will enter into force with 50 ratifications. The treaty prohibits the development, testing, production, possession, use and threat of use and stationing of nuclear weapons by a state party. So far only countries that do not have nuclear weapons and are not part of a military alliance with an NWS have signed on to the treaty. Supporters of the TPNW claim that the normative impact will gradually take hold and delegitimise nuclear weapons. Since these countries are also parties to the NPT, they maintain that it complements the NPT.

It is too early to judge the impact of the TPNW in terms of whether it will succeed in reducing the risks of nuclear use, given that all nine states possessing nuclear weapons have rejected it. The N5 members of the NPT have cautioned (in varying degrees) that the TPNW should not weaken the NPT. This is the first new development in the nuclear field which has the potential to significantly change the security calculus and demolish the myths that have come to surround nuclear weapons and deterrence theories. And this is why the NWS do not like the TPNW. There are tensions between the NPT and the TPNW and depending on how these tensions are handled, there are three possible scenarios in which this can play out.

One scenario is that either the 122 states that have supported the TPNW capitulate and revert to the status quo ante. This means that the ratification process slows down and the entry into force of the TPNW gets progressively delayed. Alternatively, the NWS can have an epiphany and decide to accept the TPNW. However, both are unlikely outcomes because the 122 TPNW supporting states have sufficient numbers to maintain the political momentum and an epiphany is unlikely.

Another scenario is about a growing shrillness in the debates between the NWS and the 122 TPNW supporting states, particularly in the run up to the NPT PrepCom meetings leading to the 2020 Review Conference. The NWS would keep the focus on non-proliferation while the 122 countries, all of whom are NPT parties in good standing, would highlight the growing nuclear risks. What would such a face-off imply for the NPT? More specifically, how credible and serious is the risk of mass defection from the NPT by an increasingly alienated cohort of states who come to believe, as has been suggested, that with the continuing failure to disarm by the NWS, mass defection would not only be legally correct but also the ethically responsible course of action?[11]

A third scenario would be to acknowledge the limitations of the NPT in addressing the risks facing the international community today while emphasising that the NPT has been largely, although not totally, successful in curbing proliferation. The twofold political challenge is first to retain the non-proliferation regime of the NPT while building up the moral authority of the TPNW; and second to bring the non-NPT possessor states inside the nuclear restraint regime tent. This requires a new approach which eschews moral censure and finger-pointing by and at the NWS, the TPNW supporters, and the non-NPT nuclear-armed states; helps to reduce nuclear risk; and at the same time, strengthens the taboo against nuclear weapons use that has held since 1945.

Learning the right lessons

How far can these diplomatic and political instruments, that evolved over seven decades, serve the purpose of ensuring nuclear stability and maintaining the taboo against nuclear use in the new nuclear age? This merits an appreciation of the shift in the strategic landscape.

During the first nuclear age, the Cold War dynamic dictated that strategic stability depended upon nuclear stability between the USA and USSR. As strategic thinkers in both countries tried to analyse nuclear stability even as a nuclear race was underway, three key concepts emerged – deterrence stability, arms race stability and crisis management stability. Underlying it was the acceptance of mutual vulnerability, which provided the impulse for cooperative management of nuclear rivalry. The acceptance of mutual vulnerability was reflected in the Anti-Ballistic Missiles (ABM) Treaty concluded in 1972 (from which the USA unilaterally withdrew in 2002) that limited the deployment of anti-ballistic-missile systems by both countries, reinforcing deterrence stability.

Other arms control agreements negotiated during the Cold War (SALT I and II, START I and II, INF Treaty) imposed limits in terms of launchers and warheads and imparted stability to the nuclear arms race. The Cuban Missile Crisis in 1962 led to the establishment of the Hot Line between Washington and Moscow and this was expanded further into Nuclear Risk Reduction Centres on both sides together with early warning systems to ensure crisis management stability. However, notwithstanding such measures, there were a number of near accidents with risks of both miscalculation and escalation.[12]

Today, the idea of cooperative management is under question. The ABM Treaty is dead; the USA considers Russia to be in violation of the INF Treaty; and, given recent statements, it is unlikely that the New START will be extended beyond 2021. There are no nuclear stability dialogues between other potential adversaries, US–China, US–DPRK, India–Pakistan, India–China, Russia–North Atlantic Treaty Organization, even as the countries proceed with their respective nuclear programmes.

With the geopolitical centre of gravity shifting from Euro–Atlantic to the Indo-Pacific, nuclear stability needs re-defining. While the US–Russian equation remains important, other equations have grown in salience. Most significantly, these equations are not limited to nuclear dyads (as was the case with the US–USSR equation) but involve strategic chains with interlinkages. The US–DPRK equation can be extended to include China and even possibly Russia. Similarly, the India–Pakistan nuclear equation cannot ignore the China factor. The US–Chinese equation could also bring in Russia. Many of these trigger points lie in a crowded geopolitical arena skirted by the Indian and Pacific oceans. Given the absence of security structures and dialogue platforms, nuclear risks are clearly on the rise.

Clearly, the deterrence equations underpinning the US–USSR dyad during the Cold War are not applicable to stability in nuclear chain relationships, raising the risks of escalation, miscalculation and deliberate use, and the cascading effects of a crisis from one dyad across the entire nuclear chain. Furthermore, these deterrence equations evolved in an exclusively bilateral context where response times were determined by the distance separating the USA and USSR. The timelines among many of the potential adversaries today are much shorter. In a situation where potential adversaries reflect asymmetries in terms of their doctrines and arsenals, the hypotheses and lessons of the Cold War become less relevant and demand a renewed realisation that any nuclear use would very quickly snowball into unmanageable escalation spiral. Furthermore, the asymmetry implies that the bean-counting approach that led to parity in terms of the numbers of launchers and warheads between the USA and USSR arms control agreements no longer works for nuclear chains.

Nuclear stability can no longer be isolated from developments in both outer space and cyberspace. So far, the regime for outer space is governed by the Outer Space Treaty of 1967 though growing space dependency has tempted major powers to develop capabilities that can militarise outer space. Attempts to build upon the 1967 treaty have stalled, both in the CD in Geneva, Switzerland and in the Committee on Peaceful Uses of Outer Space in Vienna, Austria.

Cyber-dependence has grown rapidly and offensive cyber operations will be an integral part of any future conflict. If the conflict involves NWS, it might lead to potential interference in nuclear command and control functions which would only increase risks of miscalculation. Nuclear war gaming as an exercise was always fraught with uncertainties but with these technological developments, the high unpredictability levels render them meaningless.

In hindsight, it is clear that the bilateral arms control negotiations created a semblance of nuclear stability during the Cold War but did not reduce dependence on nuclear weapons; on the contrary these agreements served to heighten the role of nuclear weapons in the security calculus of the USA and USSR. And since the two military superpowers could not do without nuclear weapons, it increased their desirability for other states thus highlighting the inherent tension between "arms control" and "disarmament."

Likewise, multilateral arms control attempts failed to achieve even a modicum of nuclear disarmament. The NPT delegitimised nuclear proliferation but failed to do the same for nuclear weapons, thereby in effect enabling the continued possession of the bomb by the five NWS. By the time the 1995 decision to extend the NPT was taken, the five permanent members of the UN Security Council were parties to the NPT. Instead of considering the Article 6 obligations as a special responsibility, these five countries converted the NPT into a certificate of legitimacy for their continued retention of nuclear weapons. Thus, if we unpack the obligations of Article 6, the TPNW is an implicit rejection of the claim that the NWS have pursued nuclear disarmament negotiations "in good faith" and for "effective measures," in order to bring about "cessation of the nuclear arms race at an early date."

In any event, today there are four countries with nuclear weapons (the DPRK, India, Israel and Pakistan) which are not parties to the NPT. Having reached its limit in terms of adherence, the NPT has exhausted its normative potential[13] and is now a victim of its success. In other words, the treaty and the regime surrounding the treaty undoubtedly deserve credit for fairly major achievements. For this reason, certainly, it should be maintained and not weakened in any way. But its limitations too must be accepted in terms of a political reality for future progress on the common agenda of avoiding a nuclear war and minimising the risks associated with nuclear weapons.

The NPT community often seeks to make a distinction between the N5 as legally recognised or licit NWS, oblivious to the political reality that all nine nuclear-armed states need to work together if nuclear risks are to be diminished. If functioning nuclear risk reduction and other restraint regimes are to be established, they will require buy-in by all possessor states who must be persuaded that the arrangements are in their individual and collective interest.

In the post-Cold War era, proliferation became the key threat. Apprehensions were heightened with the break-up of USSR and the challenge of denuclearising Belarus, Kazakhstan and Ukraine, three new countries that had inherited significant nuclear weapons capabilities. Iraq and the DPRK were found to be cheating on the nuclear safeguards system. Responses to these challenges included the push towards ensuring wider adherence and indefinite extension of the NPT, the introduction of strengthened safeguards which applied to the non-NWS that were already subject to full-scope safeguards and an expansion of export controls to cover dual use material, equipment, technologies and 'intangibles.'

After the 9/11 terrorist attacks on the USA, the threat of terrorists acquiring nuclear weapons (or other WMD) gained salience. The UN Security Council adopted Resolution 1540 which obliged all countries to tighten measures in this regard.[14] The Security Council also set up monitoring mechanisms. President Obama's initiative on nuclear security also reflected this concern. Obama did think about other measures to wean the USA off its dependence on nuclear weapons but faced domestic resistance that he could not overcome.

Increasingly frustrated with the lack of progress on nuclear disarmament under the NPT, and buoyed by the successful example of the campaign against landmines which brought together civil society and a coalition of likeminded countries, the humanitarian initiative for a nuclear ban convention took shape, resulting in the TPNW. As noted above, as the supporting states of the TPNW are parties to the NPT, they naturally see the TPNW as complementary to the NPT. According to them, the normative approach compensates for the lack of specificity in Article 6 of the NPT ('closing the legal gap') and as the moral norm gains ascendancy, it will create the legal space for negotiating a full-fledged Nuclear Weapons Convention with credible enforcement and verification (like the Chemical Weapons Convention).

One flaw in this reasoning is that it ignores the inconsistency between the NPT and TPNW which arises from the manner in which the NPT has been reinterpreted by the P5 as merely a non-proliferation norm. Thus in its only reference to the TPNW, the USA's 2018 NPR insists that the Ban Treaty "has polarised the international community and seeks to inject disarmament issues into non-proliferation fora, potentially damaging the non-proliferation regime."[15] The flip side of this is expressed by Nick Ritchie who believes that the nuclear discourse of the NWS "moves easily from" the position that the NPT permits them to possess and deploy nuclear weapons, "to the language of entitlement, legal rights and enduring legitimacy."[16] This reinterpretation, which hitherto the non-NWS have not seriously challenged, has led the P5 states to legitimise their nuclear weapons and weaken the disarmament norm.

The NWFZ approach has run its course. Positive security assurances provide the nuclear umbrella to 29 states allied to the US.[17] These 29 countries are party to the NPT as non-NWSs. Five of them (Belgium, Germany, Italy, Netherlands and Turkey) even host US nuclear weapons on their territory. Russia also says that a nuclear attack on any of Moscow's allies would be regarded as an attack on Russia itself and draw an immediate response – but has not clarified which countries are covered by that commitment.

NSAs are a counter to positive security assurances. Whatever their security value, NSAs do nothing to diminish the legitimacy of nuclear weapons. Another major limitation of NSAs is that these are unilateral gestures rather than legally binding obligations.

All measures adopted so far, with the sole exception of the TPNW, are thus in lieu of and independent of nuclear disarmament. This was best captured in the statement issued by the US, the UK and France on 7 July 2017 stating that "accession to the ban treaty is incompatible with the policy of nuclear deterrence" and further, prevailing security concerns "continue to make nuclear deterrence necessary."[18] Nuclear deterrence has been further legitimised by the myth that it has helped maintain peace since 1945.

Meanwhile, are there incremental steps consistent with the objectives of nuclear disarmament and the TPNW? To be credible these should shift away from legitimising nuclear weapons and deterrence. There are two possible approaches, one doctrinal and the other technical.

The first is the policy of no-first-use or not being the first to use nuclear weapons. In other words, nuclear weapons would be used only for retaliatory purposes. This diminishes the role of nuclear weapons. Currently, China maintains a no-first-use policy; India too has a no-first-use policy but reserves the right to retaliate using nuclear weapons in case of an attack on India or Indian forces anywhere with chemical or biological weapons. Other NWS maintain a first-use policy which implies a greater role for nuclear weapons.

The second related technical measure is de-alerting or increasing the lead time between the decision to use a nuclear weapon and the time that it takes to launch the nuclear strike. Countries that have a first-use policy consider it necessary to maintain at least a portion of their arsenals on high alert. In some countries, the authority for launching a nuclear strike is highly centralised, an issue that has become the subject of debate and discussion in the US. It is widely accepted that a crisis creates pressures on decision making, generating emotions and creating 'the fog of war', overwhelming rationality and reason.

Compressed timeframes push decision makers towards a 'use' decision. As many as 400 missiles could be launched from their underground silos in less than five minutes after an order given by the US president.[19] The idea of a hair-trigger alert status was deemed necessary to enhance the credibility of the deterrent. Taking weapons off high alert provides additional time for decision making. Separating warheads from launch vectors would introduce an invaluable time delay. Raising alert levels would become an outcome of deliberations at each level of alert. Such an approach permits a lengthening of the fuse. It does not require a no-first-use policy as a pre-condition though the two together have mutually reinforcing beneficial impact.

Neither of these two incremental measures eliminates nuclear weapons but both help in lowering the nuclear risks that are on the rise today. Most importantly, these help in prolonging the nuclear taboo that has held since 1945 but seems to be under threat today. Prolonging the nuclear taboo is vital for delegitimising nuclear weapons because any use today, especially premeditated use, would have catastrophic consequences. It could either lead to annihilation or, by eroding the taboo, make nuclear weapons an acceptable war-fighting weapon.

Moving back the Doomsday Clock is a collective responsibility. We might have maintained nuclear peace since 1945 but it has been a tenuous and a fragile peace. For too long, we have been misled into believing that arms control and non-proliferation approaches could lead to nuclear elimination. Whatever their other virtues, it is clear that these will not lead to nuclear disarmament. Accepting this reality is critical in order to make the right choices for our shared future.

Notes

1 "It is now 2 minutes to midnight," Press release, *Bulletin of the Atomic Scientists*, 25 January 2018, https://thebulletin.org/press-release-it-is-now-2-minutes-to-midnight.
2 This was most elegantly expressed in the Canberra Commission. See Report of the Canberra Commission on the Elimination of Nuclear Weapons (Canberra: Department of Foreign Affairs and Trade, 1996): 18–22.
3 Union of Concerned Scientists, "Close Calls With Nuclear Weapons Fact Sheet," April 2015, www.ucsusa.org/sites/default/files/attach/2018/02/Close%20Calls%20with%20Nuclear%20Weapons.pdf.
4 US Department of Defense, *Nuclear Posture Review*, February 2018, https://media.defense.gov/2018/Feb/02/2001872886/-1/-1/1/2018-NUCLEAR-POSTURE-REVIEW-FINAL-REPORT.PDF.
5 W. J. Hennigen, "Donald Trump is Playing a Dangerous Game of Nuclear Poker," *Time*, 1 February 2018. https://time.com/5128394/donald-trump-nuclear-poker.
6 Nikolai Sokov, "Why Russia calls a limited nuclear strike 'De-escalation'," *Bulletin of the Atomic Scientists*, 13 March 2014, https://thebulletin.org/2014/03/why-russia-calls-a-limited-nuclear-strike-de-escalation.

7 Vladimir Putin, "Presidential Address to the Federal Assembly," 1 March 2018, http://en.kremlin.ru/events/president/news/56957.
8 A/RES/1, UN General Assembly, 24 January 1946, www.un.org/en/ga/search/view_doc.asp?symbol=A/RES/1(I).
9 USA, USSR, UK, France, China (N5) who also are the P5, the five permanent members of the UN Security Council.
10 ICAN, Signature and ratification status, www.icanw.org/signature_and_ratification_status.
11 Thomas E. Doyle, "The Moral Implications of the Subversion of the Nonproliferation Treaty Regime," *Ethics & Global Politics*, 2 (2009): 131–53.
12 "Nuclear 'Command and Control': A History of False Alarms and Near Catastrophes," NPR, 11 August 2014, www.npr.org/2014/08/11/339131421/nuclear-command-and-control-a-history-of-false-alarms-and-near-catastrophes.
13 In so arguing, Ramesh Thakur notes that the non-proliferation obligations have been universalised to all non-possessor countries (other than South Sudan as a new state); the nuclear security agenda was taken over by the Nuclear Security Summit process; and the disarmament obligation has been ignored. Thakur, "The Nuclear Ban Treaty: Recasting a Normative Framework for Disarmament," *The Washington Quarterly*, 40:4 (Winter 2018), 72. Of course, should elements of a nuclear restraint regime be adopted by the NWS pursuant to their Article 6 obligation, the NPT's normative potential will be resurrected.
14 S/RES/1540, UN Security Council, 28 April 2004, https://unoda-web.s3.amazonaws.com/wp-content/uploads/2016/01/1540-fact-sheet-Jan2016.pdf.
15 US Department of Defense, *Nuclear Posture Review*, 72.
16 Quoted in Thakur, "The Nuclear Ban Treaty," 85.
17 Albania, Australia, Belgium, Bulgaria, Canada, Croatia, Czech, Denmark, Estonia, Germany, Greece, Hungary, Iceland, Italy, Japan, Latvia, Lithuania, Luxembourg, Montenegro, Netherlands, Norway, Poland, Portugal, Romania, Slovakia, Slovenia, South Korea, Spain and Turkey.
18 US Mission to the UN, "Joint Press Statement from the Permanent Representatives to the United Nations of the United States, United Kingdom, and France Following the Adoption," 7 July 2017, https://usun.usmission.gov/joint-press-statement-from-the-permanent-representatives-to-the-united-nations-of-the-united-states-united-kingdom-and-france-following-the-adoption.
19 "No-one Should Have Sole Authority to Launch a Nuclear Attack," *Scientific American*, 1 August 2017, www.scientificamerican.com/article/no-one-should-have-sole-authority-to-launch-a-nuclear-attack.

6

HOW MANY INTENSIVE CARE BEDS WILL A NUCLEAR WEAPON EXPLOSION REQUIRE?[1]

Tom Sauer and Ramesh Thakur

A novel coronavirus (Covid-19) emerged in Wuhan, China in late 2019, hopping in one way or another from other animals to humans. Initially the rest of the world thought this outbreak was a local problem and then was shocked at the brutality of the lockdown that the Chinese authorities clamped down on Wuhan to quarantine the infection cluster. Despite China's efforts at containment, soon the virus rode the highways and byways of globalisation to quickly circle the world. Other countries realised their hospital systems could be overwhelmed unless they drastically slowed the surge of new infections. No country had the number of beds in its intensive care units (ICU) to manage patient loads under worst-case scenarios of letting this new coronavirus spread through the community to acquire herd immunity.

To those of us whose primary professional interest lies in nuclear weapons and the dangers they pose, the coronavirus pandemic is a striking validation of the Humanitarian Initiative, which took off 10 years ago with three core propositions: First, no country individually has the capacity to cope with the humanitarian consequences of a nuclear war, and the international system does not have it collectively, either. Second, it is therefore in the interests of all humanity that nuclear weapons never be used again, under any circumstances. And finally: The only guarantee of non-use is the complete elimination of nuclear weapons. These precepts were the powerful impetus behind the nuclear weapons Ban Treaty that 122 states at the United Nations adopted in July 2017.

The pandemic speaks to the truth of the first proposition about the power of the bomb. The near-universal response to the panic created by Covid-19 leads us to the conclusion that the number of ICU beds needed to deal with a disaster should become a new norm, and a new way to judge when radical action is needed to respond to a global threat. So, what other types of global catastrophes could call for more hospital infrastructure and personnel than is now available? The bomb is one

DOI: 10.4324/9781003227502-8

obvious answer. Is the number of ICU beds sufficient to respond to a disaster caused by the explosion of one nuclear weapon or, in a war, many? No, it is not sufficient. Not even close.

A serious threat assessment consists of estimating the size of a threat and its probability. For the nuclear threat, estimating the size is rather straightforward; the probability is more difficult. A nuclear cataclysm is low probability in the short term, almost certain in the long run, and high impact whenever it happens. Let's put it another way: For nuclear peace to hold, deterrence and fail-safe mechanisms must work every single time. For nuclear catastrophe to occur, either deterrence or fail-safe mechanisms need to break down only once. This is not a comforting equation. Moreover, deterrence stability depends on rational decision-makers being always in office in every single nuclear-armed country. The leaders of the nine countries with the bomb today – China, France, India, Israel, the Democratic People's Republic of Korea (DPRK, or North Korea), Pakistan, Russia, the UK and the USA – do not universally reassure on this score.

So, let's take the number of available intensive care beds as the new measure and apply it to potential nuclear catastrophes. With the help of Stephens Institute of Technology researcher Alex Wellerstein's "Nukemap,"[2] we can model the approximate results of a hit on a target city by a nuclear warhead of choice. The largest bomb tested by Pakistan – which has a yield equal to 45 kilotons (kt) of TNT – would kill about 358,350 people and injure some 1.28 million, if used in an airburst over Delhi. But there would almost certainly be many more injuries; almost four million people live within the 7-km radius in which the detonation would break glass windows and create other "light" blast effects – which actually are not light and would cause major injuries. If Russia launched one of its nuclear-armed, 800-kt Topol missiles against NATO headquarters in Brussels, Belgium, 536,180 people would die and 572,830 would be injured. If a 5,000-kt Chinese Deng Fong-5 missile reaches Brussels, 839,550 will die and another 876,260 people will be seriously injured. Belgium's 1,900 ICU beds (minus those of Brussels and surroundings, which would of course be instantly destroyed or rendered unusable) could not begin to cope with a humanitarian disaster of this magnitude. And what if more than one nuclear warhead explodes? What about a nuclear war that produces dozens or hundreds of nuclear explosions?

No society is prepared for such a man-made disaster. Worse, no society can ever be prepared for such a scenario. Nevertheless, many nations (including our home countries of Belgium and Australia) base their defence policies on the threat that the United States will use nuclear weapons in their defence, if necessary.

We cannot predict when and with what ferocity the next global pandemic will hit. But we can be certain that Covid-19 will not be the last pandemic disease to afflict humanity, and we should be making preparations to forestall such a disaster. We also cannot predict when and where nuclear weapons will be used again, and by whom. But we can be grimly confident that a nuclear warhead will be detonated someday, somewhere, if not by choice and design, then inadvertently, through accidental launch, rogue launch or system failure.

Nuclear deterrence has proven itself to be anything but foolproof. Syria and Egypt attacked Israel in 1973, even though the Jewish state possessed nuclear weapons. In 1991 Iraq's Saddam Hussein also disregarded Israel's nuclear arsenal, firing Scud missiles at Tel Aviv. Argentina attacked the nuclear-armed UK in the Falkland Islands war. India and Pakistan, both nuclear powers, fought the Kargil war in 1999 (more than 1,000 people died) and had a dog-fight in February 2019. We would not call these conflicts – any one of which might have resulted in the use of nuclear weapons – expressions of security or stability. A policy based on hope and luck (as US Secretary of Defense Robert McNamara described the conduct of the Cuban Missile Crisis[3]) cannot be the basis of a serious defence policy.

What is the probability of a nuclear war or simply the explosion of a single nuclear weapon? Certainly, it is more than zero. And the probability seems to be rising rather than falling. If US President Donald Trump does not extend New START by the end of 2020,[4] for the first time in 50 years the world will end up without any bilateral arms control treaty that includes verification. The nuclear-armed countries have not negotiated one new arms control treaty since 2010. The DPRK now has nuclear weapons, and Iran could be the next in line to acquire them.

The world is facing a clear threat of an "outbreak" of nuclear weapons proliferation.

As of now, there are no treatments or preventive measures that work against the new coronavirus circling the world. But a "vaccine" against nuclear weapons use already exists – the Treaty on the Prohibition of Nuclear Weapons, often known simply as the Ban Treaty. Unfortunately, despite their legal obligations under Article 6 of the Nuclear Non-Proliferation Treaty (NPT), the five nuclear weapon states and their allies, and also the four nuclear-armed states outside the NPT, are refusing to take the prophylactic medication the Ban Treaty prescribes. The nuclear weapon "haves" refuse to give up their nuclear privileges, even though they promised to do so under the NPT. The US alone will spend $50 billion this year on the maintenance and modernisation of nuclear weapons and their delivery vehicles.

Doctors know better. They know that they will not be of any help in a nuclear war. That is why the World Medical Association stands behind the nuclear Ban Treaty since 2018. The same for the World Federation of Public Health Associations, the International Council of Nurses and the International Red Cross.

The world has experienced epidemics and pandemics before. It suffered but endured. The coronavirus pandemic too shall pass, and life will go on. But the world is unlikely to return to the pre-pandemic state of affairs. Countries will rebuild domestic manufacturing capacity for critical medical supplies and equipment and create institutional structures to manage a surge in ICU capacity for future epidemiological crises. They will rebuild some vital border protections. And they will build functional redundancy into global supply chains to reduce exposure to single points of critical supply.

But such measures will not work as preparations against a nuclear war; no infrastructure, no matter how sophisticated or extensive, could cope with the horrible injury toll. Using ICU beds as a new norm informs us that no after-the-fact response to a nuclear bomb explosion can work. So, prevention in the form of the Ban Treaty vaccine must be universally administered. In the post-pandemic world, therefore, eliminating nuclear weapons must be a top priority of the utmost urgency.

Notes

1 This article was first published in the *Bulletin of the Atomic Scientists*, 28 April 2020, https://thebulletin.org/2020/04/how-many-intensive-care-beds-will-a-nuclear-weapon-explosion-require/ and was reprinted by the Toda Peace Institution by permission.
2 Alex Wellerstein, "Nukemap," https://nuclearsecrecy.com/nukemap.
3 Hans M. Kristensen and Robert S. Norris, "The Cuban Missile Crisis: A nuclear order of battle, October and November 1962," *Bulletin of the Atomic Scientists*, 1 November 2012, https://thebulletin.org/2012/11/the-cuban-missile-crisis-a-nuclear-order-of-battle-october-and-november-1962.
4 Shortly after assuming office in January 2021, US President Joe Biden decided to extend New START by five years.

7

ON CREATING THE TPNW VERIFICATION SYSTEM

Thomas E. Shea

With the Treaty for the Prohibition of Nuclear Weapons (TPNW) having entered into force in January 2021, agreeing on its verification system will be one of the first and perhaps the most consequential decisions that the states parties will make. The greatest challenge facing the TPNW is to convince nuclear-armed states to become parties to the treaty, and then to engage in good-faith efforts aimed at peace, stability and the eventual elimination of their nuclear weapons. Given the initial responses of the nuclear-armed states to the TPNW, the parties must hope to create a different climate, in part by designing the TPNW verification system to satisfy all parties, while providing value to the nuclear-armed states. The TPNW verification system will play a crucial role in decisions by nuclear-armed states to sign the treaty, how they participate and the steps they are prepared to accept leading eventually to the elimination of all of their nuclear weapons.

The TPNW requires each nuclear-armed state party:

1. To eliminate its nuclear arsenal;
2. To eliminate, or irreversibly convert its nuclear weapon facilities to peaceful use; and
3. To commit to never again produce nuclear weapons.

The treaty stipulates that these undertakings will be verified to confirm that nuclear-armed TPNW parties honour their Article 4 obligations.

This chapter is presented in three parts.[1] The first part explores the anticipated role of the TPNW verification system in the emerging international nuclear disarmament regime, which will determine whether or not the treaty will be successful in addressing the risks posed by nuclear weapons and in achieving progress on nuclear disarmament. The second part argues in favour of creating a new verification authority responsible only to the TPNW parties to address the elimination

DOI: 10.4324/9781003227502-9

of the existing arsenals, complementing the verification missions assigned to the International Atomic Energy Agency (IAEA) in the text of the treaty. The third part presents a possible framework, methods and techniques to meet the three verification requirements noted.

The most difficult challenges foreseen for TPNW verification will be:

1. Access to known locations (especially military installations) and to clandestine locations within a nuclear-armed state or anywhere under its control where undeclared nuclear warheads might be hidden, where nuclear-weapon-related activities might be under way, or where undeclared fissile material or other nuclear material might be held;
2. Reaching agreement on verifying items containing classified[2] forms of fissile material, including nuclear warheads, warhead fissile material components, and containers holding bulk forms of fissile material containing classified properties; and
3. Obtaining accurate estimates of the amounts of fissile material that each nuclear-armed state produced or otherwise acquired for its nuclear weapons, the identification number and history of each weapon, warhead, warhead primary and secondary component produced, and the disposition of the remaining fissile material.

This chapter is intended to assist the parties as they consider this task.

The TPNW verification system and the nuclear disarmament regime

By analogy, the Non-Proliferation Treaty (NPT) and IAEA safeguards define the core of the non-proliferation regime, but that regime has grown to encompass nuclear supplier controls, the Proliferation Security Initiative and special verification arrangements created under the authority of the United Nations Security Council, for example, in Iraq, the Democratic People's Republic of Korea (DPRK, or North Korea) and Iran. So, too, the TPNW and its verification system will grow to make continuing progress on disarmament likely and sustainable. As in the non-proliferation regime, sometimes mechanisms have been added to existing bodies, sometimes new entities have been created.

The principal difference between the two is that NPT states with nuclear weapons (the UK, China, France, Russia and the USA) (referred to as nuclear weapon states, NWS, in the NPT) and the great majority of NPT non-NWS agree that proliferation is extremely dangerous. Proliferating states are historically outside the norms of national behaviour. As a result, the non-NWS have accepted demand after demand for less freedom and more intrusive inspections while the nine nuclear-armed states have managed to dismiss repeated calls for progress and the NWS have essentially ignored their NPT Article 6 obligations for some 50 years.[3]

Attracting the nuclear-armed states

The task for the parties of creating the TPNW verification system is all the more challenging given that no nuclear-armed state has signed the TPNW or voiced any positive views on its behalf. Up to now they have managed to avoid any commitments to begin a process of disarming and, regardless of the verification system adopted under the TPNW, they will probably not agree to participating in the TPNW – until they perceive that it could help their national security to do so, and when diplomatic pressure from the TPNW parties convinces them – one after another – to sign on.

In creating the TPNW verification system, the parties need to try to anticipate the national security requirements of the nuclear-armed states in order to attract them to the treaty. The first reaction of those states rejecting the treaty was no doubt a blanket wish to avoid any entanglement on this topic, continuing the tradition of the P5 to refuse any response to their commitments under NPT Article 6, with the certainty that India, Israel, the DPRK and Pakistan would follow suit, knowing that any initial step would put them on a slippery slope where they would be pressed repeatedly to do more, then more, then more. Once the TPNW verification system is fixed and is up and running, the nine nuclear-armed states might look more favourably at the costs and benefits of participating in the TPNW, taking into account its intention to work on a broad suite of issues that they, together with the international community, might support.

The scope of the TPNW verification system

Hence, the TPNW parties should consider broadening the scope of the TPNW verification system to include additional measures to enrich the role of the TPNW in securing peace and stability, and to encourage the nuclear-armed states to participate. The scope would begin with the three objectives defined in the TPNW as noted above. Recognising that there is no international mechanism for addressing the risks arising from nuclear arsenals and that all TPNW parties are potential victims should those risks be manifested, the TPNW verification system should specifically also address these risks associated with nuclear weapons, to manage threats associated with:

1. Tensions between nuclear adversaries possibly leading to nuclear war;
2. Steps taken by nuclear-armed states regarding the prevention of unauthorised use of their nuclear weapons;
3. Steps taken by nuclear-armed states to prevent sabotage or accidental detonations of their nuclear weapons;
4. Nuclear terrorism; and
5. Steps to make proliferation less attractive.

TPNW-related confidence-building measures

Not all nuclear-armed states threaten one another. Treaties and agreements between adversaries provide a common means for them to move from confrontation to stability. The international nuclear disarmament regime should encourage bilateral or trilateral treaties between nuclear adversaries, ideally within the framework of the TPNW verification system. Under such an arrangement, while allowing TPNW inspectors to verify step-by-step progress in a state, under a bilateral or trilateral accord, the parties could undertake their own verification of highly sensitive activities, including dismantling nuclear warheads and subsequent processing to remove all classified properties from the recovered fissile material.

Every nuclear weapon which includes fusion energy will require deuterium, tritium and, for thermonuclear weapons, enriched lithium. Bilateral or trilateral controls on these materials could provide another mechanism to encourage and confirm progress towards disarmament, and another mechanism to detect cheating. Bilateral or trilateral controls on warhead refurbishment and re-manufacturing would provide one mechanism for providing reciprocal transparency into an adversary's nuclear arsenal management.

Before nuclear-armed states are prepared to sign on to a treaty commitment that allows them no way out, it could be helpful if combined exercises could be held carried out by TPNW inspectors within each nuclear-armed state. The objective of such exercises would be to contribute to a realistic understanding of the steps each nuclear-armed state should expect, and to identify obstacles to implementation.

A commitment to disarmament must involve an irreversible process leading to the eventual elimination of their weapons and their production capabilities; however, it could be helpful to provide time-limited temporary arrangements under which a nuclear-armed state could submit weapons, warheads or warhead fissile material components to monitoring with the understanding that the state would maintain the right to withdraw such items if it so decided. Such a step might be helpful in convincing the adversary(ies) of a nuclear-armed state to take measured steps providing confidence in their *bona fides* and encouraging reciprocal commitments. Such steps should encourage full commitments to disarmament.

The Nuclear Suppliers Group and the Zangger Committee regulate commerce in materials, facilities, equipment and know-how within the non-proliferation regime. They control access to objects that could assist a state attempting to acquire nuclear weapons. As progress is made towards the elimination of existing nuclear weapons, it could be appropriate to introduce appropriate export/import controls as part of the nuclear disarmament regime.

TPNW verification authorities

Under Article 4.6 of the treaty:

> The States Parties shall designate a competent international authority or authorities to negotiate and verify the irreversible elimination of nuclear-weapons programmes, including the elimination or irreversible conversion of all nuclear-weapons-related facilities.

Based on my 24.5 years of service in the IAEA Safeguards Department, I can state categorically that the IAEA could – in principle – carry out any and all technical verification tasks foreseen in Article 4.6. But should it?

In favour of having the IAEA serve as the exclusive TPNW verification authority, consider the following:

a The IAEA exists and is highly regarded.
b It would be cheaper and faster for the IAEA to take on the Article 4.6 mission than to start up a new organisation for this purpose.
c Many of the existing capabilities and much of the IAEA's experience would be applicable to the Article 4.6 task.

However, in my opinion, based on the reasons cited below, the TPNW parties should create a new organisation for this all-important responsibility.

Governance. The governing structure for the IAEA dates back to 1957. In addition to directions identified within the Agency itself, the IAEA accepts requests or mandates from the UN Security Council and normally adopts agreed recommendations from NPT Review Conferences. Its governance arrangements are well established and 'set in stone.' It would be difficult to allow TPNW parties to exercise control over the Article 4.6 disarmament verification role in addition to the roles already assigned. Moreover, both the Board of Governors and the General Conference include IAEA member states who might choose to continue to remain outside the TPNW, complicating the ability of the TPNW parties to manage IAEA verification – especially in relation to Article 4.6.

Challenge Inspections. Pursuing indications of possible hidden nuclear weapons, warheads, or fissile material warhead components, or of undeclared nuclear activities or nuclear material, "challenge" inspections might be considered to be important. But there are no provisions for challenge inspections in the current IAEA safeguards system and introducing the necessary provisions would be difficult.

Competition for Attention. The IAEA is a multi-programme international organisation. If Article 4.6 verification is assigned to the IAEA, its verification requirements would need to compete with these other programmes, making it questionable whether the attention given to Article 4.6 verification would meet the intentions of the TPNW parties. In addition to its non-proliferation verification obligations under the NPT, the IAEA currently implements a host of voluntary programmes at the request of – and in support of – the needs and interests of member states. Many are financed in whole or in part through voluntary extra-budgetary funds. These include nuclear power, nuclear safety and security, application of nuclear methods to health, agriculture and industry, and technical support in all these fields to developing member states.

Controversy. It would be difficult for the IAEA to be asked to consider related tasks – such as threat reduction measures to reduce the likelihood of nuclear conflict, or nuclear weapon safety and security. These are likely to be controversial and disruptive.

Non-proliferation Consensus. The non-proliferation mission of the IAEA functions on the basis of consensus, which has held remarkably well over the years. This consensus reflects the positive role played by nuclear-armed states within the IAEA in support of its technical and financial requirements to implement safeguards in all of its capabilities.[4] Verification of Article 4.6 might undermine the non-proliferation consensus.

Requirements for Equipment Procurement & Use. The verification methods and procedures employed by the IAEA are developed and procured following agreed arrangements. The equipment used by the IAEA is accepted for common use in all relevant member states. Verification equipment for Article 4.6 will have to be developed to meet the requirements of each nuclear-armed state, in order to provide the nuclear-armed state the protection it would demand against espionage. At the same time, it will have to provide the authenticity assurance that the verification authority would demand. Assigning verification of Article 4.6 to the IAEA would saddle it with additional demands that could affect its access to practical measures for use in relation to its non-proliferation role, or to the IAEA verification responsibilities explicitly called for in the TPNW.

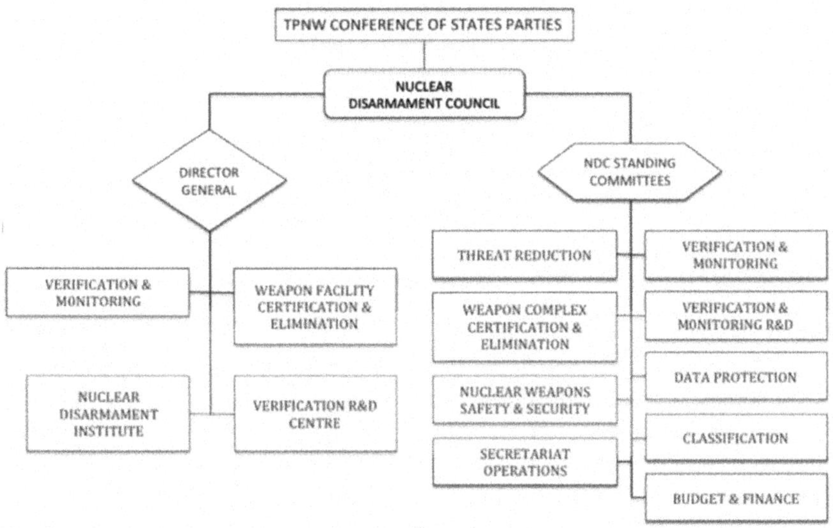

FIGURE 7.1 International Nuclear Disarmament Agency (INDA)

Military Presence. Lastly, the IAEA functions via diplomacy and technology working in unison. Adding Article 4.6 to the IAEA missions would inevitably increase military participation in the day-to-day workings of the IAEA, which could undermine the success of the IAEA in meeting its other demands.

It is for these reasons that I believe that the TPNW parties should create a new verification authority. If the TPNW parties decide on a new organisation, it might look like the hypothetical organigram in the Figure 7.1. The TPNW parties would then decide what to call it, how it should be created, where it should be headquartered, staffed, etc. Until then, the new authority might be referred to as the International Nuclear Disarmament Agency (INDA).[5] If the parties opt for INDA, the verification assignments for INDA and the IAEA might be settled as follows:

TABLE 7.1 Verification responsibilities between INDA and IAEA

INDA	*IAEA*
1. Encourage nuclear-armed states to disarm 2. Verify arms reductions and fissile material controls at four levels	1. Disposition of fissile material from disarmament
3. Detect undeclared nuclear weapons, warheads or fissile material warhead components	2. Detect diversion of declared stocks of nuclear material at declared facilities 3. Detect undeclared production, processing at declared facilities
4. Certify and eliminate mission-critical nuclear weapon facilities	4. Detect undeclared nuclear materials and undeclared nuclear activities
5. Verify non-explosive military uses of fissile material 6. Verify historical production of all nuclear weapons and their current whereabouts	5. Estimate and verify historical production of all plutonium, HEU, U-233, Np-237 and Am-241
Joint INDA/IAEA Tasks	
Detect undeclared nuclear weapon production facilities	
Convert mission-critical nuclear weapon facilities to peaceful use	

Verification methods and procedures

When a nuclear-armed state becomes a party to the TPNW, it will begin interacting with INDA and the IAEA. It will provide its official declaration on its nuclear weapons programme and the steps it commits to carrying out. A master verification dossier should be created by INDA and maintained for each nuclear-armed state, which would document all declarations made by it, all recommended steps for it to undertake and all actions taken over time toward its full and complete disarmament. It would include all activities under the three objectives cited above and be the basis for reporting progress under the treaty.

Certain aspects of the TPNW verification system will resemble current verification activities under the IAEA safeguards system in relation to the obligations of non-NWS parties to the NPT – especially in regard to objective 3, above. While the IAEA has no disarmament role at present, its assistance in relation to the TPNW will be invaluable.

In addition, owing to the extreme security surrounding nuclear weapons, new methods and procedures will be necessary for the TPNW verification system – especially in regard to Objectives 1 and 2 above, to provide clear indications of the disarmament activities undertaken by each nuclear-armed state.

Verifying the elimination of a nuclear arsenal

The focus of TPNW verification is on the possession and use of fissile material,[6] in much the same manner as the principal NPT verification focus is on the possession and use of nuclear material. TPNW verification might also include non-nuclear weapon components and weapon support activities and facilities, to increase assurances that a nuclear-armed state is honouring its TPNW obligations. Verifying the elimination of a nuclear arsenal should include – where possible – verifying the physical destruction of each warhead after its fissile material components have been removed, verifying the warheads and warhead components to confirm their authenticity, then measuring the recovered fissile material and tracking it until it is transferred to an approved disposition process, under IAEA safeguards.

TPNW verification should assure that all fissile material in all forms associated with nuclear weapons be recovered, re-committed to an approved disposition process, and be subject to IAEA safeguards thereafter. Verification of the destruction of a weapon delivery system could further enhance the verification process, if agreed by the state and the verification authority.

Figure 7.2 shows how fissile materials (plutonium and HEU) are used in a modern hypothetical thermonuclear warhead. The fission primary ignites or triggers the fusion secondary, which produces most of the explosive force. In the

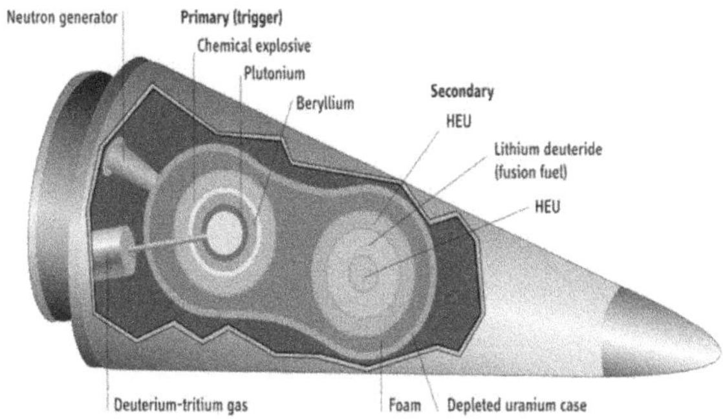

FIGURE 7.2 The Princeton cutaway diagram of a modern thermonuclear warhead
Photo: International Panel on Fissile Materials Princeton University

example shown, the explosive yield from fissioning plutonium in the primary is 'boosted' by fusing deuterium and tritium in gas form within the primary 'pit,' and the explosive yield of the secondary from fusing deuterium and tritium is increased by including HEU, causing additional fission energy to increase the overall explosive yield of a nuclear weapon.

Grouping the disarmament steps into four levels will facilitate organisation of the required verification activities.

Verification of the steps shown in Figure 7.3 could involve accepting declared objects into the verification process at any of the levels shown. If a nuclear-armed state and the verification authority are able to reach agreement on procedures that enable the authority to verify that an item declared to be a warhead is a true warhead, or if such verification were to be carried out under a bilateral or trilateral agreement between nuclear adversaries operating within the TPNW, then Level 4 verification could confirm that specific nuclear weapons have been disarmed and destroyed. At Level 3, the verification measures could confirm that specific warheads are destroyed and that the primaries and secondaries from each warhead will continue to be monitored. At Level 2, verification could confirm that the primaries and secondaries from specific warheads, or other primaries or secondaries, or other forms of fissile material are processed to remove all classified properties, noting that unclassified fissile material might be altered to block the verification authority from inferring the amounts of fissile material or the isotopic compositions of actual warhead components or warheads when unrestricted verification measures are applied at Level 1.[7]

If the state and the authority do not agree on warhead verification, then the information derived will be less immediate and the assurances less direct. Using appropriate containment and surveillance devices to maintain continuity of

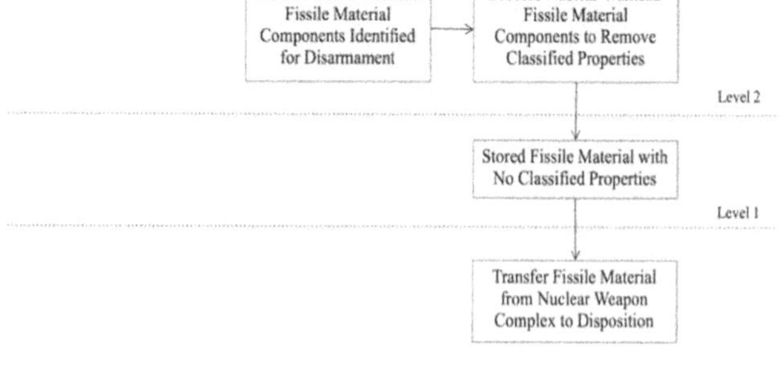

FIGURE 7.3 Four levels of nuclear disarmament verification

knowledge through warhead dismantling and the processing operations for removing all classified properties, when allowed, unrestricted measurements of the recovered fissile material can be made using IAEA measurement systems, and the verification authority might reasonably conclude that the fissile material recovered had been used in nuclear weapons.

In any case, every nuclear-armed state will have detached warheads and have dismantled warheads before the TPNW comes into force. Hence, TPNW verification will differ in each nuclear-armed state and never be as clear or as credible as IAEA safeguards verification of non-NWS' commitments.

Verifying classified forms of fissile material

A nuclear-armed state will balance its TPNW obligations with protecting its national security from possible espionage under the guise of verification by preventing access to sensitive nuclear weapon design or manufacturing information that could enable a nuclear-armed adversary to gain a military advantage, or encourage or enable a state that does not have nuclear weapons to proliferate. It would, in principle, be ideal for the purposes of verification to be able to determine that each warhead presented for verification is in fact a warhead, or that each primary or secondary is as declared. That would bring greater credibility to the verification process. In principle, it would be possible to measure the fissile material in situ, using non-destructive methods, together with the internal shapes and sizes of the inside of a warhead nose cone or a container, determining the types of fissile material that are present and how much of each is included, etc. But such measurements could clearly identify information that is considered to be sensitive to the design and/or manufacturing of a warhead or primary or secondary. Providing that sort of access could violate the nuclear-armed state's security laws and regulations, its NPT Article 1 prohibitions, and perhaps encourage proliferation, and hence TPNW verification must be restricted.

The IAEA has established competent methods for verifying unclassified forms of nuclear material which could be applied to verify all unclassified forms of fissile material. But the verification of nuclear weapons, warheads and warhead fissile material components poses a conundrum for each nuclear-armed state and the verification authority:

1. Whereas in NPT verification, the NWS and non-NWS share common interests and produce verification systems for the IAEA that are owned by and controlled by the IAEA, in disarmament verification, each nuclear-armed state is likely to be suspicious of other states and protect itself against the use of any equipment which might be capable of acquiring information in addition to its declared purpose. This concern will limit how much information the TPNW verification system is able to acquire, which physical methods are allowed to be used in the verification process, and how verification equipment will be produced and implemented. These restrictions will likely differ from state to state.

2. To be meaningful, verification of the TPNW must be independent, be based on sound scientific methods and be implemented in such a manner as to provide confidence in the authenticity of the findings.

Both must be satisfied if the verification system will include steps to assure that warheads and warhead components declared by a nuclear-armed state are, in fact, as declared. A six-year Trilateral Initiative carried out by the United States, Russia and the IAEA demonstrated that acceptable arrangements for international verification of classified forms of fissile material are possible when the parties recognise the need to co-operate fully toward that purpose.[8]

Several research institutes are looking at possible ways to 'verify' nuclear warheads, without divulging classified information, and avoiding technologies that could be vulnerable to hacking, for example. Two concepts have been considered. In one, the results of what would otherwise be revealing measurements are compared to unclassified **attributes** so that inspectors see only whether each comparison passes or fails. Under the Trilateral Initiative,[9] for example, the verification measurements on plutonium were to answer three questions about an item presented for verification:

- Is plutonium present? (Y/N)
- Is the ratio of Pu-240 to Pu-239 equal to 0.1 or less (as is typical for nuclear weapons)? (Y/N)
- Is the mass of plutonium above a value to be set for each facility where verification measurements will be made? (Y/N)

This method could be extended to include other properties, if the state and the verification authority agree.

In the other concept, the properties of an item being verified are compared to the properties of a "known" reference, i.e., a **template** comparison, or to many other items declared to be "identical." When there are many "identical" items, then the numbers themselves might provide some assurance, especially when the verification authority has the authority to select specific warheads for dismantlement. If the items are to be stored for long periods before the fissile material can be fully verified, then calibrating the templates takes on additional importance.

Recalling the security conundrum noted, avoiding or coping with potential hacking will also be necessary.

As yet, no such methods have been accepted by any party for use, even hypothetically, although some might have been tested under realistic arrangements. An ongoing TPNW research and development effort will be needed.

A suggested arsenal elimination verification process

Each arsenal will be different. For example, a nuclear-armed state might have a single type of nuclear weapon, or it might have – or have had – different types of nuclear weapons, including nuclear warheads on inter-continental ballistic missiles or shorter-range missiles, or in cruise missiles, gravity bombs, torpedoes, sea or land mines, nuclear artillery, or man-deliverable nuclear weapons.

To verify the elimination of a nuclear-armed state's arsenal, the TPNW verification system will need to address each of the nine nuclear-armed states individually or as part of a sub-group of nuclear adversaries. Each would submit official declarations on its nuclear weapons programme and a schedule identifying the steps it intends to carry out within a specified period. For each state, the TPNW verification system would organise verification methods and procedures for any deployed nuclear weapons included in the schedule, any detached nuclear warheads, fissile material nuclear weapon components, fissile material having classified warhead design or manufacturing properties that must not be shared with international inspectors, and all unclassified forms of fissile material remaining committed by a state to use in nuclear weapons.

Being able to determine that a "warhead" declared by a nuclear-armed state is in fact a real warhead and not a fake would give the verification system greater credibility and connect each to the process of disarmament. Recognising that it might take years to dismantle all warheads in an arsenal, such assurances would benefit the international community and a state's adversaries. If no such methods are approved, the ability of the TPNW verification system to identify and schedule individual warheads for dismantling would provide additional assurance.

The verification steps for the elimination of a state's arsenal should follow those shown in Appendix 7.1. These steps pertain to verifying declared actions taken by a state. These steps do not address the possibility that a state might have hidden weapons or that it might have concealed its capability to manufacture new ones. Those concerns are addressed later in this chapter.

Verifying the elimination or irreversible conversion of a state's nuclear weapons production complex

Every nuclear weapons programme will include a production chain for manufacturing nuclear warheads, warhead testing facilities, facilities for maintaining and repairing its warheads to assure that they remain reliable, plus dismantling facilities to retire warheads safely when they become obsolete or are no longer reliable. Each nuclear-armed state upon becoming a TPNW party, should, *inter alia*, provide a declaration of its nuclear weapon programme history and identify all required facilities as specified by the TPNW parties.

The nuclear weapon complexes in the nine nuclear-armed states differ significantly in terms of scale, redundancy, methods adopted to assure on-going functionality, and the ease with which a state can maintain, repair or replace its warheads over time. One might have a single complex of facilities to support its nuclear weapons program, while others might have adopted redundant facilities for security purposes. Hence, the TPNW verification system will need to be tailored to each of the nine nuclear-armed states, just as IAEA safeguards are tailored to the specific circumstances of each state.

As provided in Article 4.2 of the TPNW:

> … each State Party that owns, possesses or controls nuclear weapons or other nuclear explosive devices shall immediately remove them from operational status, and destroy them as soon as possible but not later than a deadline to be determined by the first meeting of States Parties, in accordance with a legally binding, time-bound plan for the verified and irreversible elimination of that State Party's nuclear-weapon programme, including the *elimination* or *irreversible conversion* of *all* nuclear-weapons-related facilities
>
> *(emphases added by author)*

The warhead production complex includes the fissile material acquisition element, plus the non-fissile material subsystems required for the warhead to function (such as the fusing, firing, and neutron generator subsystems). The TPNW parties will need to define which of nuclear-weapons-related facilities are to be included under Article 4.2 verification, and also define the terms "verified elimination" and "irreversible conversion." For the facilities noted, verification should include confirming the location, functions and history of each facility identified. Inspectors from nuclear-armed states with expertise related to each function will be needed to undertake this activity in a competent manner. Verification could then proceed as suggested in the table shown in Appendix 7.2.

The parties to the TPNW should consult the IAEA on its nuclear weapon acquisition path analysis system before fixing the TPNW requirements.

Verifying the absence of undeclared nuclear warheads or new production

The verification authority must assume that one or more of the nuclear-armed states parties to the treaty might intend to cheat. It must consider for each state what its most plausible means would be to hide existing warheads or make new ones and identify verification activities it could take to deter the state from proceeding, or to detect it if it did. Verifying the absence of undeclared nuclear warheads or new production would be carried out to prevent a nuclear-armed state from cheating on its TPNW obligations by intentionally omitting nuclear weapons, warheads, or fissile material warhead components from its declarations, or having undeclared weapon production capabilities that could be used by the state to produce new nuclear weapons to offset ones it dismantles.

This verification should encompass two concerns. The first would be to assure that all nuclear material declared by the state remains in peaceful use. This verification would – as specified in the TPNW – be undertaken by the IAEA, by adapting its existing methods. The IAEA is expected to detect the diversion of nuclear material committed to peaceful use to the manufacture of nuclear weapons or other nuclear explosives, or for unknown purposes, and to detect undeclared activities in facilities committed to peaceful use. While this would no doubt bring some new challenges to the IAEA, adapting existing practices should be relatively straightforward.[10] Note that the IAEA might wish to introduce a new form of safeguards agreement for this mission, which could emphasise the disarmament nature of this undertaking and include the substance of the Additional Protocol as reflected in INFCIRC/540.

The second concern would require the TPNW verification system to gain knowledge of a nuclear-armed state's efforts to hide nuclear warheads and/or establish a clandestine warhead programme or the concealment apparatus to avoid its discovery. To address such threats, the TPNW verification system must allow for the introduction of so-called "third-party information" – including national intelligence information.[11] The TPNW parties should consider whether to include *challenge inspections* as part of the verification system, when it is deemed to be necessary.

Notes

1 Much of what is included in this chapter is drawn from Thomas Shea, *Verifying Nuclear Disarmament* (London: Routledge, 2019).
2 In this chapter, classified forms or properties means that knowledge of the shape, dimensions, physical form, chemical and/or isotopic composition of specific fissile material are restricted because that information would convey secret information on the design or manufacturing of nuclear weapons.
3 See, for example, John Carlson, Vladimir Kuchinov and Thomas Shea, *The IAEA's Safeguards System as the Non-Proliferation Treaty's Verification Mechanism* (Washington DC: NTI Paper, May 2020, https://media.nti.org/documents/NTI_Paper_Safeguards_FINAL_5-8-20.pdf.
4 Ibid.
5 Shea, *Verifying Nuclear Disarmament*, chapters 1 and 2.
6 For TPNW verification, *fissile material* means plutonium with 90% or more of the isotope Pu-239 or highly enriched uranium (HEU) containing more than 20% U-235. Other nuclear species could be used in lieu of plutonium or HEU, including plutonium containing lower amounts Pu-239, U-233, Np-237 and Am-241, but each has properties that make it less suitable than weapon-grade plutonium or HEU. *Nuclear materials* are broader in scope than *fissile material*. Whereas TPNW verification is focused primarily on *fissile materials* essential for nuclear weapons, NPT verification focuses on *nuclear materials* from which nuclear weapons could be produced. *Fissile material* is nuclear material that is ideally suited to nuclear weapon use.
7 In 2000 the USA and the Russian Federation signed a Plutonium Management and Disposition Agreement under which each would convert 34 tonnes of plutonium from nuclear weapon use under IAEA safeguards. Under this agreement, Russia would be allowed to blend this plutonium so as to conceal the isotopic concentration of the plutonium it uses in its nuclear weapons. This agreement never went into force and is now defunct. http://fissilematerials.org/library/PMDA2010.pdf.
8 Thomas E Shea and Laura Rockwood, *IAEA Verification of Fissile Material in Support of Nuclear Disarmament* (Cambridge, Mass: Belfer Center for Science and International Affairs, Harvard University, May 2015). Under the Trilateral Initiative, Russian experts informed their U.S. and IAEA counterparts that if the IAEA would bring its equipment to Russia to use for verifying classified forms of fissile material, Russian security experts would have to examine each item, that each examination could take up to 18 months, that if some problems were identified, the IAEA would be informed, but not of the specific problems, and the equipment would likely not be returned to the IAEA after the examinations. If the items were determined to be acceptable for the IAEA to use they would be returned to the IAEA, but the IAEA would not be allowed to open the

equipment to confirm that the equipment had not been modified such that it would not function in the manner intended.

9 Shea and Rockwood, *IAEA Verification of Fissile Material in Support of Nuclear Disarmament.*

10 Carlson, Kuchinov and Shea, *IAEA's Safeguards System as the Non-Proliferation Treaty's Verification Mechanism.*

11 The IAEA Statute encourages member states to provide such information as would, in the judgement of the Member, be helpful to the Agency (Article 8.A.). In relation to safeguards in Iran, at one point the Director General reported that more than ten States had provided such information.

12 Note that as the warheads are to be dismantled, making permanent markings on the nose cone and base should be included in the scheme of containment and surveillance to facilitate tracking a warhead through transportation and interim storage until the dismantling operation can be carried out.

13 Verification measurements will require that the State agrees that the information obtained and the access granted would not pose a risk of espionage, and that the verification authority is able to make use of methods based on sound science, under arrangements that ensure the results are authentic. Attribute verification and template matching are described in Verifying Nuclear Disarmament, including an Annex identifying promising methods.

Appendix 7.1: Inspection activities for the elimination of a state's nuclear arsenal

Category	*Inspection Activities*
Deployed nuclear weapons under military control designated for disarmament.	Visual examination of mounted warheads *in situ*; Observation of de-mating the warhead; Identification of warhead ID markings; Application of seals and surveillance methods to establish and maintain a chain of custody;[12] Use of allowed radiometric measurement systems to confirm agreed warhead characteristics, as allowed by state;[13] Re-verification during transport & storage.
Complete nuclear warheads detached from delivery systems, under military control, as above, or additional warheads within the production complex, or on reserve, in maintenance or repair, under production, or in dismantlement.	Identification of warhead ID markings; Application of seals and surveillance for establishing or confirming chain of custody; Use of allowed radiometric measurement systems to confirm agreed warhead characteristics, as allowed by state; Verification of warhead dismantlement by perimeter control, perhaps supplemented by bi- or trilateral inspections; Verification of fissile material warhead components inside of storage/shipping containers by use of ID confirmation, application of seals and surveillance to establish and maintain the chain of custody, and use of allowed radiometric measurement systems to confirm each item, according to protocols approved by the verification authority and by the state; Re-verification of fissile material warhead components during transport & storage.

Category	*Inspection Activities*
Fissile material components recovered from nuclear warheads during dismantling containing plutonium and/or highly enriched uranium, and any process, scrap or waste materials containing these fissile materials having classified properties.	Examine and record ID markings; Application of methods establishing or confirming chain of custody; Verification of fissile material warhead components by use of allowed radiometric measurement systems to confirm each item, as allowed by state; Verification of processing of fissile material warhead components to remove all classified properties by perimeter control, perhaps supplemented by bi- or trilateral inspections; Use of existing IAEA-type radiometric assay systems to verify the elemental and isotopic content of all fissile material with no classified properties, use of seals and surveillance to establish and maintain the chain of custody on unclassified fissile material; Re-verification fissile material during transport & storage.
Fissile material committed by the state to use in nuclear weapons remaining within the nuclear weapon production complex, not containing any classified properties.	Identification of container ID markings; Use of IAEA-type radiometric assay systems to verify the elemental and isotopic content of all fissile material having no classified properties; Use of seals and surveillance to maintain the chain of custody on unclassified fissile material; Re-verification fissile material during transport & storage until transfer to disposition under IAEA supervision.
Verification of the absence of any undeclared nuclear weapons or nuclear warheads or fissile material nuclear warhead components, once a NASP has declared that its entire arsenal has been eliminated.	Unannounced access to specific locations; Visual examinations, perhaps under managed access arrangements; Use of passive radiometric measurement systems to detect fissile material; Use of neutron generators to stimulate fission from fissile material.

Appendix 7.2: Inspection activities for the elimination of a state's nuclear weapon capabilities or irreversible conversion of certain of a state's nuclear weapon capabilities to peaceful use

Category	*Inspection Activities*
Verification of mission-critical nuclear weapon facilities.	Examination of information provided by the state to determine location, functions, historical record of operations, and current capabilities; Visual examination of each facility, including essential equipment as required for the declared nuclear weapon support functions performed.
Verification of the destruction of each designated mission-critical nuclear weapon facilities following verification under Step 1 above.	Review of plan for destruction and enabling actions; Verification of disposition of sensitive equipment; Verification of actual destruction; and Ongoing verification of satellite imagery.

Category	*Inspection Activities*
Verification of the irreversible conversion of designated mission-critical nuclear weapon facilities to peaceful use following verification under Step 1 above.	Review proposed modification and submit plans to IAEA Board of Governors for approval; Verify disposition of designated sensitive equipment identified under Step 1 above; Verify modifications; Institute ongoing monitoring program, as determined by IAEA Board of Governors.

8

NUCLEAR PROHIBITION

The long night's journey into day

Joseph Camilleri

The fiftieth ratification by Honduras, which brought the Treaty on the Prohibition of Nuclear Weapons (TPNW) into effect in January 2021, was a momentous occasion. It does not eliminate a single nuclear warhead, but it strengthens the principle that nuclear weapons are ethically indefensible and contrary to international law.

That none of the nine nuclear-armed states, including the five permanent members of the UN Security Council, has signed or ratified the treaty is hardly surprising. None of the governments in question favoured the adoption of the treaty in July 2017, and several of them, notably the Trump Administration, strenuously opposed it.

More telling is the fact that no member of the G7 group and none of the North Atlantic Treaty Organization (NATO)'s 28 members has signed the treaty, and none is likely to do so in the foreseeable future. In the case of the G20, only six of the 20 member states voted in favour of adoption (Argentina, Brazil, Indonesia, Mexico, Saudi Arabia and South Africa), and of these, only South Africa has signed and ratified, with Indonesia the only other signatory.

The response of two other international actors is worth noting. Only five relatively uninfluential members of the European Union (Austria, Cyprus, Ireland, Malta and Sweden) out of a membership of 27 supported its adoption, and three years later, only Ireland and Malta have become states parties to the treaty,

In the case of the Organisation for Economic Cooperation and Development, of the 37 member countries, only seven voted for adoption, and as yet only three have deposited their ratifications: Austria, Ireland and New Zealand.

Why is this analysis significant? Because it tells us that economically and militarily powerful states have almost universally refused to join the drive to outlaw the development, possession, threat and use of nuclear weapons. True enough, though they tried hard, the nuclear-armed states have not managed to derail the treaty.

DOI: 10.4324/9781003227502-10

Aided and abetted by faithful allies and client states, they are now intent on ensuring the treaty remains a toothless tiger.

This pernicious strategy need not succeed. That the treaty took only three years to gain the necessary ratifications is encouraging. The aim must now be to double the number of ratifications over the next three years. This will add to the moral force of the treaty and increase the pressure on governments and publics alike to let go of their nuclear addiction.

Increasing support for the treaty is critical. But it is not enough. Well before they accede to the treaty, states, in particular those that view nuclear deterrence as holding the key to their security, can nevertheless act in ways that enhance the prospects of substantive, verifiable and time-bound nuclear disarmament agreements.

Other important steps include:

- Measures by the nuclear-armed states on nuclear-risk reduction and transparency, including lowering the operational readiness to use nuclear weapons, and adoption of no-first-use policies;
- Agreement by the nuclear-armed states to cut their respective nuclear stockpiles and halt their nuclear modernisation programmes;
- Relaunching of the United Nations (UN) process for establishing a Middle East Nuclear-Weapon-Free Zone;
- Confidence-building measures as a prelude to the establishment of a North East Asian Nuclear-Weapon-Free Zone.

The responsibility of nuclear weapon states to move towards nuclear disarmament is indisputable. There is nevertheless a crucial role which influential allies and friends of the United States can play. In Russia's and China's case, allies and friends are fewer in number and generally less influential, which is not to say they should be overlooked.

These small and middle powers are virtually all parties to the Nuclear Non-Proliferation Treaty. Many have at different times portrayed themselves as enthusiastic advocates of nuclear disarmament. At this point, only two US allies, New Zealand and the Philippines, have ratified the TPNW. As for the Russian led Collective Security Treaty Organization, only one member state, Kazakhstan, has ratified the TPNW.

To elicit a degree of support from at least some of these states is strategically important and politically feasible. What the TPNW currently lacks is the kind of muscular support which European countries have provided other multilateral agreements, in particular the Ottawa Treaty, the Cluster Munitions Convention and the Rome Statute. Much the same holds for climate change, from the Kyoto Protocol to the Paris Accord.

When it comes to nuclear weapons, the position of some US allies, notably France and to a lesser extent the UK, will be difficult to shift. But within NATO, a good many governments, including Canada, Norway, the Netherlands, Greece, Italy and even Germany and Turkey, might over time be open to persuasion. In Asia-Pacific, much the same could be said of Japan, South Korea and Australia.

To get one or more of these countries to break ranks with the senior ally and sign up to the treaty should be regarded as a strategic priority. It would provide the treaty with much needed geopolitical muscle, set a precedent for other allies to follow and heighten the pressure on nuclear-armed states to reconsider their attitude to the treaty and support a substantive nuclear disarmament agenda.

Little or none of this will happen in the absence of a major shift in the public mood (as distinct from "public opinion"). Several organisations, it is true, have launched wide-ranging educational and advocacy campaigns. Among them are the International Physicians for the Prevention of Nuclear War, Prague Vision, Parliamentarians for Nuclear Non-Proliferation and Disarmament, the Basel Peace Office, the Global Security Initiative, Mayors for Peace 2020 Vision, and Abolition 2000. The most effective of these is the International Campaign to Abolish Nuclear Weapons, established only a decade ago and winner of the 2017 Nobel Peace Prize. They have engaged in intensive lobbying of potentially sympathetic governments, intruded with varying success into intergovernmental processes and even negotiations, and developed a stronger profile within the UN.

They have not, however, managed to recreate the mass enthusiasm and mobilisation of the late 1970s and early 1980s, which heralded the end of the Cold War. The proposition that nuclear weapons pose an existential threat is widely accepted in the abstract, but not as a call to urgent collective action. The question then is: how does one activate a public that is weary with so many dark, ominous clouds gathering overhead? For this we need a sustained national conversation, especially in countries closely allied to the USA, both in Europe and the Indo-Pacific region.

Such a conversation must cultivate bold and creative thinking. It must explore the causes of our nuclear predicament, not just its symptoms. It must make it clear that the nuclear threat is closely entwined with other problems and crises, not least climate change, and that none of these can be adequately understood, let alone acted upon, in isolation. Most importantly, we must identify the roadblocks that obstruct a sane approach to security and be prepared to question the mindsets and institutions that are not fit for purpose. And all this we must do as part of a comprehensive outreach programme that connects with the professions, business, trade unions, community and religious organisations, sporting and cultural networks, and much else.

The journey has only just begun.

9

THE POWER OF A BAN

Outlawing nuclear weapons practices

Joelien Pretorius

The Treaty on the Prohibition of Nuclear Weapons (TPNW) that entered into force in January 2021 bans nuclear weapons by outlawing a number of practices. These include possessing nuclear weapons, developing, testing, stockpiling, transferring, using, threatening to use, encouraging and stationing them. To understand why the ban on nuclear weapons is a watershed moment in history that will bring about a psychological shift in how people think about nuclear weapons, we have to understand what it means to outlaw something.

Outlawing a practice means that it is deemed unacceptable by a community, which then creates law to put an end to (or abolish) the practice by making it illegal and illegitimate. This does not mean that no one will ever engage in the practice again, but when they do, they will be on the wrong side of the law (or "outside" the law). When a person is outlawed,[1] he/she is no longer entitled to the protection or benefits provided by the laws of that community. Herein lies the power of the Ban Treaty. It changes the incentives for those who are engaging or thinking of engaging in the practices that make nuclear weapons (and by extension nuclear war and accidents) possible.[2] It creates consequences that will be on the minds, not only of state leaders, but also of individuals along the decision-making, support and operational chain of nuclear weapons. These include nuclear scientists, academics, politicians, business people, engineers, military commanders, and others that assist in nuclear weapons practices.

To begin with, most individuals and even states as communities of individuals want to be on the right side of the law and do what is morally acceptable. The moral suasion of the humanitarian approach on which the Ban Treaty is built provides the foundation to stigmatise practices that make nuclear weapons possible, as well as those who engage in those practices. However, the TPNW's impact goes beyond moral suasion by having material consequences for those who take part in practices that make nuclear weapons possible. Whatever is acquired as a result of

DOI: 10.4324/9781003227502-11

outlawed practices can be confiscated, destroyed or lost in the future. A state that invests billions in producing or modernising nuclear weapons could be condemned and sanctioned by the international community and end up having to give up their nuclear weapons eventually. A company that invests in nuclear weapons technology could be sued for profiteering from illegal and immoral activities. A nuclear weapons engineer could lose a chosen career and a reputation.

The TPNW's power to change incentives for states and individuals goes even further than material and reputational risks. It has punitive consequences for all involved. Individuals can be tried in international courts or by tribunals when they engage in nuclear weapons practices. We must remember that the Ban Treaty fits into a system of international law. The practices it prohibits are therefore judged not just in the context of the TPNW, but in the context of complementary branches of international law. These branches include the law of armed conflict that requires distinction between military and civilians in conflict, the proportional use of force, and the limitation of suffering, as well as human rights law that protects the right to life and a safe environment. The TPNW bans weapons on the humanitarian grounds already codified in these branches of law.

The impact of international law that banned two other international practices on humanitarian grounds, namely slavery and wars of aggression, illustrates the power of a ban. Once commonplace and legitimate, slavery and wars of aggression have been turned into aberrations. More specific examples exist of how international law functions in this area. In 1961 Adolf Eichmann was tried in Israel for his role in the Holocaust, after being captured in Argentina by Israeli special agents. His capture and trial were justified under the guiding principle established by law that abolished slavery and piracy, namely that enemies of humanity can be captured and tried by any nation. Eichmann was found guilty and executed. As an outlaw (an enemy of humanity), he could not claim protection under any law. Both the Nuremberg and the Tokyo tribunals, in addition to charges of wartime atrocities, tried individuals for crimes against peace drawing on the 1928 Kellogg-Briand Treaty that outlaws wars of aggression. Russia's annexation of Crimea has incurred sanctions and international condemnation for Russia and, importantly, non-recognition of its sovereignty over Crimea, because it was acquired by an outlawed practice – a war of conquest.

These legal precedents should induce powerful disincentives for individuals and states, even major powers, to engage in the practices that the TPNW outlaws. It might seem unthinkable now that the leaders of the USA and Russia, or those individuals, who operate nuclear weapons and think up nuclear strategy, will end up being tried for crimes of nuclear weapons practices in The Hague. But, let's not forget that Germany was a major power prior to the end of World War II. As the Nazis learned, today's untouchables can be tomorrow's defeated having to face the law. Imagine a state and its leaders responsible for a nuclear war, intended or not, and the unthinkable humanitarian disaster that results from it. In the aftermath of such an event, public opinion will not accept the defence that nuclear deterrence justified the risk of such horror and neither will the courts.

It is true that at this point the TPNW is likely only binding on the states that have joined the treaty. However, the power of the Ban Treaty can grow over time to become customary international law, general practice accepted as law and binding on everyone, everywhere. How does this work? Customary international law concerns patterns of practice, as well as patterns of legal expectation, what can also be deemed the acceptance of something as law.[3] The nuclear weapon states have been at pains to refute that the TPNW contributes to customary international law against nuclear weapons.[4] But here's the catch: it is not just about what official state elites have to say. It is about what human beings in general think about nuclear weapons that counts towards the development of customary international law. Paust argues: "a particular nation-state might disagree whether a particular norm is customary and might even violate such a norm, but it would still be bound if the norm is supported by patterns of generally shared legal expectation and conforming behaviour extant in the community."[5]

The foundations to make the Ban Treaty binding on those states that have not acceded to the TPNW have indeed already been laid. The norm against nuclear weapons is concrete in the Nuclear Non-Proliferation Treaty (NPT) that came into force in 1970 – a treaty that is close to universal. Unfortunately, the NPT has a legal loophole that allows the nuclear weapons states to continue postponing nuclear disarmament indefinitely (since the treaty was extended indefinitely in 1995). It does not set a date for states that have tested nuclear weapons by 1967 to negotiate nuclear disarmament, even though the treaty makes such negotiations a binding obligation in Article 6. The nuclear weapon states have disingenuously interpreted the NPT as therefore giving them a sovereign right to possess nuclear weapons and to control them on their own terms. Four states that are not members of the NPT have followed the nuclear weapon states' example and acquired nuclear weapons. These practices and interpretation work against the Ban Treaty and its customary law status. The only way I see for states that are serious about nuclear abolition to invalidate this interpretation of the NPT, reclaim its original intent and strengthen the customary law status of the Ban Treaty is to withdraw from the NPT and join the TPNW. Withdrawal will be legitimately based on the grounds that the nuclear weapon states are in breach of Article 6.

The Ban Treaty's customary law status is also built on the many times that world leaders have publicly deplored nuclear weapons, like Ronald Reagan and Mikhail Gorbachev did at the Reykjavik Summit in 1986. The times that leaders could have used nuclear weapons, but didn't, because of the humanitarian consequences (the nuclear taboo), is clearly a pattern of state behaviour against the use of nuclear weapons.

The TPNW is an instrument around which activist states and civil society are doing the political work necessary to strengthen the legal case that nuclear weapons practices are generally unacceptable to humanity at large. The recent open letter by 56 former presidents, prime ministers, foreign ministers and defence ministers from 20 North Atlantic Treaty Organization member states, as well as Japan and South Korea, calling on current leaders to join the TPNW,[6] is an example of this work.

Notes

1 Philip Kerr, "The Outlawry of War," *Journal of the Royal Institute of International Affairs*, 7:6 (1928): 361–88, www.jstor.org/stable/3014936.
2 Oona Hathaway and Scott J. Shapiro, "What Realists Don't Understand About Law," *Foreign Policy*, 9 October 2017, https://foreignpolicy.com/2017/10/09/what-realists-dont-understand-about-law.
3 Jordan J. Paust, "Customary International Law: Its Nature, Sources and Status as Law of the United States," *Michigan Journal of International Law*, 12:1 (1990): 59–91, https://repository.law.umich.edu/cgi/viewcontent.cgi?article=1638&context=mjil.
4 "P5 statement on the TPNW," Permanent representation of France to the Conference on Disarmament, 22 October 2018, https://cd-geneve.delegfrance.org/Statement-P5-on-the-TPNW-10-22-2018.
5 Paust, "Customary International Law," 64.
6 ICAN, "56 former leaders and ministers of US allies urge states to join the nuclear weapon ban treaty," 21 September 2020, www.icanw.org/56_former_leaders.

10

SOVEREIGNTY AS RESPONSIBILITY AND THE BAN TREATY[1]

Ramesh Thakur

In 1984 President Ronald Reagan noted the nuclear emperor had no clothes:[2] "The only value in our two nations [US and Soviet Union] possessing nuclear weapons is to make sure they will never be used. But then would it not be better to do away with them entirely"? Indeed, it would. The Treaty on the Prohibition of Nuclear Weapons (TPNW) tries to do so through a new normative settling point[3] on the ethics, legality and legitimacy of the bomb.

The TPNW entered into force on 22 January 2021, 90 days after the ratification by Honduras (the 50th state to do so) and three-and-a-half years after adoption by the United Nations (UN) General Assembly. Shortly before ratification by the 50th state, which triggered the countdown to entry into force of the first legally binding treaty with a comprehensive prohibition of possessing, using, deploying, testing nuclear weapons etc., the Associated Press obtained a copy of a US letter to treaty states parties.[4] Washington described the TPNW as "dangerous" for the continued viability of the Nuclear Non-Proliferation Treaty (NPT) as the cornerstone of global non-proliferation efforts, said signatories had made "a strategic error," and called on them to rescind their ratification.

The letter recognised "the sovereign right" of NPT states parties to accede to the TPNW. The correct response is it's also their sovereign responsibility. According to Article 6 of the NPT, nuclear disarmament is the responsibility of every state party, not just the five nuclear weapon states (NWS: China, France, Russia, the UK and the USA): "**Each of the Parties to the Treaty** undertakes to pursue negotiations in good faith on effective measures relating to cessation of the nuclear arms race at an early date and to nuclear disarmament" (emphasis added). In the famous Advisory Opinion delivered on 8 July 1996, the World Court unanimously strengthened the nature of disarmament obligations under Article 6 from a commitment to pursue negotiations, into an obligation "to pursue in good faith and bring to a conclusion" such negotiations.[5]

DOI: 10.4324/9781003227502-12

In the 50 years that the NPT has been in operation since entry into force in 1970, the NWSs have in practice brought about a redefinition of Article 6. Not one nuclear warhead has been dismantled nor a single multilateral disarmament negotiation session been convened under NPT auspices. The failure to action Article 6 was accompanied by a subversion of the original NPT bargain. The five NWSs quietly transitioned from claiming that the NPT permitted them to possess and deploy nuclear weapons, to behaving as though the NPT entitled them to possess the bomb in perpetuity and legitimised their monopoly status indefinitely. A good example of this "NWS with attitude" syndrome is the derision on open display when, in a speech in London on 11 February 2020, the Trump administration's top arms control official Chris Ford belittled the arms control community as naive virtue-signallers.[6]

Given this reality, what's a responsible sovereign NPT state party to do? One option is to exit the NPT as indeed has been suggested by Tom Doyle[7] and also Joelien Pretorius and Tom Sauer.[8] That would certainly kill off the NPT. Instead, the good-faith non-NWSs have chosen to make one last stand to complete the NPT Article 6 agenda on nuclear disarmament by means of a supplementary and reinforcing treaty. In Chapter 1 of this volume, Alexander Kmentt asks two related questions: how can the risks that are inherent and inescapable in nuclear deterrence "be considered a responsible policy? Conversely, if nuclear-armed states are apparently trapped in a vicious circle … what is then the *responsibility* of non-nuclear weapon states?" (emphasis in original).

To grasp the argument for the ban treaty as an expression of sovereign responsibility by NPT states parties, it's helpful to refer to the reconceptualisation of sovereignty as responsibility in the context of the Responsibility to Protect (R2P) principle, adopted unanimously at the World Summit at UN headquarters in 2005. This was the largest gathering of world leaders until then. R2P was formulated and adopted as a replacement for the new norm of "humanitarian intervention" proclaimed by North Atlantic Treaty Organization (NATO) leaders to justify the Kosovo war in 1999, which was widely criticised across the non-Western world, for example by the Non-Aligned Movement.

Of course, R2P has itself been very controversial since the UN-authorised and NATO-led intervention in Libya in 2011. But the controversy is limited in the UN community to the manner of – and accountability for – implementation. The principle itself, including the reconceptualisation of sovereignty as responsibility as the normative underpinning, remains almost universally accepted. Some of the key distinctions between the old humanitarian intervention and the new R2P are relevant to the NPT-TPNW differences.

To start with, any norm or law typically can have a permissive ("licence") and/or a restraining ("leash") function. With humanitarian intervention, the major powers asserted a right to intervene inside the sovereign borders of other states alleged to be engaged in committing humanitarian atrocities as the enabling attribute of the norm, but without any corresponding obligations or restrictions with respect to who made the decision to intervene, the extent and types of force that could be employed, the duration of the intervention, and what they could and could not do as intervening powers. By contrast R2P requires Security Council authorisation for any international intervention for human protection and imposes the new normative framework on all states.

With the NPT, the NWSs have similarly asserted their right, as the five permanent members of the UN Security Council (P5), to enforce non-proliferation obligations on all other non-NWS. In 1998 they even did this with sanctions on India and Pakistan, which never signed the NPT, because they had allegedly violated the global norm against nuclear proliferation with their nuclear tests. But the NWSs have steadfastly rejected any binding obligations under Article 6 to begin and complete their own nuclear disarmament. The TPNW moves beyond the NPT in imposing legally binding requirements to disarm and cease and desist from all nuclear-weapon-related activities on all states parties.

Second, humanitarian intervention attempted to redefine the relationship between the intervening powers and the countries that were the objects of their use of military force. In insisting they had the right to such unilateral intervention, they forcefully rejected any role for the UN as the representative of the international community to govern their actions. In complete contrast, R2P redefined the relationship between any individual state, on the one hand, and the UN as the agent and site of the international community, on the other. But R2P leaves untouched the relationship between states directly. Thus, while humanitarian intervention is a violation of national sovereignty, R2P amounts to a temporary suspension of the exercise of the functions of sovereignty without violating the principle of state sovereignty.

The justification for this is the redefinition of sovereignty as responsibility which imposes obligations on states, as an inalienable part of their sovereign privilege, to protect all persons living within their territorial jurisdiction from life-threatening harm. All other states have a responsibility to assist any vulnerable state to develop the capacity and the will to carry out its responsibility to protect. Should the state prove manifestly unable or unwilling to uphold its responsibility and atrocities are committed on a mass scale, or the state itself perpetrates mass atrocities, then the responsibility to protect populations subject to, or at imminent risk of atrocities, trips upwards to the international community which is called upon to take decisive and timely action through the UN Security Council.

Again, the TPNW is remarkably analogous. Every state party has a legal duty and all states have a moral responsibility to promote nuclear disarmament. After 50 years of the NPT being in force, the NWSs have manifestly failed to acquit their responsibility to disarm. Their insistence that nuclear disarmament is a matter solely for them in negotiation with one another, and others have neither voice nor vote on it, is akin to the major powers asserting a right to unilateral intervention with no regulatory role for the UN. Moreover, a nuclear war would be an atrocity on an unimaginable mass scale. No state individually, nor the international system collectively, has the capacity to cope with the humanitarian consequences of such a catastrophic event.

Consequently, as part of its responsibility to protect all life and lives, the international community acting through the UN is fully justified in adopting a new treaty to ban nuclear weapons and associated activities. In the language of the humanitarian consequences initiative that led to the TPNW, it is in the interests of the very survival of humanity that nuclear weapons are never used again, and the only guarantee of non-use is non-possession by anyone. Of course, the Ban Treaty cannot impose legal obligations on non-parties, including all nine bomb-possessing states and their allies sheltering under the nuclear umbrella. But it will reorder the envelope of humanitarian laws, norms, practices and discourse on nuclear weapons.

The TPNW could have one other unintended but significant consequence. While the P5-controlled Security Council is the geopolitical cockpit of world order, the General Assembly is the normative centre of gravity owing to universal membership. In practice this translates into a norm and standard-setting division of responsibility for the General Assembly and enforcement role for the Security Council. Once the international community has successfully stigmatised nuclear-weapon possessors, how can the P5 continue to function as the enforcement authority on nuclear issues? As there is no other body that can lawfully and legitimately substitute for the Security Council on this function, what will fill the enforcement gap with regards to nuclear threats to international peace and security?

Notes

1 This article is a revised and extended version of an article first published in the *Bulletin of Atomic Scientists* (22 January 2021) that has its origins in a Toda Peace Institute webinar held on 8 December 2020.

2 Bernard Gwertzman, "Reagan reassures Russians on war," *The New York Times*, 26 January 1984, www.nytimes.com/1984/01/26/world/reagan-reassures-russians-on-war.html.

3 Ramesh Thakur, "The Nuclear Ban Treaty: Recasting a normative framework for disarmament," *The Washington Quarterly*, 40:4 (2017): 71–95.

4 Edith M. Lederer, "US urges countries to withdraw from UN nuke ban treaty," *AP News*, 22 October 2020, https://apnews.com/article/nuclear-weapons-disarmament-latin-america-united-nations-gun-politics-4f109626a1cdd6db10560550aa1bb491.

5 ICJ, Advisory opinion, *Legality of the threat or use of nuclear weapons*, 8 July 1996, www.un.org/law/icjsum/9623.htm

6 The video of the speech is available at: www.iiss.org/events/2020/02/the-politics-of-arms-control.

7 Thomas E. Doyle II, "The moral implications of the subversion of the Nonproliferation Treaty regime," *Ethics & Global Politics*, 2:2 (2009): 131–53.

8 Joelien Pretorius and Tom Sauer, "Is it time to ditch the NPT?" *Bulletin of the Atomic Scientists*, 6 September 2019, https://thebulletin.org/2019/09/is-it-time-to-ditch-the-npt.

PART II

Country perspectives

11

UNHINGED LEADERS AND NUCLEAR WEAPONS

It's time to act

Tanya Ogilvie-White

I have spent my life studying the risks posed by nuclear weapons. I have always worried that one day an unhinged leader would emerge in a nuclear-armed country, with the authority to launch a nuclear attack. The assumption that nuclear-armed leaders will act rationally has always seemed fundamentally flawed and dangerous. Robert McNamara, former US Secretary of Defense, highlighted this problem when he warned: "The indefinite combination of human fallibility and nuclear weapons will destroy nations."[1] Today, I worry about this more than ever and wish more people would wake up to the problem and push for change.

Until Donald Trump was elected President, I never considered the USA would feature so prominently in my assessments of nuclear risk. Granted, the USA has a patchy record of nuclear decision-making (including accidents and close calls[2]), but in terms of relative nuclear risk, other nuclear-armed states have tended to sound more alarms. Over the past few years, however, I watched President Trump's behaviour with growing alarm, with an eye on the potential domestic and global consequences of his unchecked narcissism.

His presidency was disturbing for so many reasons: his irresponsible approach to the pandemic; his encouragement of racism, extremism, sexism and corruption; his flagrant incitement of political violence; his fuelling of conspiracy theories and blatant disregard for the truth…I could go on. Perhaps most disturbing, though, is his enablement by those who would normally be expected to check irrational and irresponsible behaviour – and this despite their knowledge that Trump had sole authority in the US to launch nuclear weapons.

Even putting Trump's erratic behaviour aside, it is incredible to me that the "sole authority" nuclear decision-making procedure, which is a relic of the Cold War, still exists in the USA. It was introduced to allow the president to employ nuclear weapons within minutes of receiving warning of an attack, without needing to consult others. Decades later, this procedure remains in place,[3] with US

DOI: 10.4324/9781003227502-14

nuclear forces kept ready for prompt launch and with no statute limiting the president's nuclear authority. To drive this point home, this means the US president can order a nuclear attack without briefing Congress and without even informing the Executive Branch, including the Secretary of Defense, Secretary of State, Chairman of the Joint Chiefs of Staff, Commander of the US Strategic Command, or the Attorney General. Ultimately, the decision to use US nuclear weapons is the President's and the President's alone.

When the sole authority procedure was introduced, the idea of a rogue US president assuming office and recklessly abusing his presidential authority would have seemed like a 'black swan' (unexpected and fanciful) event or even science fiction. But such confidence has sometimes waned (as it did during the Watergate Scandal when President Richard Nixon's advisers doubted his sanity[4] and tried to limit his nuclear authority), and it would be fair to say that during the Trump presidency it has slumped to an all-time low.[5] Among his many awful lessons, Trump has taught us that nothing can be taken for granted: the unexpected does happen; political leaders do behave irrationally; and the reckless actions of unhinged leaders can and do go unchecked, including in democracies once held up as beacons to the world.

All of this has profound implications for global security. I am not arguing that the world is facing an imminent nuclear threat from the USA; my point is that we need to wake up from the type of nuclear complacency that has allowed Cold War relics to remain a key feature of our rapidly changing world. Today, it is more important than ever that political decisions reflect our shared responsibility to maintain strategic stability, and that threats to that stability are dealt with, with the future of humanity and the planet in mind.

The upcoming entry into force of the Treaty on the Prohibition of Nuclear Weapons on 22 January was a timely and important step on our long-term path towards nuclear disarmament, but it will have little impact on current nuclear risks, including those posed by unhinged leaders. More significant would be a decision by the administration of President Joe Biden to introduce statutory limits on the president's launch authority. Given Trump's abuse of power, it is critical that the Biden administration takes this step. If it does, the media interest it would generate would provide an opportunity for interested parties to draw unprecedented global attention to the issue of nuclear risk reduction, including providing a powerful platform to promote the shared security benefits of reducing the alert status of nuclear weapons and pledging not to be the first to use them. It could also encourage the nuclear-armed states and their allies to reassess the logic and ethics of nuclear deterrence in our unpredictable world.

A final word on the Trump presidency and the chaotic political transition in Washington, DC: if even the US leadership cannot be relied upon to prevent a descent into chaos, surely it adds weight to the argument that the risks from the continued existence of nuclear weapons are just too great for us not to ban and eliminate them.

Notes

1 "Robert McNamara," Belfer Center for Science and International Affairs, Harvard University, www.cubanmissilecrisis.org/lessons-policymakers/robert-mcnamara.
2 Zaria Gorvett, "The nuclear mistakes that nearly caused World War Three," BBC Future, 10 August 2020, www.bbc.com/future/article/20200807-the-nuclear-mistakes-that-could-have-ended-civilisation.
3 Ernest J. Moniz and Sam Nunn, "The President and nuclear weapons: Implications of sole authority in today's world," NTI, December 2019, https://media.nti.org/documents/The_President_and_Nuclear_Weapons_Implications_of_Sole_Authority_in_Todays_World.pdf.
4 Galen Jackson et al., "Policy Roundtable: Nuclear first-use and presidential authority," *Texas National Security Review*, 2 July 2019, https://tnsr.org/roundtable/policy-roundtable-nuclear-first-use-and-presidential-authority.
5 Ibid.

12

THE TREATY ON THE PROHIBITION OF NUCLEAR WEAPONS

Russia's perspectives

Vladimir Baranovsky

Russia's assessment of the Treaty on the Prohibition of Nuclear Weapons (TPNW) seems *grosso modo* similar to the approaches of other opponents to this endeavour. Moscow is by no means a leader in forging the common front against the nuclear ban; however, to a certain extent, Russia puts forward its arguments even more consistently. Thus, it tends to substantiate them with some basic requirements with respect to the international system (the current one or the one in the making) – and in doing so, to raise the quality of its opposition to the TPNW and to make this opposition more fundamental than if it resulted only from the situational conjuncture. This vision is often formulated as the official policy stand; but Moscow could also refrain from proclaiming its negativity publicly and express it in a 'hidden' way, outside the official framework.

Altogether, Russia's arguments, directly or indirectly raised against the TPNW, could be categorised within four clusters:[1] as a matter of principles; as a challenge to Russia's place in the international arena; the prevailing trends in nuclear-weapons thinking and planning in the possessor states differ from the normative and ethical underpinnings of the TPNW; and objections to numerous concrete setbacks for the project rather than opposition in principle to a ban.

Russia's negativity

First, the issue is presented as a matter of principles. It is stressed that the very idea of the TPNW should be assessed against the background of two major requirements: the total elimination of nuclear weapons, and general and complete disarmament. The TPNW, according to Russia, points to this link only formally and superficially – which is absolutely insufficient. In the absence of these conditions, to ban nuclear weapons is simply unrealistic. "No state considering possession of nuclear arsenal as a guarantee of its statehood and national security would ever

DOI: 10.4324/9781003227502-15

agree to make such a step,"[2] says Nikita Danyuk of the Institute for Strategic Studies and Forecasts, People's Friendship University of Russia.

At this 'conceptual' level, another substantive objection points to the fact that the nuclear ban, as it is promoted nowadays, does not take into account the principle of equal and indivisible security of all states. In particular, one should not disregard the security of states possessing nuclear weapons. This is, for instance, envisaged by the Non-Proliferation Treaty (NPT), whereas it is bypassed in the TPNW. The latter, according to such logic, becomes discriminatory towards states relying on nuclear weapons for their security.

In a broader sense, according to critics, the TPNW could undermine the very idea of nuclear non-proliferation. The latter requires, *inter alia*, the concerted actions of those who possess nuclear weapons or rely on the nuclear umbrella, and those who do not. If they operate as opponents and not as co-operative partners, the non-proliferation of nuclear weapons becomes a dead letter, a pure slogan without any chance of implementation. The TPNW would devalue and undermine the fundamental principle of integrity of the international community, deepening the divide on the issue of nuclear weapons. Strategically, this would not only call into question the perspectives of the non-proliferation process, but also destabilise the future of the international system at large.

Also, when addressing the problem of elimination of nuclear weapons, Russia believes it is necessary to consider all other major factors affecting strategic stability. Because the latter could be defined, understood and interpreted within a very large spectrum, this reference to strategic stability allows unlimited space for criticism towards the nuclear ban. According to Russia's Foreign Ministry, factors to be considered include *inter alia* non-nuclear strategic weapons, US plans to develop outer space weapons, global ABM system, and non-entrance into force of the Comprehensive Nuclear-Test-Ban Treaty (CTBT). The TPNW fails to take these factors into account.[3]

Second, the TPNW is believed to be a challenge to Russia's specificity as an international actor. The nuclear ban would appear in sharp contradiction with a number of essential characteristics that Moscow believes existentially important for the country's place in the international arena. Thus, although Moscow officially endorses the nuclear-free world idea, politically and psychologically nuclear weapons play a significant (if not irreplaceable) role in forging the great power status of Russia. Some key parameters in this regard, such as permanent membership of the Security Council and the ability to compete for global leadership, are believed to be credible only to the extent that they are supported and promoted by the possession of nuclear weapons.

The latter is believed to be a key factor of military security. Nuclear weapons are its core component – insofar as Russia is a country with vast territory, direct neighbourhood to China which is a growing world giant and relative weakness in conventional forces. Whether the nuclear factor could be a full-size reliable compensation for conventional deficiencies remains an unanswered question. But the opposite theoretical model of a large-scale conflict – a purely conventional one without a nuclear component – is hardly considered as deserving serious attention.

The compensatory role of the nuclear factor could be interpreted in a broader sense as well. On the one hand, despite Russia's considerable potential in science, technologies, resources and human capital, the country's various weaknesses remain numerous and significant, whereas nuclear weapons appear as a great equaliser with respect to those who are stronger. On the other hand, it is also an important psychological factor in Russia's ongoing search for self-identification.

Third, the prevailing trends in the nuclear weapons area are considered to have a different vector in comparison to the TPNW. The latter, if viewed from this perspective, appears to be born of the normative and ethical desiderata, a kind of wishful thinking rather than the result of objective social, political and technical developments. Nuclear policies of states possessing nuclear weapons are different. But they all proceed from the considerable role of the nuclear factor, both security-wise and politically. Within this group of states, the attitude towards the nuclear weapon could be defined, in most cases, by ascending rather than descending line. This concerns doctrines and military build-up alike, as well as nuclear-related rhetoric and declaratory policy.

The changing emphases with respect to some specific aspects of nuclear-weapons thinking and planning seem especially remarkable. In particular, this concerns, for instance, the first use, escalation-de-escalation dynamics and the conventional-nuclear threshold in case of conflict. Some approaches which were officially or tacitly accepted and observed in the past have been rejected or reconsidered. Sometimes, the decades of debates on nuclear arms control seem to be consigned to oblivion.

Paradoxically, the TPNW could be assessed sceptically even within the logic of nuclear arms control. According to some proponents of this logic, in practical terms, it is important to focus upon minimising the instability factors of nuclear deterrence, rather than upon the illusory task of creating a nuclear-free world. On the contrary, it is argued that while moving to the latter (in particular, via the TPNW), problems could appear because of the destabilising consequences of minimal deterrence. Indeed, in the 1980s, this issue was debated within the arms control community, but remained inconclusive. However, nowadays, analysing the relationship between the total nuclear ban and minimal deterrence might mean multiplying two uncertainties by each other rather than getting an analytically and politically relevant result.

Fourth, among opponents of the TPNW, there are also those analysts and politicians who do not reject the idea of a total nuclear ban in principle or because it is at odds with what they consider to be Russia's political interest. Rather, the negative reaction of many of them proceeds from numerous concrete setbacks for the project as it was conceived and implemented.

In particular, the TPNW is regarded as differing significantly from most other serious arms control treaties. It covers almost all aspects of an eventual nuclear ban, but disregards numerous details that deserve serious attention, owing to their importance and sensitivity for participants. The TPNW pretends to be a document addressing the most devastating weapons of mass destruction – those that have been at the centre of debates, analytical battles and negotiations for decades. Meanwhile, the text of the treaty is surprisingly short. In comparison to practically all other documents of this kind (with very few exceptions), it looks more like an explanatory note than an international treaty on arms control. Both at first glance and after thorough reading, it seems insufficiently substantive and deprived of analytical depth. It clearly lacks the description of how to begin moving to a world without nuclear weapons and what means and mechanisms would guarantee the full mutual elimination of nuclear arsenals.

In particular, the treaty actually passes over the problem of verification. Critics stress that the latter is of key importance for any arms control endeavour and has always been one of the central elements in both the negotiation and the process of implementation of treaties. Also, the TPNW does not say what should be done in case of non-compliance. Meanwhile, it is well known that the decline of arms control in recent years was, to a very significant degree, the result of contradictions on precisely these two fields: verification and non-compliance.

There is also a problem of reversibility of the ban, if and when a participating state would decide to withdraw from the treaty.[4] In this regard, Russia's grievances refer to the US practice of withdrawing from the arms control agreements that used to be considered cornerstones of international stability – such as the Anti-Ballistic Missile (ABM) and Intermediate Range Nuclear Forces (INF) treaties. Two other cases could be mentioned in this regard as well: the participation/non-participation of the Democratic People's Republic of Korea (North Korea) in the NPT and Iran's eventual withdrawal from it.

Finally, traditional arms control assumes that a treaty has to be the result of serious negotiations which seek to find a broadly acceptable balance between various approaches. This was not so in the case of the TPNW, according to its critics. Indeed, many countries did not take part in discussions and might find it impossible to sign the document which has been prepared without their involvement. Russia shares this argument in its criticism towards the TPNW.

Broader optic

The above description shows Russia's obvious negativity regarding the TPNW. This is undoubtedly the predominant feature of the country's position nowadays. However, in the longer term, it is worth looking at this problem through a more multifaceted optic. The sources of variability in Russia's attitude towards a total nuclear ban do exist.

Within each of the four 'anti-nuclear ban' clusters, as outlined above, one could also find some counterbalancing arguments – if not in favour of the TPNW, then at least allowing for a more compromise-oriented attitude. For instance, coming back to principles, it is recognised (although not very energetically) that the initiative for a total nuclear ban proceeds from good intentions and deserves positive assessment. And when entering this path, analysts could easily come to alternative conclusions.

In particular, this concerns the rhetoric on general and complete disarmament. Actually, referring to it was probably not the best idea of those who aimed at discrediting the total nuclear ban. Without discussing here how convincing the arguments on general and complete disarmament are, it seems obvious that what was perhaps relevant in the 1950s or 1960s is not so any longer, looking both outdated and deprived of concrete substance that would allow operation and implementation. Not surprisingly, direct appeals to this logic as an anti-TPNW argument, without bringing the desired results, could become counterproductive.

Also, attitudes towards the nuclear ban as undermining the goal of nuclear disarmament become less relevant if one puts aside the immediate political considerations and keeps in mind a longer timeframe. Independent analysts, while reproducing the official criticism with respect to the 'fast track' way towards a nuclear weapons-free world, at the same time might consider the TPNW not only compatible with the officially shared goal of nuclear disarmament but even opening the most direct vector thereto.

Within more balanced assessments of the total nuclear ban, the positive context of analysis could have an even broader character, referring to the problem of prohibiting the weapons of mass destruction in general. According to Vladimir Kolzin, an expert of the Moscow State Institute of International Relations: "The TPNW is a concrete specific step forward to denuclearise the world on the global scale, and to add nuclear arms to two other international treaties on elimination of the WMD, namely conventions banning biological and bacteriological weapons and chemical weapons which entered into force respectively in 1975 and 1997."[5]

There are no signs of intensive intellectual debate on the total nuclear ban in the Russian expert community. But the reluctance both to raise the issue and to formulate attitudes thereto is not necessarily explained by the lack of interest towards denuclearisation or scepticism with respect to its practical implementation. There could be another plausible explanation – namely, that the TPNW was overtaken by the prevailing negative dynamics in Russia's relations with the West, as well as by what is considered the most acute aspects of degradation in international arms control. Also, the reverse side of the lack of debate is the lack of excessive criticism towards the nuclear Ban Treaty.

Some Russian experts pay attention to a number of positive changes that were introduced into the treaty in the process of its elaboration. According to Dmitry Stefanovich: "The authors of the TPNW were able to abandon the assessment of nuclear weapon as contradicting to the international law, as well to specify formal procedures for the future signatories, including in regard to the interaction with the International Atomic Energy Agency."[6] Such observations seem meaningful – they do not only point to the minimisation of the potential contradiction between the NPT and the TPNW, but also assume the possibility of including the latter into a future innovative arms control architecture.

It is true that in order to present a more adequate picture of nuclear-weapons related discussions in the country, one has also to point to a noisy campaign aimed at reconsidering in a radical way traditional arms control and pro-denuclearisation attitudes thereto. According to this line of thinking, nuclear weapons should be assessed as a great stabiliser of the international system. This extremist approach stops short of proclaiming a crusade against eventual denuclearisation, says Sergey Karaganov: "It is certainly bad when nuclear weapons stockpiles grow, but it is even worse to have this factor of deterrence disappeared."[7] Rejection of the TPNW stems directly from this kind of logic. That's why it is noteworthy that the latter has not been endorsed by the official policy line and in fact remains an exotic intellectual exercise rather than a serious factor of domestic debates on nuclear issues in Russia.

The overall political context could also work in different ways. Commentators operating within the official policy would undoubtedly have been able to promote the arguments of the latter more energetically. Their lack of enthusiasm in doing so is probably explained by the fact that drawing such a line around an 'anti-Western' pillar is in fact impossible. In a sense, a more supportive attitude towards the TPNW could be a politically motivated line of a broader allies/clients-oriented strategy aimed at forging alternative non-western coalitions/patterns.

But not only opportunistic and situational motives could push in this direction. Of key importance is the fact that nuclear arms control remains on Russia's agenda. Some experts, when looking into the future, believe that sooner or later Russia will become more receptive to total nuclear ban arguments – because the deterrence logic will be assessed as increasingly outdated and requiring a valuable substitute.[8]

Notwithstanding all Moscow's irritation with respect to pro-nuclear ban enthusiasts, Russia seems to be anxious that the TPNW could become a divisive factor in the non-proliferation efforts and, in particular, in the context of the forthcoming NPT Review conference.[9] This concern paves the way for attempts to reduce contradictions and to find common approaches. Joint/common positions could be required within other patterns as well – such as, for instance, relations between Russia and Kazakhstan (with the latter supporting the TPNW while being at the same time the closest ally of Russia).

When discussing the TPNW, Russian experts usually stress that it is necessary not to keep the conceptual and political discussions within the narrow limits of the total nuclear ban problem. It is also expedient to focus upon other important and practically achievable goals – such as the post-New START developments, the entry into force of the CTBT, the search for a substitute for the INF treaty, the (re) launching of conventional arms control and confidence and security building measures in various regional patterns, the inclusion of 'unofficial' nuclear-weapon states into the multilateral co-operative patterns, and so on.[10] Strengthening international security in these sensitive areas requires broader approaches.

Options

By and large, Russia seems to have chosen a low-profile attitude towards the TPNW. Its approach could be summed up in the following way: 'We do not like the treaty, but it has been signed, passed ratification (even if at the lowest possible level) and become a fact of life. It is expedient to have this phase behind us and to have the whole issue, if not forgotten as soon as possible, then at least deprived of its problem-generating potential'. Such is the logic which apparently looks predominant (although not often proclaimed by Moscow publicly). Thus, the overall Russian attitude towards a nuclear ban in its current incarnation, even if not tending to present this project overdramatically, seems to be rather sceptical.

With the entry into force of the TPNW in January 2021, the overall context around the total nuclear ban is not changing in a radical way. But the changes do appear – even if only in the form of some minimalist political, ethical and normative messages *urbi et orbi*. Russia might disregard them and continue its current line – or, alternatively, alter it by choosing among a number of available options. They seem to vary within the following spectrum:

1. To sign the TPNW and to become its full-fledged participant. This option is only a theoretical one; its implementation would require considerable (and perhaps radical) alteration within the triad 'Russia – international system – nuclear weapons' (affecting at least two of its three elements, if not all of them).
2. To support the TPNW politically and in the media without signing it. This could be accompanied by a statement on partial or conditional involvement in the project. Russia could explain, in the former case, what provisions of the treaty it is ready to observe. In the latter one, Russia would outline the amendments it considers desirable or what changes in the international circumstances it is awaiting in order to consider formally joining the TPNW. The plausibility of this scenario seems questionable since its premises are rather artificial and unrealistic.
3. To oppose the TPNW actively and energetically. This option seems next to impossible. It would require the readiness of Moscow to operate as the leader of the anti-non-proliferation trend, as well as Russia's self-identification on the side of the old-type international establishment and against the 'new wave' – something which clearly goes against recent trends in the international system and the country's policy therein.
4. To combine the non-acceptance of the TPNW with refraining from vocal and strident opposition thereto; on the contrary, to promote dialogue between the opponents and supporters of this document to make them more receptive and tolerant towards each other's arguments.
5. To promote constructive engagement with TPNW parties and advocates with the aim of achieving common approaches to the nuclear ban and/or other nuclear weapons-related issues.

Russia's political developments, both domestically and in relation to the outside world, generate prerequisites for all presented options/scenarios. The first three could result in more or less radical approaches (pro- or anti-TPNW). Whether

Moscow is willing (or able) to add radical innovations to its already radicalised foreign policy remains an open question. The last two options would hopefully make the negative implications of debates around the total nuclear ban less salient or even allow for Russia's constructive role in the overall nuclear weapons related area.

Notes

1 See: "Events with the participation of the Minister of Foreign Affairs of the Russian Federation," Ministry of Foreign Affairs of the Russian Federation, www.mid.ru/web/guest/meropriyatiya_s_uchastiem_ministra/-/asset_publisher/xK1BhB2bUjd3%20/content/id/2913751; "Briefing of the spokesman of the Russia Ministry of Foreign Affairs M. V. Zakharova, Moscow, October 29, 2020," Ministry of Foreign Affairs of the Russian Federation, 29 October 2020, www.mid.ru/web/guest/foreign_policy/news/-/asset_publisher/cKNonkJE02Bw/content/id/4411063; "Lavrov explained the refusal to sign a treaty banning nuclear weapons," RBC, 17 March 2018, www.rbc.ru/rbcfreenews/5aad4e799a79479fd56b6a6e; "Prohibition Agreement Nuclear Weapons: Formation of a New Regime?" Ministry of Science and Higher Education Russian Federation, Ural Federal University, Yekaterinburg Ural University Publishing House, 2020, www.pircenter.org/media//content/files/14/15838241570.pdf.

2 "Political scientist: the scenario of a ban on nuclear weapons is utopian," Radio Sputnik, 19 January 2018, updated 3 March 2020, https://radiosputnik.ria.ru/20180119/1512909733.html.

3 "Lavrov explained the refusal to sign a treaty banning nuclear weapons", "Interview of the Minister of Foreign Affairs of the Russian Federation Sergey V. Lavrov to the TV and Radio Complex of the President of the Republic of Kazakhstan, Astana, March 16, 2018," Ministry of Foreign Affairs of the Russian Federation, 17 March 2018, www.mid.ru/ru/foreign_policy/news/-/asset_publisher/cKNonkJE02Bw/content/id/3126872.

4 "Speech by Mikhail Ulyanov, Director of the Department for Non-Proliferation and Arms Control of the Russian Foreign Ministry, Representative of the Russian Federation in the First Committee of the 72nd session of the UN General Assembly in the framework of a general political discussion," Ministry of Foreign Affairs of the Russian Federation, 4 October 2017, www.mid.ru/web/guest/general_assembly/-/asset_publisher/lrzZMhfoyRUj/content/id/2887054.

5 Vladimir Kolzin, "UN Treaty to Ban Nuclear Weapons," YouTube, 27 October 2020, www.youtube.com/watch?v=S18aiJlNRNM.

6 Dmitry Stefanovich, "Nuclear Weapons Ban and International Security," Russian Council for International Affairs, 19 September 2017, https://russiancouncil.ru/analytics-and-comments/analytics/zapret-yadernogo-oruzhiya-i-mezhdunarodnaya-bezopasnost/?sphrase_id=64759952.

7 "God gave nuclear weapons to man as a deterrent to world wars," Sergey Karaganov, Russian Council for International Affairs, 7 October 2017, https://russiancouncil.ru/analytics-and-comments/comments/bog-dal-yadernoe-oruzhie-cheloveku-kak-faktor-sderzhivaniya-mirovykh-voyn.

8 "Vladimir Kolzin – UN Treaty to Ban Nuclear Weapons."

9 Ekaterina Mikhailenko, "'Spirit of the NPT' or 'Let us be realistic'?," Russian Council for International Affairs, 13 June 2019, https://russiancouncil.ru/analytics-and-comments/analytics/dukh-dnyao-ili-let-us-be-realistic/?sphrase_id=64514882.

10 Stefanovich, "Nuclear Weapons Ban and International Security."

13

NATO ALLIES, DON'T DISMISS THE TPNW[1]

Tom Sauer

The entry into force of the Treaty on the Prohibition of Nuclear Weapons (TPNW) on 22 January 2021 produced strong and mixed emotions. Advocates expect an acceleration of the climb to the summit of Mount Global Zero. Opponents repeat that the nuclear-armed states will never sign the treaty. If the nuclear-armed states are not willing to ban nuclear weapons, though, the odds are that others will not believe their promises to eliminate nuclear weapons, as required by the Nuclear Non-Proliferation Treaty (NPT). That does not bode well for the NPT, the "cornerstone" of the nuclear non-proliferation and disarmament regime.

The TPNW is a manifestation of the frustration on behalf of the non-nuclear weapon states about the very slow rate of nuclear disarmament by the nuclear weapons states and their allies under the NPT, especially over the last two decades. If the signal of the TPNW[2] is not picked up by the nuclear weapons states and their allies, these frustrations will come back like a boomerang. This time, these frustrations will not be canalised by another treaty. Done that, been there. A possible next step is to withdraw from the NPT.[3] Iran has already threatened to do so. If that threat is carried out, the odds are that Saudi Arabia and possibly Turkey and Egypt will follow. At the United Nations (UN) General Assembly in September 2019, the Turkish President Recep Tayyip Erdogan made clear that he did not like the discriminatory nature of the NPT, for which he got a lot of applause. Egypt has already walked out of one of the NPT PrepComs. Other non-nuclear weapon states also ask themselves why they have to fulfil their NPT obligations, while the nuclear weapon states do not, at least in their perception. Threatening to leave the NPT is the leverage the non-nuclear weapon states have. If they really believe that the nuclear-armed states and their allies are not willing to give up their nuclear weapons, they have not much to lose by withdrawing from the NPT. The discriminatory NPT regime would be left behind, and one can start building a more equal regime from scratch.

DOI: 10.4324/9781003227502-16

Is that desirable? Certainly not. It might lead to more proliferation. Luckily, this scenario can still be prevented. The ball is now in the camp of the nine nuclear-armed states – the five formal nuclear weapon states and Israel, India, Pakistan and the Democratic People's Republic of Korea (North Korea) – and in the next phase even more their allies. Do they remain dismissive of the TPNW and do they continue modernising their nuclear weapons arsenals for the coming 80 years for trillions of dollars, or do they understand the signal?

It is in the first place up to the allied non-nuclear weapon states to make a decision. Do they keep hiding behind the nuclear-armed states or do they start acting as non-nuclear weapon states under the NPT? Worse, the allies do not only hide behind the nuclear-armed states, they help the nuclear-armed states to hide behind them[4] and they are probably not even aware of it. The USA, the UK and France continue to legitimise their nuclear weapon arsenals and doctrines not only by pointing to the outside threats, but also to the demands of the allies. That is already a long-term practice going back long before the invasion of the Crimea by Russia. Without the European allies, the US advocates of the expensive modernisation programme of the B-61 bomb – costing more than US$10 billion for 400 bombs – might not have won the debate. Without Japan and the European allies, the Obama administration in all likelihood would already have announced a no first use or a sole purpose doctrine. The allies are at least as much responsible for the current status-quo with respect to the North Atlantic Treaty Organization (NATO)'s nuclear weapons policy than the three NATO nuclear-armed states.

Given that public opinion in the allied states[5] is highly in favour of nuclear disarmament and the TPNW, and given the fragile nature of the NPT, it is time to switch gears. In my own country, Belgium, there is a clear majority in favour of the withdrawal of the US tactical nuclear weapons, and 77% favour signing the TPNW. As a result, the allies should delegitimise nuclear weapons in the upcoming NATO Strategic Concept. Under the TPNW, stationing nuclear weapons on other states' territory is regarded as illegal. Each additional day that the American tactical nuclear weapons remain on European territory, NATO's legitimacy in countries like Belgium, the Netherlands and Germany crumbles further. But also, Poland and the Baltic States (and Russia's President Vladimir Putin) are aware that NATO is never going to use nuclear weapons to "protect" these states. They should be reassured with a credible (non-nuclear) deterrent. That is a win-win.

The withdrawal of the tactical nuclear weapons in turn would also make it easier to announce a NATO no first use policy. Alternatively, tactical nuclear weapons (and probably also missile defence) should be included in follow-up New START negotiations between the US and Russia.

Ideally, the allies should also sign the TPNW as soon as possible, as recommended by 56 former Prime Ministers, Ministers of Foreign Affairs or Defence, and two former NATO Secretaries-General,[6] all from allied states. Here are some steps the allies could take in the interim phase:

- Change the rhetoric and tone vis-à-vis the TPNW[7] from being dismissive to at least a neutral or positive tone, like the Belgian government declaration of 30 September 2020, and a resolution by the Spanish parliamentary Foreign Affairs Committee in December;
- Establish a "Group of Friends of the TPNW" in the alliance;
- Be present as an observer at the first meeting of the States Parties in March 2022 to engage with the TPNW member states without having to commit themselves to anything yet;
- Contribute financially to the assistance of victims of nuclear weapon tests (as demanded by the TPNW);
- Vote in favour or abstain on TPNW resolutions at the UN General Assembly in autumn 2021.

With the entry into force of the TPNW, the international community stands at a crossroads with respect to the future of nuclear weapons. The non-allied non-nuclear weapon states have done their part. It is now up to the allies to put pressure on the nuclear-armed states, not limited to the USA, the UK and France. Otherwise, a world without nuclear weapons will indeed become a utopian goal and nuclear weapons will further spread. Under that scenario, the only hope that remains is that nuclear weapons will never be used. Just like we hoped that a global pandemic à la Covid would never arise.

Notes

1 This article was first published by European Leadership Network (ELN) on 21 January 2021, www.europeanleadershipnetwork.org/commentary/nato-allies-dont-dismiss-the-tpnw.

2 Paul Meyer and Tom Sauer, "The Nuclear Ban Treaty: A Sign of Global Impatience," *Survival*, 60:2 (2018): 61–72, www.tandfonline.com/doi/abs/10.1080/00396338.2018.1448574.

3 Joelien Pretorius and Tom Sauer, "Is it time to ditch the NPT?" *Bulletin of the Atomic Scientists*, 6 September 2019, https://thebulletin.org/2019/09/is-it-time-to-ditch-the-npt.

4 Kjølv Egeland, "Spreading the Burden: How NATO Became a 'Nuclear' Alliance," *Diplomacy & Statecraft*, 31:1 (2020): 143–67.

5 ICAN, "New poll: Europeans reject US nuclear weapons on own soil," www.icanw.org/new_poll_europeans_reject_us_nuclear_weapons_on_own_soil.

6 ICAN, "56 former leaders and ministers of US allies urge states to join the nuclear weapon ban treaty," www.icanw.org/56_former_leaders.

7 Tom Sauer and Claire Nardon, "The softening rhetoric by nuclear-armed states and NATO allies on the Treaty on the Prohibition of Nuclear Weapons," *War on the Rocks*, 7 December 2020, warontherocks.com/2020/12/the-softening-rhetoric-by-nuclear-armed-states-and-nato-allies-on-the-treaty-on-the-prohibition-of-nuclear-weapons.

14

DISARMING THE UNARMED

Current reality of the Nuclear Ban Treaty[1]

Manpreet Sethi

Honduras became the 50th country to ratify the Treaty on the Prohibition of Nuclear Weapons (TPNW) on 24 October 2020. Ninety days later, the Ban Treaty, as it is popularly called, entered into force. At a time when arms control treaties are falling by the wayside, this should have been a heartening move. However, despite the landmark event, TPNW is unlikely to achieve its goal of ushering in a nuclear-weapon-free-world. While it valiantly outlaws the development, testing, production, manufacture, acquisition, transfer, possession, stockpiling and use or threat of use of nuclear weapons, it presently bans the bomb for those who do not have it!

The current 50 ratifications and 84 signatures for TPNW come from countries that do not possess nuclear weapons. The nine nuclear weapons possessors (NWP) and North Atlantic Treaty Organization states have rejected the treaty. At the time of its conclusion, the USA, the UK and France had said they do not intend to sign, ratify or ever become party to it. China, Russia, and the four non-Nuclear Non-Proliferation Treaty (NPT) countries fault it for lack of definitions, verification and compliance processes.

So, as far as the possessor states are concerned, nothing changed after 22 January 2021 when the treaty became operative. Each of them remains wedded to nuclear deterrence and engaged in upgrading its nuclear arsenal. In fact, it was their unwillingness to change course that led some frustrated non-nuclear weapons states to move the United Nations (UN) General Assembly to mandate negotiations for the treaty in 2016. Two sessions were convened. Nuclear possessors refused to participate. Consequently, when the treaty was adopted by a vote in July 2017, it revealed a deep rift between the possessors and the rest. The treaty that had set out to stigmatise the nuclear weapon and seek its elimination had ended up stigmatising the nuclear-armed states and creating fractious camps.

Since the treaty opened for signature, supporter nations and non-governmental organisations including the Nobel Peace Prize winner International Campaign to

DOI: 10.4324/9781003227502-17

Abolish Nuclear Weapons, have actively and successfully worked for its entry into force. However, while the treaty has entered into force, it will not mark the exit of nuclear weapons until such time as possessor states agree to action.

The focus, therefore, of the supporters of nuclear elimination should now be on trying to find ways of nudging nuclear possessors in this direction. One way of doing so would be to empathetically examine their points of opposition to the treaty. India, for instance, had raised two pertinent issues while explaining its position on TPNW in 2017. These resonate with others too and addressing them can help engage these countries.

New Delhi had rejected the treaty for two main reasons. First, because it was not negotiated in the right forum or in the right manner. India believes that the appropriate forum for negotiating complex dimensions of nuclear elimination is the Conference on Disarmament, a UN body comprising 65 nations, that follows consensus-based decision making. India considers it critical to take all stakeholders along on this subject. Not doing so could result in an outcome unacceptable to key players, as seems to have happened with the TPNW.

India's second criticism has been on lack of attention to issues of verification and compliance. The treaty exhorts NWPs to join by removing nuclear weapons "from operational status immediately and to destroy them in accordance with a legally binding, time-bound plan." However, these terminologies are not defined. Nor does the treaty establish who would monitor and certify progress of elimination as per schedule, or how non-compliance would be addressed. With such fundamental questions left unanswered, India found the treaty insufficient to promote real disarmament.

Given the current high trust deficits amongst multiple adversarial nuclear dyads, it would be impractical to expect nuclear elimination unless a verification regime was woven in. But to do so will require not only innovative technologies but also inclusive political negotiations. Festering divisions would be counter-productive. Consensus building through small, doable measures has to be the key.

Movement towards nuclear elimination might best be started through steps that seek to reduce the salience of nuclear weapons. Human nature rebels against giving up anything to which it attaches value. So, by reducing the worth of nuclear weapons, nations might be persuaded to eliminate their arsenals. Such value reduction might be possible by encouraging doctrines that constrict the role of nuclear weapons to nuclear deterrence alone; by showcasing the military futility of use of such weapons; by universalising no first use; or, by first prohibiting the use or threat of use of nuclear weapons. As weapons fall into disuse as a result of these measures, their elimination will become possible.

Interestingly, India's nuclear doctrine is a practitioner of these measures. It shows how deterrence can be effectively maintained while keeping a narrow role for nuclear weapons, building low numbers, and severely restricting circumstances of employment to retaliation only. Through such a doctrine, India has managed to simultaneously deter both a conventionally weaker and stronger nation. Therefore, its practice of nuclear deterrence is a practical demonstration that, if adopted by others, could set us towards an nuclear weapon-free world.

The occasion of entry into force of the TPNW can be best utilised to give serious thought to steps that help attain its deeper objective. This would be in the interest of all states – nuclear and non-nuclear.

Note

1 This chapter was published originally by *The Sunday Guardian* and has been reproduced with permission, www.sundayguardianlive.com/opinion/disarming-unarmed-current-reality-nuclear-ban-treaty.

15

HOW NUCLEAR-DEPENDENT STATES COULD RESPOND TO THE ENTRY INTO FORCE OF THE TPNW[1]

Alexander Kmentt

Since the dawn of the nuclear age in 1945, perceptions and strategic positions among states regarding nuclear weapons have always differed. The 2017 Treaty on the Prohibition of Nuclear Weapons (TPNW) has thrust these existing divisions to centre stage. The treaty is the result of increasing emphasis placed by non-nuclear weapon states on the humanitarian consequences of nuclear weapons and the persisting risks[2] posed to all humanity by these weapons. The TPNW is also the consequence of concern about the absence of credible nuclear disarmament steps and actions to which all State parties to the Nuclear Non-Proliferation Treaty have committed themselves by consensus. Through the TPNW, supporting states take an unequivocal stance on the nuclear weapons issue. The humanitarian consequences of nuclear weapons explosions are too grave, unacceptable and potentially global, and the risks of nuclear weapons and the practice of nuclear deterrence postures are too high. Hence these weapons must be prohibited to avert these contingencies and as a conceptual precondition allowing the world to move away from a nuclear weapons-based concept of security.

Not surprisingly, the TPNW is heavily criticised by nuclear-armed states that show no inclination to relinquish these weapons. The nuclear weapons debate, as led by these states over the past decades, is preconditioned and subordinated with the "need" to maintain nuclear deterrence; the value and the necessity of nuclear deterrence is posited and taken for granted. Thus far, any notion or initiative that questions the veracity of the assumptions on which nuclear deterrence is based is objected to as naïve or heretical and not considered on its merits. Breaking through the wall of the nuclear deterrence dogma has been impossible so far. This is demonstrated by the fact that since the first international conference in Oslo in 2013 that focused on the humanitarian consequences and risks of nuclear weapons, nuclear-armed states have not been able or prepared to engage on the substantive arguments raised. As these arguments do indeed challenge the veracity of nuclear

DOI: 10.4324/9781003227502-18

deterrence, the tactics of nuclear-armed and nuclear-dependent states have been to deflect, by criticising instead the idea of a ban and then the TPNW itself.

The underlying rationale of the TPNW also puts the nuclear-dependent states, those states that are under extended nuclear deterrence arrangements with nuclear-armed states, into a difficult position. Nuclear dependent states find it more difficult to argue their professed support for nuclear disarmament while, at the same time, criticising the TPNW and defending the "necessity" of nuclear weapons and the nuclear status quo. As none of the nuclear-armed states participated in the process leading up to the TPNW, such as the 2016 United Nations open-ended working group and the 2017 TPNW treaty negotiations, it was left to the nuclear-dependent states to speak out at these meetings in favour of the security value of nuclear weapons and the need to keep them. As such, the TPNW has exposed a credibility issue for nuclear-dependent states between supporting nuclear disarmament and multilateralism more broadly, at the same time as acquiescing to the current nuclear weapons and nuclear deterrence policies of military alliances, such as NATO, to which they belong. This situation is poised to become even more of a challenge as the entry into legal force of the TPNW will inevitably bring about a broader and more public discourse on the TPNW and its rationale in their own countries and, with it, mounting civil society engagement.

There are, however, steps that nuclear-dependent states could take to acknowledge this challenge and to build a constructive bridge towards support of the TPNW. For example, nuclear-dependent states could declare their understanding of the nuclear risks and the threat perceptions faced by the vast majority of non-nuclear weapon states because of current nuclear deterrence policies. They could declare that they too wish to move away from a nuclear deterrence-based security architecture and understand that this is not a sustainable security policy in the long run. While nuclear-dependent states might think that they cannot sign the TPNW right now for political reasons, reducing their reliance on and moving away from nuclear deterrence and replacing it with other forms of deterrence could be formulated as a clear policy goal and an urgent priority. Nuclear dependent states could, individually or collectively, set such a political objective, opening the door for a more constructive dialogue on the sustainability of nuclear deterrence, one in which the humanitarian consequences and risks of nuclear weapons for all humanity would be weighed against their perceived security benefits.

This broader and more inclusive discussion on nuclear weapons and collective security is needed and should be pursued at the international level at a pace and with a sense of importance commensurate with the global threat that nuclear weapons constitute.

In 2010, in its strategic concept, the North Atlantic Treaty Organization (NATO) stated that "as long as nuclear weapons exist, NATO will remain a nuclear alliance."[3] This is an often-cited quote to underscore NATO's opposition to the TPNW. The logical corollary of this statement is, of course, that "nuclear weapons will exist as long as NATO remains a nuclear alliance."[4] However, the preceding sentence in NATO's strategic concept "commits NATO to the goal of creating the conditions for a world without nuclear weapons." Arguably, initiating credible movement away from reliance on nuclear weapons and nuclear deterrence creates these conditions, probably more than anything else. Thus far, there has not been much movement among more pro-disarmament nuclear-dependent states to initiate or engage in such a broad discussion on nuclear deterrence. This is in part for political reasons that go beyond the nuclear weapons issue, including the larger question of the future of the transatlantic alliance and US security guarantees. It remains to be seen whether, with different political circumstances in Washington and after the entry into force of the TPNW, some of the nuclear-dependent states will see more of a possibility for engaging in such bridge-building efforts.

Notes

1 The views expressed in this article are those of the author and do not necessarily reflect the positions of the Austrian Foreign Ministry.
2 Alexander Kmentt, "Nuclear deterrence perpetuates nuclear risks: The risk reduction perspective of TPNW supporters," European Leadership Network, 4 December 2020, www.europeanleadershipnetwork.org/commentary/nuclear-deterrence-perpetuates-nuclear-risks-the-risk-reduction-perspective-of-tpnw-supporters.
3 NATO, *Strategic Concept 2010: Active Engagement, Modern Defence*, 19 November 2010, www.nato.int/cps/en/natohq/topics_82705.htm.
4 Paul Meyer, "Between a rock and a hard place: NATO's non-nuclear weapons states, the NPT and the TPNW," *Toda Peace Institute Global Outlook*, No. 13, 26 November 2020, https://toda.org/global-outlook/between-a-rock-and-a-hard-place-natos-non-nuclear-weapon-states-the-npt-and-the-tpnw.html.

16

FOLDING THE UMBRELLA

Nuclear allies, the NPT and the Ban Treaty

Paul Meyer

To fold the metaphorical "nuclear umbrella" it will be necessary to convince those sheltering under it that it is safe to come out and to recognise that the umbrella might be more of a danger than a protection. To understand why the advent of the Treaty on the Prohibition of Nuclear Weapons (TPNW) represents such an existential dilemma for those non-nuclear-weapon states party to the Nuclear Non-Proliferation Treaty (NPT), but under a nuclear umbrella, it is necessary to consider the antecedents to the TPNW. This paper will briefly review the diplomatic developments that led up to the conclusion of the TPNW, the predicament posed by this new direction in nuclear affairs for those allied to nuclear-weapon states (NWS), and what prospects exist for the non-NWS concerned to take actions that would enable eventual adherence to the TPNW. Particular attention will be paid to the nuclear policies of the North Atlantic Treaty Organization (NATO) as a constraint on non-NWS members of that alliance, but there is much similarity with how non-NATO non-NWS, such as Australia, Japan and South Korea, have reacted to these new developments, with the common factor being the reliance of all these non-NWS on US nuclear guarantees.

Origins of the Humanitarian Impact movement

The NPT which entered into force in 1970 and currently boasts 191 states parties has for decades been the foundational treaty governing global nuclear affairs. Its core tripartite bargain provided for the non-NWS to foreswear ever acquiring nuclear weapons; for the five NWS party to the treaty (the USA, the USSR, the UK, France and China) to commit to nuclear disarmament; and for all to co-operate in the peaceful uses of nuclear energy. The quinquennial review conferences of the NPT provided opportunities for the states parties to express, if they could agree by consensus on a text, further understandings or commitments with respect to the treaty.

DOI: 10.4324/9781003227502-19

As part of the consensus outcome document of the NPT review conference held in 2010, there was an important, if underappreciated at the time, statement that acknowledged "its deep concern at the catastrophic humanitarian consequences of any use of nuclear weapons" and reaffirmed "the need for all states at all times to comply with applicable international law, including international humanitarian law."[1] This statement introduced into the usual, dry strategic discourse of NPT review conferences the language of humanitarian concerns. The statement further recalled for states their obligation to comply "at all times" with the provisions of international humanitarian law. This latter represented a thinly veiled challenge to the doctrine of nuclear deterrence with its provision for the use of nuclear weapons under certain circumstances. Given the requirements of international humanitarian law for discrimination between combatants and civilians and for proportionality in response, it is difficult if not impossible to envision how the use of a nuclear weapon could be rendered compatible with compliance under international humanitarian law.

As the International Red Cross and Red Crescent Movement, the guardian of international humanitarian law, put it in a resolution adopted at a meeting in November 2011: the Council of Delegates "finds it difficult to envisage how any use of nuclear weapons could be compatible with the rules of international humanitarian law, in particular the rules of distinction, precaution and proportionality." The resolution further appealed to all states "to ensure that nuclear weapons are never again used" and "to pursue in good faith and conclude with urgency and determination negotiations to prohibit the use of and completely eliminate nuclear weapons through a legally binding international agreement."[2]

The combination of the 2010 Review Conference outcome, the efforts of the International Red Cross and Red Crescent movement and the mobilisation of civil society via the International Campaign to Abolish Nuclear Weapons, a broad coalition of hundreds of non-government organisations (NGO) provided fertile ground for a handful of non-NWS to begin to exercise a leadership role in challenging the existing nuclear orthodoxy. Three states, Norway, Mexico and Austria in particular, came forward to organise and host a series of three conferences on the humanitarian impact of nuclear weapons in 2013–14. The three conferences, which gathered greater numbers of states and NGO delegations as they proceeded, shared the common goal of highlighting the humanitarian, as opposed to the strategic, consequences of nuclear weapon use. The conference featured an array of presentations that demonstrated the inadequacy of any humanitarian response to nuclear weapon use, the severe effects on global climates of even a limited nuclear exchange, the history of close calls regarding nuclear force accidents and the recognition that the only sure protection from the threat of nuclear weapons was to ensure their complete elimination.

The nuclear-weapons-possessing states declined to participate officially in the three conferences, although the USA and the UK did send representatives to the last of the series of conferences which was held in Vienna, Austria in December 2014. Non-NWS including nuclear allies generally participated in the conferences, but the implications of this process with its stress on humanitarian considerations and the increasing civil society support it was attracting was causing some discomfort amongst nuclear-dependent states. "Where is this going?" was a frequently heard question in exchanges with officials of these states. As it happened, these states did not have long to wait for an answer. No sooner had the Vienna conference concluded than the Austrian chair set out a national "pledge" to fill the "legal gap" on the prohibition of nuclear weapons and called upon others to follow suit.

The failure of the NPT Review Conference of May 2015 to agree on an outcome document and the evident clash of views on the state of nuclear disarmament in the statements made at that meeting provided further impetus for advancing the nuclear disarmament aims of the leading non-NWS. This attitude was reinforced by the protracted impasse at the 65-nation Conference on Disarmament in Geneva, Switzerland, ostensibly the United Nations' (UN) venue for negotiating multilateral arms control and disarmament agreements, that meant that no programme of work had been adopted in this forum since 1998. By the time of the annual meeting of the UN General Assembly's First Committee (Disarmament and International Security), Austria and over forty co-sponsors were able to introduce a resolution entitled "Humanitarian Pledge for the prohibition and elimination of nuclear weapons." The resolution's preamble contained an affirmation "that it is in the interest of the very survival of humanity that nuclear weapons are never used again, under any circumstances." In the operative section the resolution called upon "all states to identify and pursue effective measures to fill the legal gap for the prohibition and elimination of nuclear weapons." Moreover, it appealed to "all relevant stakeholders … to cooperate in efforts to stigmatize, prohibit and eliminate nuclear weapons in the light of their unacceptable humanitarian consequences and associated risks."[3]

When put to a vote in the First Committee on 2 November 2015, the resolution was adopted with 128 yes, 29 no, and 18 abstentions (the subsequent vote by the General Assembly was 139–29–17). The five NWS parties to the NPT all voted 'no' along with Israel. A 'no' vote was also cast by all the NATO non-NWS, except Albania and Portugal, which abstained. Nuclear allies Australia and South Korea voted against the resolution while Japan abstained. The other nuclear-weapons-possessing states outside the NPT (India, Pakistan and North Korea) abstained. The "Humanitarian Pledge" resolution generated a new division within the international community on the issue of nuclear weapons policy which has continued to the present day and foreshadowed the stance states would take to the subsequent initiation of a negotiating process under UN auspices and to the TPNW which resulted from that process in July 2017.

The essential dilemma posed by the "Humanitarian Pledge" resolution for the NWS and the non-NWS in alliance with them was its rejection of nuclear deterrence, a doctrine upheld by the NWS and enshrined in alliance policy. The resolution brought into sharp relief the tension inherent in advocating nuclear disarmament on the one hand and affirming nuclear deterrence on the other (with its attendant doctrinal and practical manifestations). The resolution did not allow for this tension to be fudged over as it specifically challenged the basis of the allied nuclear policies.

In particular, its advocacy that nuclear weapons "are never used again, under any circumstances" directly contradicted allied nuclear policy which envisages, under certain circumstances, that nuclear weapons are used. The resolution's call for "effective measures to fill the legal gap for the prohibition and elimination of nuclear weapons" also hit a neuralgic point as allied policies denied that any form of "legal gap" existed with respect to nuclear weapons, and that the NPT was a sufficient legal framework. Finally, the resolution's appeal to all stakeholders to co-operate "to stigmatize, prohibit and eliminate nuclear weapons" suggested a campaign to delegitimise nuclear arms and to depict them in the same category as chemical weapons, landmines and cluster munitions, weapons subject to comprehensive prohibition treaties. Given that for nuclear-reliant allies this was an all-out assault against a weapon system still deemed essential for alliance defence, it was evident that the resolution would have to be opposed, if these same allies were not to put themselves into a contradictory position.

At the General Assembly, the nuclear-dependent non-NWS decided on joint statements (both prior to and after the actual vote, something of a departure from normal procedure which limits states to one or the other) to voice their dissent. The statements on behalf of 27 non-NWS, delivered by Australia and Germany respectively, were an effort to explain the opposition, but in terms considered more palatable for the majority of non-NWS supporting the resolution, as well as for domestic constituencies which would be sympathetic to the resolution in the minority group of states.

The statements reaffirm the recognition by the concerned states of "the grave humanitarian consequences of a nuclear weapons detonation" and "our common and unshakeable commitment to the ultimate elimination of all nuclear weapons." At the same time the statements assert that "security and humanitarian principles co-exist" and decry that the resolutions "do not reflect these realities and imperatives" and are contributing to "increasing international divisions with regard to nuclear disarmament, including by seeking to marginalize and de-legitimize certain policy perspectives and positions."[4]

This stance implies a dichotomy between humanitarian and security goals that many concerned with nuclear disarmament would dispute. For the supporters of the "Humanitarian Pledge," the elimination of nuclear weapons makes sense for both humanitarian and security reasons. The dissenting minority of non-NWS are obliged by the logic of their statements to affirm that nuclear weapons have security benefits, which sits uneasily with traditional support for nuclear disarmament under the NPT including the 2000 NPT Review Conference's "unequivocal undertaking by the nuclear-weapon states to accomplish the total elimination of their nuclear arsenals." The nuclear-reliant non-NWS also had to contest the stigmatisation of nuclear weapons put forth in the resolution, as otherwise they would be perceived as supporters of an illegitimate weapon. This compounded the problem for non-NWS which prefer to be seen as supporters of international law, including international humanitarian law. These factors underscored the inherent ambiguity of these non-NWS' declaratory policy in favour of nuclear weapons abolition. It began to resemble St. Augustine's cry for God to make him chaste, but just not yet.

The NATO factor

In order to appreciate the dilemma faced by the non-NWS which did not support the "Humanitarian Pledge" resolution when it was put to the vote in the autumm of 2015, it is necessary to consider what NATO's nuclear policy consisted of at the time (25 of the 27 delegations behind the joint statement on their opposition to the resolution were NATO member states).

NATO's nuclear policies have evolved significantly over the years since its creation in 1949. The approach of the NATO NWS has been instrumental in defining these policies especially on the part of the USA, although there is no monolithic allied NWS stance. France for example has always maintained its distance from the rest of the alliance on nuclear weapon matters and has not participated in the Nuclear Planning Group forum at NATO.

Nuclear policies of the alliance are most authoritatively presented in the "Strategic Concept," a comprehensive policy document last issued in 2010, and in the communiqués released after the biennial NATO summits, of which the most recent is the 2016 Warsaw Summit statement. Although the overall trend in the nuclear policy as expressed in these documents is towards a lessened reliance on nuclear weapons, they are still depicted as an "essential" component of NATO's deterrence stance. At the same time, NATO asserts that it is strongly committed to the NPT, pointing out that all its members are NPT states parties and that "Allies have repeatedly emphasized their strong commitment to full implementation of the Nuclear Non-Proliferation Treaty."[5]

Following the lead of the USA and echoing the words of President Barack Obama's speech in Prague, Czech Republic, in April 2009, NATO in its 2010 "Strategic Concept" pledged to help "create the conditions for a world without nuclear weapons." Although the alliance has failed to articulate subsequently what it considers those conditions to be, or how it intends to contribute to their creation, the impression was made that NATO recognised the need to work towards total elimination of nuclear weapons in alignment with undertakings all the allies had made in the NPT context. Ambiguity has at times featured prominently in nuclear weapons policies, and NATO in the same "Strategic Concept" that endorsed the goal of a world without nuclear weapons also seemed to caveat this by proclaiming that "NATO will remain a nuclear alliance as long as nuclear weapons exist." [6] This Mobius strip of a declaration can of course be read "as long as NATO remains a nuclear alliance, nuclear weapons will exist."

NATO nuclear policy therefore provided useful political cover for all allies, who, like with scripture, could cite the elements that suited them best. The advent of the humanitarian imperative movement with its express aims to delegitimise nuclear weapons and to frame them as immoral weapons of mass destruction that should never be used again, posed such a direct challenge to NATO's core doctrine of nuclear deterrence that member states could not ignore it. The rift already evident in the fall of 2015 within the non-NWS bloc (between nuclear-reliant states and the others) was only going to widen as proponents of the "Humanitarian Pledge" moved to operationalise their commitment to fill the "legal gap" by initiating negotiation of a treaty prohibiting nuclear weapons.

The Open-Ended Working Group: The debate is joined

At the same session of the General Assembly that adopted the "Humanitarian Pledge" resolution, a further resolution entitled "Taking forward multilateral nuclear disarmament negotiations" was passed by a wide margin. This resolution established an Open-Ended Working Group (OEWG) to "substantively address concrete effective legal measures, legal provisions and norms that will need to be concluded to attain and maintain a world without nuclear weapons."[7] Importantly, this OEWG, which would meet over three weeks in 2016, would operate under General Assembly rules of procedure that permit voting as opposed to the consensus rule that had paralysed the Conference on Disarmament for so long. This provision for outcomes that would be voted upon rather than subjected to consensus (and hence vulnerable to negation by any opposing state) was sufficient to lead the nuclear-armed states to boycott the process. Nuclear-reliant states in the main opted to participate in the OEWG with a view to influencing the proceedings in a manner aligned with their preferences.

Over the three sessions of the OEWG the nuclear-reliant allies were noticeably active in contributing to the discussions. They submitted seven working papers to the OEWG, the most important of which was a paper entitled "A progressive approach to a world free of nuclear weapons: revisiting the building blocks paradigm" sponsored by 17 non-NWS allies including Australia, Canada, Germany and Japan. This paper dropped the discredited, to many, term "step-by-step" approach to disarmament in favour of a "progressive" approach that spoke of "identifying concrete and practical 'building blocks' to reach that shared goal" of a world free of nuclear weapons.[8]

The paper argued the need to take into account the prevailing international environment, which required "as an immediate priority the promotion of practical and effective confidence building measures."[9] The paper enumerates a lengthy list of such effective practical measures both in the legal and non-legal realms, while making it clear that the NPT remains the only authoritative legal agreement for nuclear matters and that any further legal arrangements for the prohibition of nuclear weapons among nuclear-weapons-possessing states would only be feasible as "the final building block." As if to underscore this point, Canada and the Netherlands both submitted separate working papers essentially contesting the existence of any "legal gap" with respect to the prohibition and elimination of nuclear weapons (a central tenet of the "Humanitarian Pledge" enterprise).[10]

The non-NWS allies were obliged to operate as advocates of the NWS throughout the OEWG given the latter's decision to boycott the proceedings. It is not clear to what extent the principal NWS attempted to direct the actions of the allied non-NWS during the OEWG. There was considerable speculation that Australia was acting as a proxy for the USA, when on the last day of the session it called for a vote on the final report of the OEWG which had up to that point had been considered as an agreed text. While accurately incorporating the various proposals presented by delegations during the OEWG, the report's primary recommendation was for the General Assembly to convene in 2017 a conference to negotiate a legally binding instrument to prohibit nuclear weapons. The Australian manoeuvre, whatever its motivation, failed to derail the outcome as the report was adopted with 107 votes for and 22 against.[11] Momentum was building to translate aspiration into reality and the non-NWS allies were finding themselves fighting a futile rear-guard action against the negotiation of a new treaty on the prohibition of nuclear weapons.

The TPNW and the impact of a new reality

With the conveyance of the OEWG report to the 2016 session of the General Assembly it was only a matter of time before a resolution was introduced to authorise the negotiation recommended in the report. The resolution provided for four weeks total of negotiation in March and June–July 2017 with a view to concluding "as soon as possible a legally binding instrument to prohibit nuclear weapons, leading towards their total elimination."[12] Significantly, the negotiations were to be open to all states and would utilise General Assembly rules of procedure (thus avoiding the strictures of consensus decision-making).

The move to operationalise the negotiation elicited a hardening of the positions of the nuclear-reliant states. The resolution was adopted with 113 in favour, 35 opposed and 13 abstentions: a marked increase in opposing votes from the 12 voting against the resolution establishing the 2016 OEWG. The boycott tactics practised by the nuclear-armed states were now emulated by their nuclear dependants which, with the singular exception of the Netherlands, whose government had been mandated by its Parliament to attend, refused to participate in the negotiation sessions. Just in case there were any doubts as to where official Dutch sentiments lay, the Netherlands was the only country calling for a vote and then voting against the adoption of the TPNW, providing further evidence for ban supporters of the wisdom of not adopting a consensus-based decision-making procedure for the negotiations.

Given the fact that these negotiations were part of a duly authorised UN process, the decision of the umbrella states not to attend tarnished the public image of these non-NWS long considered as epitomes of good multilateralism. This was not merely a case of rejecting the outcome of a multilateral process deemed incompatible with their national interests (which had been done in the past), but a deliberate effort at delegitimising the very negotiation and its expected product.[13] This overt shunning of the negotiation came with a cost: the lack of any opportunity to influence the negotiations in a direction more aligned with the interests of the non-NWS supporters of the "progressive approach."

In the absence of NWS and nuclear-reliant states, it was to be expected that the negotiators present would work to elaborate as comprehensive a prohibition on nuclear weapons as possible. These prohibitions included the commitments never under any circumstances to "use or threaten to use nuclear weapons" or "allow any stationing, installation or deployment of any nuclear weapons or other nuclear explosive devices in its territory."[14] Such prohibitions were direct rejections of the nuclear deterrence doctrine with its threat of use of nuclear weapons, as well as of existing nuclear sharing arrangements under which at least five non-NWS were providing bases for US nuclear weapons. At a minimum, for nuclear-reliant allies to sign on to the TPNW would entail disavowing such policies and practices.

The NATO NWS were quick off the mark with their rejection of the TPNW. On the very day the treaty was adopted by 122 states at the UN headquarters in New York, the US, UK and France issued a joint statement declaring that "We do not intend to sign, ratify or ever become party to it." The statement also confirmed that in the view of these NWS "Accession to the ban treaty is incompatible with the policy of nuclear deterrence, which has been essential to keeping the peace in Europe and North Asia for over 70 years."[15] NATO officially dismissed the TPNW in a press release as disregarding "the realities of the increasingly challenging international security environment" and referred to the communiqué from the 2016 NATO Summit and its recognition "that progress on arms control and disarmament must take into account the prevailing international security environment. We regret that the conditions for achieving disarmament are not favourable today."[16]

Of course, this claim does beg the question as to whether the security environment was any better during the Cold War when NATO member states were involved in negotiating a series of arms control and disarmament agreements. Is it really a worsening of the international security environment that is preventing progress – or rather a lack of political will and diplomatic energy to seek agreed arrangements to reduce nuclear risks and advance disarmament objectives?

Variations of this theme of hand-wringing and lamentation in the face of an apparently nasty international security context characterised the statements by nuclear-reliant non-NWS at the UN General Assembly's First Committee in October 2017, the first opportunity for those who boycotted the TPNW negotiation to voice their views in a UN security forum. Typical in this regard was the statement delivered by the Australian Ambassador on behalf of 29 states (all the NATO member non-NWS plus Australia, Japan and South Korea) during the thematic debate on nuclear weapons. Under the banner of the "Progressive Approach" the statement declared that "effective, sustainable disarmament must take into account the international security environment." Such disarmament must also be "inclusive, and engage NWS" as well as promote "practical and effective confidence-building measures."[17]

No new legally binding measures were cited or recommended, but the statement saw practical progress represented by the convening of an expert preparatory group on a fissile material production ban and the establishment of another expert group on nuclear disarmament verification. Both steps are of marginal utility compared with the initiation of actual negotiation or action on nuclear arms reduction. The bar of ambition has been dramatically lowered by these non-NWS. Their statement, by ignoring the fact of the TPNW, seems to reflect a blinkered hope that if the nuclear-reliant non-NWS only pretend it does not exist, this troublesome treaty will just go away.

A house divided: The TPNW elephant in the NPT room

The adoption of the TPNW by 122 states has created a schism within the NPT and its 191 states parties. Suddenly, a super majority of non-NWS parties have recovered their agency in rejecting a global nuclear order in which the tempo and scale of nuclear disarmament was solely determined by the NWS. In contrast to the sclerotic "step by step" approach a 'fast track' to fulfilment of Article 6 obligations has been embraced by a new "moral majority" within the NPT ranks. While all concerned might continue to pay lip service to the NPT's importance, the rift amongst its members over the right approach to achieve nuclear disarmament will inevitably have a corrosive effect on the NPT's authority. It might provoke defections de facto or de jure from the NPT as some non-NWS switch to a treaty embodying higher disarmament standards.[18]

Although the NWS and their dependents might continue to ignore the TPNW's presence in the series of NPT meetings leading up to its Review Conference in 2020 (postponed to 2021, owing to the coronavirus pandemic), this might well prove to be a counter-productive tactic, likely only to exacerbate the alienation of TPNW supporters. Equally unhelpful would be the continued accusation against the "moral majority" by the "dissident minority" of having created disunity in the NPT family.

A more constructive approach for the NWS to adopt in the NPT context would be to demonstrate fulfilment of the many agreed, if still unimplemented, commitments on nuclear disarmament and risk reduction generated by successive Review Conferences. Among the most salient of such measures would be:

1. Unilateral reduction of existing arsenals similar to the presidential initiatives of the early 1990s;
2. Elimination of escalatory aspects of nuclear force modernisation plans and the exercise of restraint in any essential force maintenance;
3. Further negotiated reductions in nuclear warheads either bilaterally or through the launching of a multilateral process by the NWS;
4. Major steps in "de-alerting" strategic nuclear weapon delivery systems;
5. A significant diminishment in the role of nuclear weapons in security policy and doctrine (for example adoption of a "sole purpose" pledge on nuclear deterrence);
6. Ratification by "hold-out" states of the Comprehensive Test Ban Treaty;
7. Initiation of negotiations on a treaty banning the production of fissile material for nuclear weapons; and

8. Operationalisation of discussions of nuclear disarmament verification to a degree commensurate with the resources devoted to nuclear weapons development and maintenance.

Bridging options

In addition to lobbying NWS to realise some tangible nuclear disarmament goals as per the listing in the previous paragraph, the nuclear-dependent states could also play a major role in bridging the gap within the non-NWS opened up by the TPNW. A key diplomatic vehicle potentially towards this end is the Non-Proliferation and Disarmament Initiative (NPDI) grouping of states. This grouping of twelve states has the unique advantage compared with other associations within the NPT membership of including both nuclear-dependent non-NWS (for example, Australia, Canada and Japan) and pro-TPNW states (Brazil, Mexico, Philippines and Nigeria). The NPDI has already been active within the NPT context in promoting transparency initiatives and other steps to strengthen the effectiveness of the regime and encourage realisation of its agreed objectives (for example promotion of the Action Plan adopted at the NPT's 2010 Review Conference). If the NPDI could intensify its efforts to identify areas of common ground between the two non-NWS camps it could conceivably play a significant role in rebuilding a degree of solidarity and common purpose within the NPT community. Such an effort would require an investment of political-diplomatic energy on the part of the NPDI states.

To succeed, it would also have to be more than a mere attempt to paper over the cracks and project a frail solidarity. The root causes of the rift among NPT members lies in the failure to make sufficient progress on nuclear disarmament and all the goodwill and well-intentioned initiatives of the non-NWS will be in vain unless that situation is fundamentally altered.

Conclusion

The TPNW has introduced a potent new dynamic into a global nuclear governance regime that has stagnated for years. The TPNW is no sudden "bolt out of the blue" but evolved over several years of intensifying non-NWS frustration with an NWS-dominated NPT-based regime which was unresponsive to their concerns. If the NPT's relevance is to be sustained it will require the NWS and their nuclear-reliant allies to develop a positive agenda regarding the TPNW and demonstrate that they are able to actually deliver on neglected Article 6 commitments.

Notes

1 Final Document, Parties to the Treaty on the Non-Proliferation of Nuclear Weapons, UN, New York, May 2010, www.un.org/en/conf/npt/2010.

2 "Working towards the elimination of nuclear weapons," Resolution 1, Council of Delegates of the International Red Cross and Red Crescent Movement, Geneva, 26 November 2011.
3 "Humanitarian pledge for the prohibition and elimination of nuclear weapons," UN General Assembly Resolution A/70/48, 7 December 2015.
4 "Pre-voting statement on the three Humanitarian Impact of Nuclear Weapons resolutions, delivered by Australia on behalf of 27 delegations," UNGA First Committee, 2 November 2015, www.reachingcriticalwill.org.
5 "NATO and the Non-Proliferation Treaty," *Fact Sheet*, March 2017, www.nato.int/nato_static_fl2014/assets/pdf/pdf_2017_03/20170323_170323-npt-factsheet.pdf.
6 "NATO and the Non-Proliferation Treaty." Original statement in "Strategic Concept" 2010, paragraph 17.
7 "Taking forward multilateral nuclear disarmament negotiations" UN General Assembly resolution, A/70/33, 11 December 2015.
8 "A progressive approach to a world free of nuclear weapons: revisiting the building blocks paradigm" OEWG, A/AC.286/WP.9, 24 February 2016, www.reachingcriticalwill.org/images/documents/Disarmament-fora/OEWG/2016/Documents/WP09.pdf.
9 "A progressive approach to a world free of nuclear weapons."
10 See "The existence of a 'legal gap'" submitted by the Netherlands, OEWG, A/AC.286/WP.16 and "Reflections on the 'Legal Gap for the elimination and prohibition of nuclear weapons'." A/AC.286/WP.20, submitted by Canada, both dated 12 April 2016.
11 For an account of the concluding day of the session see "OEWG Report," 2:19 (19 August 2016), www.reachingcriticalwill.org. Additional commentary on Australia's role contained in Michael Slezak, "Australia attempts to derail UN plan to ban nuclear weapons," *The Guardian*, 21 August 2016 and Richard Lennane "Australia writes itself out of nuclear disarmament diplomacy," *The Interpreter*, 23 August 2016, www.lowyinstitute.org/the-interpreter/australia-writes-itself-out-nuclear-disarmament-diplomacy.
12 "Taking forward multilateral nuclear disarmament negotiations," UNGA resolution, A/71/258, 23 December 2016.
13 It has been argued that this boycott constituted noncompliance with Article 6 obligations under the NPT. See Ramesh Thakur "The Nuclear Ban Treaty: Recasting a Normative Framework for Disarmament," *The Washington Quarterly*, 40:4 (2017), 80.
14 See Article 1 Prohibitions, Treaty on the Prohibition of Nuclear Weapons, UN General Assembly, 7 July 2017.
15 "Joint Press Statement from the Permanent Representatives to the UN of the United States, United Kingdom and France Following the Adoption of a Treaty Banning Nuclear Weapons," 7 July 2017, https://usun.usmission.gov/joint-press-statement-from-the-permanent-representatives-to-the-united-nations-of-the-united-states-united-kingdom-and-france-following-the-adoption.
16 "North Atlantic Council Statement on the Treaty on the Prohibition of Nuclear Weapons," 20 September 2017, www.nato.int/cps/en/natohq/news_146954.htm.
17 "Statement on the Progressive Approach UNGA 72" delivered by H.E. John Quinn, Australian Ambassador for Disarmament, UN First Committee, 11 October 2017, www.un.org/disarmament/wp-content/uploads/2018/11/statement-by-australia-on-behalf-of-a-group-of-countries-72-nw.pdf.
18 For a fuller discussion of this theme see Paul Meyer, "The Nuclear Nonproliferation Treaty: Fin de Régime?" *Arms Control Today*, 47:3 (April 2017).

17

THE NUCLEAR UMBRELLA REVISITED

Sverre Lodgaard

On 21 September 2020 a total of 56 former leaders of 22 umbrella states published an open letter in support of the 2017 Treaty on the Prohibition of Nuclear Weapons (TPNW, or the Ban Treaty).[1] The treaty obliges member states to never, under any circumstance, assist or encourage use, threats of use or possession of nuclear weapons. It entered into force on 22 January 2021, 90 days after submission of the 50th instrument of ratification.

The five nuclear weapon states (NWS) explain their failure to live up to their disarmament obligations under Article 6 of the Nuclear Non-Proliferation Treaty (NPT) with reference to the international security environment. Big power relations are too strained and complex to permit new arms control and disarmament agreements. Old agreements have been terminated and arms racing is picking up. Contrary to their NPT commitments, the leading nuclear weapon states are planning to keep and upgrade their arsenals for the foreseeable future. Moreover, the NPT does not cover four non-NPT nuclear-armed states (Israel, Pakistan, India and the Democratic People's Republic of Korea – North Korea).

The Ban Treaty builds on a different narrative emphasising the risks of nuclear war, the humanitarian consequences if it happens and the obligations under international humanitarian law. It says no to any use, use in retaliation included. In so doing, it challenges the ingrained belief in nuclear deterrence. The narrative pointedly disassociates itself from the miserable state of the international security affairs. Instead, it calls for elimination of nuclear weapons in its own right as a common global good and as a matter of urgency.

In recommending accession to the Ban Treaty, the 56 leaders noted the growing risks posed by nuclear weapons and called for a reconsideration of policies. In their view, business as usual is a recipe for disaster and therefore no tenable alternative. It only makes a precarious security situation worse:

DOI: 10.4324/9781003227502-20

> By claiming protection from nuclear weapons, we are promoting the dangerous and misguided belief that nuclear weapons enhance security. Rather than enabling progress towards a world free of nuclear weapons, we are impeding it and perpetuating nuclear dangers – all for fear of upsetting our allies who cling to these weapons of mass destruction.

Therefore, they denounced any role for nuclear weapons in the defence of their countries, mainly on humanitarian grounds.

The same conclusion can be drawn from *within* the international security paradigm. For European umbrella countries, the humanitarian approach and the international security paradigm are not competing narratives paradigms, but mutually supporting ones. A key issue is the purported credibility of the roles assigned to nuclear weapons. In the history of the North Atlantic Treaty Organization (NATO), which harbours the great majority of umbrella states, this has always been a critical question.

The link to US strategic forces

During the Cold War, nuclear weapons were deployed in Europe to offset a perceived Soviet conventional superiority in the region. The rationale, furthermore, was that the use of forward-based nuclear forces would activate US intercontinental systems, projecting a credible threat of escalation to the strategic level. Often referred to as the nuclear umbrella, this would be the most effective deterrent. However, ever since the Soviet Union achieved a retaliatory capability vis-à-vis the US, this assumption has been questioned and increasingly so as the Soviets achieved parity on important dimensions of nuclear capability. This led to deployment of new weapon systems to convey a sense of superiority and bolster the credibility of the umbrella, but without escaping the dilemma.

Charles de Gaulle questioned if the USA would risk New York for Paris, or Chicago for Bonn.[2] In his view, only a national finger on the trigger would be credible. In 1979 Henry Kissinger tuned in, cautioning that "European allies should not keep asking us to multiply strategic assurances that we cannot possibly mean or if we do mean, we should not want to execute because if we execute, we risk the destruction of civilization."[3] The Euromissile debate of the 1980s shed ample light on the problem. Cruise and Pershing missiles could hit targets in the Soviet Union with greatly improved accuracy, but if they were used that way, retaliation against the USA would follow. The reaction could not be assumed to depend on the launching point or the physical characteristics of the delivery vehicles.

In the 1980s, the targeting policy was more nuanced depending on the war scenario. Had a war broken out in Europe between NATO and the Warsaw Pact, Western intermediate range nuclear forces (INF) could have been used against Soviet and Warsaw Pact targets in Eastern Europe. Had the scenario been one of strategic warfare between the USA and the USSR, the same INFs would have been precious assets for use against Soviet targets because of their accuracy, stealth characteristics (cruise missiles) and short flight times (Pershing). In no case would the USA willingly escalate a regional war to the strategic level, exposing the continental USA to nuclear warfare.

In Europe of today, NATO extending to the borders of Russia, there is no place for such a differentiation. New US intermediate-range systems on European soil would be strategic. Should it happen, they would probably be conventionally armed. Conventional weapons are more usable than nuclear ones and could be directed at targets in Russia on the questionable assumption that Russia would not retaliate against the USA, at least not with nuclear weapons. Still, the escalation risks would be significant depending on the nature of the conflict and the specifics of the targeting policy.

The logic permeating these issues is unambiguous and its strength is overwhelming: both powers would do their very best to keep their own territories out of a nuclear war in Europe. We do not have to read public statements and war manuals to know that this is so. That commonality of interests works perfectly well by tacit understanding. This is, *nota bene,* not to say that a nuclear war in Europe will actually be so confined, only that the USA and Russia will try to confine it. No one can know whether they will succeed: a chaotic battlefield, breakdown of command, control and communications facilities and human behaviour under extreme stress defy prediction. Therefore, as long as the likelihood of escalation to the strategic level is a figure above zero, the coupling argument cannot be totally dismissed. There remains a remnant of credibility to the umbrella, not by design but because events might get out of control. That is small comfort, however.

The sharing arrangements

Today, the USA keeps of the order of 150 gravity bombs in Europe, down from a peak of 7300 in 1971, spread on six storage sites in five countries (Belgium, the Netherlands, Germany, Italy and Turkey). The weapons are B61–3 (yield: 0.3–170 kt) and B61–4 (yield: 0.3–50kt), for delivery by US F-15E and F-16 and NATO F-16 and PA-200 (Tornado). Sharing arrangements still exist, meaning that some weapons might be transferred to the above-mentioned countries and used by their nuclear-certified aircraft.

In view of the sea-and air-based US nuclear capabilities that are available for use in European contingencies and that are currently being upgraded, the double key arrangements are of little military significance. Their value is mostly symbolic and political, signalling common belief in the coherence of NATO and the US nuclear umbrella. Visible forward-basing and sharing is assumed to be more effective in this role than US sea- and air-based systems. The claim is also that the sharing arrangements provide a necessary glue to keep the alliance together. However, if these arrangements fail on the credibility test – coupling to the strategic level is not supported by logic and reason – is it not time to forget about make-believe politics and drop the physical arrangements that allegedly sustain it? Assertions about the necessary glue likewise: had the integrity of the alliance depended on such hollow symbols it would have disappeared a long time ago. The reality, however, is quite the opposite: the bonds across the Atlantic are historical, cultural, economic and political and have made NATO the most durable military alliance in modern history.

Still, the rigid commitment to nuclear sharing and forward deployment makes it hard to discuss alternatives. There has been significant public opposition to the presence of nuclear weapons for years and the numbers of weapons and host countries have gone down, but there is little attention to the broader question of the credibility of the umbrella. In official circles, there is an aversion to discussing it, probably for fear that it would raise severe issues of contention in the alliance. This is where the 56 former leaders, among them two former secretaries-general of NATO, are breaking ice by openly asking their non-nuclear countries to leave all nuclear arrangements and stake their security on conventional means. The fact that so many leaders were ready to support such a radical departure so shortly after leaving government suggests that they had developed a certain restiveness and discomfort with the state of affairs during their time in office. The open letter was not only a reaction to growing risks of nuclear weapon use, but these were the developments that triggered a dam to burst.

Still, land-based weapons remain in Europe and many more are available from a distance. Nuclear weapons are a regular feature in NATO military exercises. They usually end the same way: what should be defended would be destroyed. In the 1980s there was the distinct fear that Europe would be the prime battlefield and victim and, with the demise of the INF Treaty and the looming prospect of new intermediate-range weapons, those worries have been brought to life again.

This time, the worries go deeper than saying no to new weapons. The global setting poses new risks asking for new solutions, and the Eastern adversary is less imposing and perhaps more amenable to reduction of tensions and political solutions than during previous rounds of arms racing. Russia, which tries to reassert itself as regional big power, is not the Soviet Union after all, its economy being the size of Spain's and its military budget only a fraction of NATOs. Its military shadow is not what it used to be. To stick to traditional action-reaction thinking in such an environment, known for its inbuilt security dilemmas, and without comparative analyses of other options, is woefully inadequate.

The USA and NATO maintain an option to use nuclear weapons in response to an attack with non-nuclear means, i.e., to be the first to do so. Will the Europeans be ready to sign off on initiating nuclear war on their own soil? Presumably, the threshold for doing so is very high. If it cannot be a shared decision – time pressures might not allow it, and disagreements might prevent it – it would be for the Americans to decide. For them, the threshold might be lower but still high, especially if many Europeans are known to oppose it. The credibility and legitimacy of the current posture is therefore wide open to doubt.

Escalate to de-escalate

A scenario often alluded to is one where Russia intrudes on the territory of a state in its "near abroad" and tries to establish a fait accompli by threats of escalation to the nuclear level, resorting to demonstrational use of one or a few weapons to make it credible. The Trump Administration's Nuclear Posture Review assumed that Russia has such an "escalate to de-escalate strategy" and that it might work if there is no suitable capability to deter it. In its immediate neighbourhood, Russian stakes are higher than those of its adversaries, so they might be less risk-averse. In response, the USA is introducing new weapons suited for nuclear warfighting on the argument that by widening the spectre of deterrence, the risk of war is reduced.

To "escalate in order to de-escalate" is a fanciful construct, and there is no mention of it in Russian nuclear strategy. That apart, there is a certain logic to it, so in the hypothetical case that NATO is confronted with such an aggressive strategy, what would be the best response?

It could use its non-nuclear capabilities to repel the attack and perhaps hit assets inside Russia that have been used in the offensive. Generally, NATOs conventional capabilities are assumed to be superior to the Russian ones, but geographical proximity would be in Russia's favour. If more resources are needed in areas where NATO is at a short-term conventional disadvantage, elimination of forward-based nuclear weapons could cover part of the cost. More important, conventional forces can be used where nuclear weapons cannot because of the indiscriminate nature of the latter or because of the risk of escalation or both. To go for more nuclear warfighting capabilities would be the wrong response, for they make nuclear war more thinkable and therefore more likely to actually happen. If the goal is to reduce the role of nuclear weapons and encourage disarmament, such capabilities are among the ones to be removed as a matter of priority.

Two narratives; same conclusion

The basic premises of NATO's nuclear strategy fail on the credibility test. The international security narrative leads to the same conclusion as the humanitarian approach. The open letter of the 56, which is phrased in humanitarian terms, is corroborated by international security analysis. The narratives are not contradictory, but mutually supportive.

The credibility of the US nuclear umbrella is long gone, and the remaining US weapons in Europe have little or no military meaning. The sharing arrangements, officially heralded as political expressions of a coherent "nuclear alliance," are empty symbols. It is simply not credible that the Europeans, mindful of the outcome of military exercises, would use nuclear weapons against targets on their own soil. Still, the USA might do so in the face of Russian aggression, but on the understanding that they would treat each other's territories as sanctuaries. Europe would be the battleground. In the fog of war, developments could certainly get out of control and escalation follow, but that is small comfort. None of this is entirely new, but it is worth updating and repeating.

In another scenario – war starting as a strategic exchange between the big nuclear powers – the interests of umbrella states are much the same. They could be drawn into the war, directly and certainly indirectly – there can be no guarantee – but if they cut all involvement in nuclear weapon planning, they are less likely to be targeted. By withdrawing from the nuclear segment of the alliance, they would also send a signal to the nuclear powers that, far from being prestige items, these weapons detract from their standing.

Such a move by umbrella states would put Russia on the political defensive for maintaining large stocks of non-strategic weapons. Moscow could be challenged to reduce the numbers and return the rest to central storage as part of a wider arms control deal including a ban on new land-based INFs and limitations on missile defence. This would be a bonus, but the argument that umbrella states are better served by non-nuclear postures is not premised on it.

The strength of argument and the power of inertia

To most civil servants and decision-makers in allied ministries of defence and foreign affairs, the Ban Treaty is an alien bird. Drilled in alliance doctrine and strategy and echoing each other in opposition to the new treaty, open discussion of established positions is hard to generate.

The humanitarians always emphasised the importance of the NPT, which is the cherished platform of the NWS. Rather than letting the leadership of NPT affairs rest with the NPT's five NWS, however, they are claiming agency of their own to better press for implementation of it. The relationship between the camps was not bound to be bitter and hostile. The Ban Treaty challenges the nuclear-armed states – the special status of the five NWS in particular; it lists them on the same line as the other four – but there was no reason to portray the Ban Treaty as a threat to the NPT. When it nevertheless happened, the human instinct to brandish what is new and threatening accounts for much of it.

The NPT is in miserable shape, betrayed on the disarmament dimension, stuck in the Middle East and mostly irrelevant to the Asian nuclear-armed states, but it has proven resilient and lingers on. In January 2021 it was joined company by the TPNW. Hopefully, the wrangling between the respective treaty supporters will calm down and enable a new consensus on the normative basis for non-proliferation and disarmament consisting of a combination of both treaties. That will not happen overnight, however. There is a long way from mutual recriminations to passive co-existence to bridge-building to exploitation of synergies – if it ever happens.

The dilemma facing the umbrella states is a hard one. On the one hand, it is in their interest not to be defended with nuclear weapons. On the other hand, they deem it important to remain members of NATO. These propositions might or might not be compatible. Some believe they are, emphasising that the alliance is a conglomerate of nuclear and non-nuclear states; of states that are hosting nuclear weapons and others which do not; and that France left the military part of NATO but remained part of the political co-operation without rocking the rest. Others claim they are not and note that in the face of big power pressure, small states tend to balk at running the risks involved – especially if they cannot agree to act together.

Business as usual is the problem, not the solution. In view of current trends in international security affairs, there can be little disagreement about that. If so, much is achieved, because it encourages reflection and re-examination of established positions. If not, the strength of argument will remain posited against the power of inertia.

Notes

1 The European signatories are from Albania, Belgium, the Czech Republic, Croatia, Denmark, Germany, Greece, Hungary, Iceland, Italy, Latvia, the Netherlands, Norway, Poland, Portugal, Slovakia, Slovenia, Spain and Turkey. Other signatories are from Canada, Japan and South Korea. Two former Secretaries General of NATO signed: Willy Claes and Javier Solana. ICAN, "56 former leaders and ministers of US allies urge states to join the nuclear weapon ban treaty," 21 September 2020, www.icanw.org/56_former_leaders.

2 Orion Noda, "Risking New York for Paris? The Illusion of the US Nuclear Umbrella," STRIFE, 1 May 2020, www.strifeblog.org/2020/05/01/7577/; Fred Kaplan, "Warring over new missiles for NATO," *The New York Times*, 9 December 1979, www.nytimes.com/1979/12/09/archives/warring-over-new-missiles-for-nato-missiles.html; Drew Middleton, "The de Gaulle military doctrine is alive in Paris," *The New York Times*, 6 May 1981, www.nytimes.com/1981/05/06/world/the-de-gaulle-nuclear-doctrine-is-alive-in-paris-military-analysis.html.

3 Quoted by Earl C. Ravenal, "Coupling and Decoupling: The Prospects for Extended Deterrence," in *Rethinking the Nuclear Weapons Dilemma in Europe*, edited by P. Terrence Hopmann and Frank Barnaby (London: Macmillan, 1988), 61.

18

THE NUCLEAR BAN TREATY IS A FACT

Jorge Hersschens

On 24 October 2020 Honduras – a country of almost 10 million people with a gross domestic product less than 5% of Belgium's – was the 50th country to sign and ratify the Treaty on the Prohibition of Nuclear Weapons (TPNW or the Ban Treaty). Under international law, this treaty prohibits, among other things, the use and threat of use of nuclear weapons as well as their development and stationing. This treaty had already been adopted by the General Assembly of the United Nations (UN), yet still needed to meet the threshold of 50 ratifications to enter into force 90 days later. The ratification by Honduras thus entailed that the Ban Treaty became legally binding on 22 January 2021.

The vast majority of the 50 countries that ratified the treaty are situated geographically below the equator; they are also economically below the global median income, notable exceptions being Austria, Ireland, New Zealand and Vatican City. All of these countries have a large chip on their shoulder with respect to the Non-Proliferation Treaty (NPT) that dates from 1968. At that time, the NPT, which has been signed by 189 of the 193 UN member states, was established primarily to halt the spread of nuclear weapons and related technology. It was also intended to facilitate the ensuing negotiations about eventual nuclear disarmament – an additional pillar of the treaty. However, even though this treaty explicitly recognises the danger a nuclear war would pose to humanity, it does not contain any article that would make nuclear weapons illegal.

The spread of nuclear weapons to other countries has been relatively limited, so that the main objective of the NPT has been achieved. Yet there has been no progress whatsoever on the critical issue of nuclear disarmament by the nuclear-armed states (the 'haves') – which are all situated above the equator and are predominantly rich countries, except for Pakistan, the Democratic People's Republic of Korea (North Korea) and, arguably, India and China. It is also precisely these rich countries that refuse to negotiate, let alone sign the Ban Treaty. Over the

DOI: 10.4324/9781003227502-21

years, this lack of progress has been addressed time and time again by the 'have-nots' and consequently the NPT's relevance is increasingly being questioned. As such, the TPNW is both a reaction to the NPT's failures and a logical extension of its stated objective of nuclear elimination.

On the brink of destruction

At the same time, all of the important nuclear arms control treaties that were established since the 1970s have expired. Only the New START Treaty between the United States and Russia is still in force but, unless extended, this is set to expire on 5 February 2021. Moreover, after 70 years, the horrors of total war and the use of nuclear weapons seem to have all but disappeared from our collective memory. The implication of this is that the taboo against the use or threat of nuclear weapons is weaker than ever and therefore the so-called deterrence effect – insofar as it has ever really worked – could easily switch in a conflict and lead to a rapid escalation. Just over a year ago, for instance, at least one fighter jet was downed in a tit-for-tat border conflict escalation between India and Pakistan. Two nuclear-armed states were clearly not deterred from engaging in airstrikes against targets in each other's territories for the first time in almost four decades. Luckily, both sides appeared to recognise the risks of miscalculation in a war and showed restraint.

Instead of disarming and decommissioning existing nuclear weapons as agreed in accordance with the NPT, all of the nuclear-armed states are modernising their nuclear arsenals. In the absence of arms control treaties, it will be impossible to legally enforce any limitations to those arsenals. Finally, the risk of a terrorist organisation obtaining and using nuclear weapons technologies and materials is real, if not with a fully developed nuclear device, then with a radioactive 'dirty' bomb. The combination of these factors means that we are once again living in a world that is extremely dangerous and potentially on the brink of destruction.

Belgium and the North Atlantic Treaty Organization

The coalition agreement that was signed by the newly formed Belgian government on 30 September 2020 vows to investigate how the Ban Treaty "can give a new impulse to multilateral nuclear disarmament." That makes Belgium the only North Atlantic Treaty Organization (NATO) member state to recognise this treaty, even though the federal government's policy statement that was delivered about a month later failed to repeat the vow. Belgium is a small country and a military minnow, but for a number of reasons it would be wrong to conclude that this country's actions – or inaction – with respect to the Ban Treaty are irrelevant for the Atlantic alliance.

First, as a founding member state, it has been the host country for NATO's political and military headquarters since 1966, after France decided to withdraw from the organisation's integrated military structure. As such, a fair amount of turbulence could be expected if the Belgian government projected a stance that is fundamentally at odds with that of the alliance it hosts. And since the capital Brussels is also the main political centre of the European Union (EU), the country functions as a co-ordination and co-operation hub between the two institutions. This function has increased significantly over the years, as the EU and NATO currently have 22 member countries in common. This implies that any decision taken by Belgium with regard to the Ban Treaty will have a direct impact on both organisations. Consequently, it should not take its decisions lightly either way.

Second, even though it is only one of the alliance's 30 member countries and a small one in terms of both population and territorial extent, it plays an important role in NATO's nuclear posture. After all, American nuclear weapons have been stationed in Belgium since 1963 – just over a year after the Cuban missile crisis ended – and there currently remain about 20 of the tactical version B61 with an explosive yield range of 0.3–170 kilotons. Such forward deployments started in Europe in 1954 in the United Kingdom, peaking in 1971 at approximately 7,300 nuclear warheads spread across Europe in seven additional countries: Belgium, the Netherlands, Germany, France, Italy, Greece and Turkey. The deployment in France ended upon its withdrawal from NATO's integrated military command in 1966, and the warheads in Greece were discreetly removed in 2001.

As reiterated in the 2016 Warsaw Summit, NATO's nuclear posture relies on solidarity between the member countries, the indivisibility of security, and the cohesion of the alliance itself. The relinquishing of forward deployment by any of the de facto nuclear-armed states could therefore seriously undermine the alliance. Other NATO members might then feel compelled to place them even further eastward, e.g., in Poland or one of the Baltic states, which would be perceived by Russia as extremely provocative. Most importantly, no NATO member state, least of all those just listed, is currently willing to even consider signing the TPNW, because the stationing of nuclear weapons on their territory would directly contravene it. However, by working constructively with the Ban Treaty, Belgium could persuade its peers that it is not necessarily in conflict with the multilateral disarmament clauses of the NPT. Belgium's allies might then be more willing to follow in its footsteps by signing the TPNW and to revitalise nuclear disarmament without undermining NATO as a collective security organisation.

Third, a closer look at the situation within Belgium reveals some interesting details that are mirrored among its neighbouring host states, and perhaps other EU or NATO member states as well. A November 2020 YouGov poll commissioned by the International Campaign to Abolish Nuclear Weapons indicates that a majority of Belgium's population firmly opposes nuclear weapons, with 57% of the public in favour of and only 23% against removing the forward-deployed nuclear weapons from Belgian territory (up from 49% in favour just one year ago), and 77% in favour of signing the Ban Treaty (up from 66%). For decades, the country's four major peace movements have condemned the presence of nuclear weapons on its territory, and weapons of mass destruction in general. In what was to become the country's largest demonstration in its history, they were critical actors in mobilising around 400,000 protesters in October 1983 against the extremely risky stationing of ground-launched cruise missiles in Europe.

Despite having failed to stop the deployment of these missiles, the protests probably did help to intensify the public debate about nuclear weapons in Europe, leading to the eventual removal of the missiles five years later. Of course, almost 40 years later the B61 gravity bombs have still not been removed. Very similar events unfolded in other European countries where these bombs were deployed, such as the Netherlands, Germany and Italy. Tellingly, the earlier 2019 YouGov poll indicated almost identical public opinion ratios with regard to the presence of nuclear weapons on their respective territories and the Ban Treaty (except for the Netherlands, where 32% of the public is in favour of forward deployment).

Since only a minority of Belgium's population is in favour of hosting US nuclear weapons, many of the country's political parties are in something of a bind. On the one hand, they have a responsibility to uphold the state's commitments to the Atlantic alliance; yet on the other, they need to be responsive to public opinion and especially their respective voter bases. A survey undertaken among the major parties of the northern region of Flanders in 2019 by #NoNukes.be, the Belgian coalition against nuclear weapons, shows that the government's position in favour of the status quo stands in stark contrast with national public opinion. In the northern region of Flanders, only the greens, the socialists and the far-left worker's party are in favour of signing the Ban Treaty and removing all nuclear weapons from Belgian territory.

All the parties on the right side of the political spectrum, i.e., the liberals, the conservative-nationalists, and the Christian Democrats, are against. One might wonder how the Christian Democrat party can still logically justify its position after the Vatican stated in 2014 that the use of nuclear weapons is absolutely prohibited, and that their very possession was morally problematic – not to mention Pope Francis's explicit support for the TPNW in 2020. The arguments used by the parties in favour of maintaining the nuclear status quo in Belgium (and, hence, in Europe) broadly echo NATO's stipulations in its Warsaw Summit Communiqué. Essentially, the alliance will retain its nuclear capabilities as long as nuclear weapons exist in the world. At the same time, it emphasises its strong commitment to the full implementation of the NPT. After having dramatically reduced the number of nuclear weapons in Europe since the height of the Cold War, it claims that conditions today are not favourable for additional reductions. Especially in light of the perceived threat posed by Russia's military capabilities and the fact that NATO does not expect any significant reciprocity from Russia, any removal of forward-deployed nuclear weapons would be neither realistic nor pragmatic.

A community of peace, human rights and democracy

The Atlantic alliance upholds its mission to maintain a community of peace, human rights and democracy, and reiterated its global role in projecting stability. These last words sound particularly hollow, since either the member states appear woefully ignorant of recent history or they are using Orwellian doublespeak. NATO interventions in Afghanistan and Libya have caused extreme regional instability (with large population displacements and a vicious political backlash in Europe in their wake), and its Eastern extension might have led to a simmering war in the Ukraine. As for the pro-democratic credentials of NATO, the forward deployment of nuclear weapons in Belgium was arranged by a series of secret agreements between the US and Belgian governments without having been preceded by a parliamentary debate, let alone a public one. Almost half a century later, it is still not possible to verify the actual process that led to the nuclear weapons being placed there. This lack of transparency and accountability is duplicated by the current new Belgian government's 'pending' decision of whether the 34 F-35s, the first of which are expected to be delivered in 2023, will be capable of carrying B61 warheads. It appears that the decision has already been made by the Ministry of Defence or its Air Force without any parliamentary participation whatsoever. It is most unfortunate, therefore, that the Belgian political parties collectively sharing the majority of seats are unable or unwilling to critically assess the country's official position with regard to NATO, the forward deployment of nuclear weapons and the Ban Treaty.

Belgium has had a pioneering role as the first NATO country to ban anti-personnel mines in 1995, cluster munitions in 2006, and weapons containing depleted uranium in 2009. It should take on this role once again and be the first NATO member state to sign the Ban Treaty, thus showing its solidarity with the rest of the world – all those 'have-nots,' those global 'deplorables.' It should stick its neck out and signal to its neighbours and allies that a new security structure can and must be created. The YouGov polls referred to earlier did not measure how salient the nuclear weapons issue is today, but other reports point towards a revived global anti-nuclear movement. By taking this opportunity to support the TPNW, Belgium can show the non-nuclear armed states that NATO's projections of solidarity and security could reach beyond its borders. By thereby increasing pressure on the nuclear-armed states to uphold their part of the NPT, it could help resolve the current gridlocked condition of that treaty. The persistent Covid-19 pandemic has demonstrated a striking lack of solidarity, in both individuals hoarding toilet paper and disregarding safety measures, and states hijacking face masks from each other. One could be justified in being doubtful about international solidarity once effective vaccines are mass-produced. But there is no question that global nuclear solidarity is of perennial importance for a meaningful survival of our societies. According to the Doomsday Clock, it is 100 seconds to midnight: time to wake up.

19

BANNING NUCLEAR WEAPONS

A role for Germany, the Netherlands and Belgium?[1]

Moritz Kütt, Jan Hoekama and Tom Sauer

On 22 January 2021 the Treaty on the Prohibition of Nuclear Weapons (TPNW) entered into force. The new agreement, also called the Ban Treaty, prohibits member states from developing, producing, testing, and stockpiling nuclear weapons. It similarly restricts the use and the threat of use of these weapons. The treaty has 54 member states; 32 more have signed the treaty. Additional states are expected to join. The treaty puts into law a prohibition of a substantial threat to the planet: the use of nuclear weapons in warfare that has catastrophic humanitarian and environmental consequences.

Our governments – Belgium, Germany and the Netherlands – have not signed the Ban Treaty. The Netherlands was part of the negotiating conference; the two others stood aside. All three governments publicly voice that they are in favour of a world free of nuclear weapons, as stipulated by the Nuclear Non-Proliferation Treaty (NPT). Clearly, this is not an easy task, but constant repetition of a goal does not get us closer to it. This can be done only through substantive governmental and public action.

We would like to see Belgium, the Netherlands and Germany support the TPNW with the goal of joining it at an appropriate time. There are good reasons for such a move. First, it would align the countries' actions with their proposed political agenda of reaching a world without nuclear weapons. Second, it would enable them to influence the future development of the treaty. Furthermore, it is in the interest of the people, as public opinion polls in each country have repeatedly shown strong majorities in support of such a step. Lastly, it would contribute to mutually reinforcing the Ban Treaty and the NPT.

The three countries are also in a special situation. Currently, they host American nuclear weapons on their soil as part of nuclear sharing agreements. The weapons are supposed to be used by Belgian, Dutch and German pilots using national aircraft. This practice has been frequently criticised and, in all three countries,

DOI: 10.4324/9781003227502-22

parliamentary resolutions have called for the withdrawal of these weapons. The Ban Treaty explicitly prohibits the stationing of nuclear weapons on foreign soil. We believe that the nuclear weapons stationed on our territories today are a remnant of the Cold War, without any military utility. Our governments should request the removal of nuclear weapons by the USA as soon as possible and end the potential involvement of their citizens in nuclear war.

Relying on the threat of use of nuclear weapons through North Atlantic Treaty Organization (NATO), our governments try to guarantee security with inhumane weapons of devastating effect. Such a posture cannot provide sustainable security for a long time. NATO should start discussing effective non-nuclear strategies of deterrence. We also encourage the USA and Russia to begin bilateral negotiations for a follow-up New START treaty to reduce the nuclear arsenal, including tactical nuclear weapons.

Unfortunately, our three governments today voice strong criticism of the Ban Treaty. The treaty is often described as a mere symbolic measure, sometimes even considered a danger for international security. In our view, these arguments are wrong. The treaty is an actual legal instrument, by which all member states are bound. For example, it is the first instrument to effectively ban nuclear testing while the Comprehensive Nuclear Test Ban Treaty awaits entry into force because the USA and China have not ratified it. There is also no legal incompatibility between the Ban Treaty and the NPT. This has been confirmed in a recent report by the Research Services of the German Parliament. The report considers both treaties to be part of a joint disarmament architecture.

There are substantial effects beyond member states, too. Financial actors like pension and investment funds (like in the Netherlands) and banks (like KBC in Belgium and Deutsche Bank in Germany) already consider and enact withdrawal of money invested in companies involved in nuclear weapon production, directly as a result of the Ban Treaty. And we can see from the action of opponents how seriously they take the "symbolic measure." In December 2020 NATO published a statement voicing opposition. Why would they do so, if the treaty had only symbolic value?

The first event of the treaty will be the meeting of states parties in the first year after entry into force. Belgium, the Netherlands and Germany should take up the opportunity to engage with the Ban Treaty members by participating as observers. Such an engagement does not commit our states to anything yet. However, it would already be a significant departure from the current dismissive attitude towards the new agreement and its members. The Belgian coalition agreement of September 2020 is a good start in that regard. International diplomacy will benefit from a more constructive tone. This might also help in obtaining a successful outcome at the upcoming NPT Review Conference.

To conclude, the Ban Treaty should be seen in Western Europe as a signal by the rest of the world to take the promise of nuclear elimination much more seriously. Belgium, the Netherlands and Germany should work together to get rid of the American nuclear weapons on our soil, and sign the Ban Treaty as soon as politically possible.

Note

1 This chapter appeared in several European newspapers in their respective languages on the day of the entry into force of the TPNW: In the Netherlands in *De Volkskrant*, (www.volkskrant.nl/columns-opinie/opinie-kernwapens-de-wereld-uit-maar-nederland-doet-niet-mee~b3e11fb6/), in Belgium in Le Soir (https://www.volkskrant.nl/columns-opinie/opinie-kernwapens-de-wereld-uit-maar-nederland-doet-niet-mee~b3e11fb6/), and *De Morgen* (www.demorgen.be/meningen/kernwapens-bannen-een-rol-voor-belgie-nederland-en-duitsland~b4bf9de9/), as well as in Germany in *Spiegel Online* (www.spiegel.de/politik/ausland/atomwaffen-sind-jetzt-verboten-halten-wir-uns-daran-a-d00a0906-bcc3-44b0-8ac8-edaebbe2e3be).

20

CANADA ACKNOWLEDGES REASON FOR THE TPNW

Douglas Roche

PROHIBITION TREATY[1]

In a subtle diplomatic move, the Government of Canada has ceased its opposition and now "acknowledges" the reason for the Treaty on the Prohibition of Nuclear Weapons (TPNW), which entered into force on 22 January 2021.

The new treaty, which has been ratified by 50 states, has been denounced by the Trump administration and also rejected by the North Atlantic Treaty Organization (NATO). Canada is betting that the expected election, on 3 November, of Joe Biden as president will bring the USA back into more co-operative multilateral work and that NATO will gradually recognise that the global norm against the possession of nuclear weapons is rising.

Only the states that join the treaty will be bound by it, but its central provision – the prohibition of the possession of nuclear weapons – is a direct attack on the military doctrine of nuclear deterrence.

Canada is not joining the treaty – at least at this moment in history. But its policy is shifting. In 2017, when negotiations for the treaty were under way, Prime Minister Justin Trudeau called the exercise "useless." Then, when 122 states adopted the treaty at the UN, government spokespeople dismissed it as "premature." Now Global Affairs Canada says: "We acknowledge the widespread frustration with the pace of global efforts toward nuclear disarmament, which clearly motivated the negotiation of the Treaty on the Prohibition of Nuclear Weapons."

Some might argue that this is not a clear-cut endorsement of the treaty, but given that Global Affairs Canada did not want to directly contradict the prime minister or directly challenge NATO, which still claims that nuclear weapons are the "supreme guarantee" of security, the statement is a diplomatic expression of a shift in policy. Doubtless, the recent rebuke to NATO's nuclear policies by two former Canadian prime ministers (Jean Chrétien, the now late John Turner), three former foreign ministers (Lloyd Axworthy, Bill Graham, John Manley) and two

DOI: 10.4324/9781003227502-23

former defence ministers (Jean-Jacques Blais, John McCallum) – all of them Liberals – made an impression on the Pearson Building. The prohibition treaty is now treated with respect in Canada. The logical next step is for Canada to open a dialogue with NATO to bring the organisation's nuclear weapons policies into conformity with the prohibition treaty.

The government statement adds that, for 50 years, Canada has pursued a "pragmatic, inclusive approach to nuclear disarmament," which is "anchored" in the Non-Proliferation Treaty (NPT). But, with nine states still holding 13,865 nuclear weapons, the NPT has clearly not produced a nuclear weapons-free world.

Reacting to this failure to eliminate nuclear weapons, a new movement, composed of activist governments and civil society leaders, began to warn of the catastrophic humanitarian consequences of the use of nuclear weapons. The Prohibition Treaty resulted.

The treaty, driven by the International Campaign to Abolish Nuclear Weapons, which won the Nobel Peace Prize in 2017 for its efforts, does not pretend to eliminate nuclear weapons. Nor does it seek to replace the NPT, which the treaty hails as the "cornerstone" of nuclear disarmament. What it does is stigmatise nuclear weapons as standing outside international humanitarian law and prepare the ground for comprehensive negotiations by all states for the elimination of nuclear weapons as called for by the NPT.

At the same time, the treaty is more than an exercise in public education. It is an international legal reality, binding on all those who join it. The combined educational, political and legal value of the treaty, taking the world a step closer to the end of nuclear weapons, is what the USA fears most.

In a letter to supporters of the treaty urging they recant, the USA claimed that the treaty is divisive and "will detract from realistic and practical efforts to advance the cause of nuclear disarmament." It is quite hard to see how the USA is advancing nuclear disarmament when it plans to spend $1.7 trillion over the next quarter-century modernising its fleet of nuclear missiles.

Whether President Biden will butt heads with the military-industrial complex, driving such outrageous expenditures, remains to be seen. But he did say in his campaign, "I will work to bring us closer to a world without nuclear weapons." And he emphasised his respect for treaties: "For decades, American leaders of both parties have understood that the United States has a national security imperative and a moral responsibility to reduce nuclear threats, including by negotiating treaties and agreements to control and eventually eliminate these weapons."[2]

It will take a lot of pressure on a Biden presidency to "acknowledge" the prohibition treaty, but even if he only stops the US attack on it, the treaty might come to be seen as a reinforcement of the NPT. In a renewed political atmosphere, the paralysis that has plagued nuclear disarmament for so long could be broken.

With a becoming modesty, Canada has nudged this process forward.

Statement issued to Doug Roche from Global Affairs Canada 26 October 2020

- Canada unequivocally supports global nuclear disarmament.
- We acknowledge the widespread frustration with the pace of global efforts toward nuclear disarmament, which clearly motivated the negotiation of the Treaty on the Prohibition of Nuclear Weapons.
- For more than 50 years, Canada has actively pursued a pragmatic, inclusive approach towards nuclear disarmament, which we believe is the best way forward for creating the conditions for a world free of nuclear weapons.
- Canada's nuclear disarmament and non-proliferation policy is anchored in the Treaty on the Non-Proliferation of Nuclear Weapons (NPT), the cornerstone of the international non-proliferation and disarmament regime.
- Since its entry into force, Canada's commitment to the NPT has been unwavering.

Notes

1 This article was first published in *The Hill Times* on 30 October 2020 (www.hilltimes.com/2020/10/30/269583/269583) and reprinted by the Toda Peace Institute with permission.

2 In a statement issued to mark the 75th anniversary of the atomic bombing of Hiroshima. Kyodo News, "U.S. presidential candidate Biden vows to work toward nuke-free world," 7 August 2020, https://english.kyodonews.net/news/2020/08/fde0f299de44-us-presidential-candidate-biden-vows-to-work-toward-nuke-free-world.html.

21

LATIN AMERICA AND THE QUEST FOR NUCLEAR ABOLITION

From the Treaty of Tlatelolco to the Ban Treaty

Cesar Jaramillo

On 14 February 2014, as the Second Conference on the Humanitarian Impact of Nuclear Weapons came to an end, conference Chair Juan Manuel Gomez Robledo – then deputy Minister of Foreign Affairs of Mexico – captured the sentiment in the room in the powerful last few words of his closing remarks: in global efforts towards the elimination of nuclear weapons, this conference marked a "point of no return."[1] His optimistic conclusion was met with a roar of applause.

Hosted by the Government of Mexico in the coastal state of Nayarit, this was the second of three conferences specifically focused on highlighting the catastrophic consequences of any nuclear weapons use – the first and third hosted, respectively, by the governments of Norway and Austria. A key recognition that emerged from this cycle was that a legal prohibition was necessary to remedy the anomaly under international law whereby every other category of weapons of mass destruction had been explicitly prohibited, except nuclear weapons, the most devastating of all.

As Gomez Robledo explained at the Nayarit conference, "we need to take into account that, in the past, weapons have been eliminated after they have been outlawed. We believe this is the path to achieve a world without nuclear weapons."[2] Against all odds and despite the direct opposition of nuclear weapons states and their allies, that path was indeed followed. Nearly three and a half years after Nayarit, on 7 July 2017, the Treaty on the Prohibition of Nuclear Weapons (TPNW) was adopted by 122 nations at the United Nations (UN) in New York, with Latin America having influenced both process and outcome.

Not only had Mexico played a decisive role in laying the groundwork that led to the historic adoption of the TPNW, but every single state in Latin America participated in the negotiations and voted in favour of adopting the treaty. Moreover, treaty negotiations were presided over by ambassador Elayne Whyte Gomez of Costa Rica, a country that continues to be among the TPNW's strongest advocates.

DOI: 10.4324/9781003227502-24

More recently, on 24 October 2020 Honduras secured a place in nuclear disarmament history by becoming the 50th state party to ratify the TPNW.[3] When it deposited its instrument of ratification at the UN, Honduras triggered the process that led to the treaty's entry into force 90 days later on 22 January 2021. The TPNW has now formally become part of international law and it bears an indelible Latin American mark.

Honduras brought to 12 the number of Latin American states among the first 50 states parties to the TPNW.[4] It joined Paraguay, Mexico, Cuba, Venezuela, Costa Rica, Nicaragua, Uruguay, El Salvador, Panama, Bolivia and Ecuador. Several others, including Guatemala, Chile and the Dominican Republic, have signed and are undergoing the domestic legislative process towards ratification.

To be sure, the strong Latin American support for the TPNW was hardly surprising. In fact, it was a natural step, entirely consistent with earlier, treaty-based commitments to renounce nuclear weapons.

States in the region were already party to the Treaty for the Prohibition of Nuclear Weapons in Latin America and the Caribbean,[5] more commonly known as the Treaty of Tlatelolco. Under the auspices of the Agency for the Prohibition of Nuclear Weapons in Latin America and the Caribbean (OPANAL), this treaty establishes a regional nuclear weapons free zone which includes prohibitions on the possession, transfer and use of nuclear weapons, as well as an obligation to use nuclear material solely for peaceful purposes.

Opened for signatures in 1967, the Treaty of Tlatelolco is a compelling testament to the longstanding regional commitment to nuclear abolition. It predates the nearly universal Nuclear Non-Proliferation Treaty (NPT), to which all states in the region are also party. The resolve with which Latin American states have engaged with nuclear disarmament underscores the fact that nuclear disarmament is a shared international responsibility and that all nations, big or small, can make a positive contribution to this enterprise.

The conviction by Latin American states that nuclear weapons must and can be eliminated does not seem to be based on a naive or crude understanding of international relations. It is abundantly clear that nuclear weapons states and many of their allies enshrine nuclear weapons in their national security doctrines and strategies. But the case has been made, repeatedly and convincingly, that any perceived benefits of nuclear weapons possession are based on fallacious arguments and, in any case, are far outweighed by the threat posed by these weapons to human civilisation itself.

The renewed attention in recent years to the humanitarian impact of nuclear weapons has been critical for Latin American states' involvement in nuclear disarmament efforts and was vital to the adoption of the Treaty on the Prohibition of Nuclear Weapons in 2017. It has also signalled a shift in the traditional attributes of power that shape multilateral arms control and disarmament processes. This is not to say that military and economic power have suddenly become irrelevant. But the humanitarian imperative to disarm can serve as an effective catalyst and rallying point for states in the region.

The TPNW was a response to the many failures and shortcomings of the global nuclear disarmament and non-proliferation regime, including the NPT's inability to bring about nuclear abolition. The NPT was designed to prevent non-nuclear weapon states from acquiring nuclear weapons and to compel nuclear weapon states to eliminate them, yet those that hold nuclear weapons have resisted, avoided or ignored not only their treaty obligations, but the groundswell of support for nuclear abolition from all corners of the planet. But if the history of nuclear abolition efforts for the past half century is any indication, Latin American states will not stop pushing.

Notes

1 Chair's Summary, Second Conference on the Humanitarian Impact of Nuclear Weapons, 2014, www.reachingcriticalwill.org/images/documents/Disarmament-fora/nayarit-2014/chairs-summary.pdf.
2 Ibid.
3 "UN treaty banning nuclear weapons set to enter into force in January," UN News, 25 October 2020, https://news.un.org/en/story/2020/10/1076082.
4 Signature and ratification status, ICAN, www.icanw.org/signature_and_ratification_status.
5 Treaty for the Prohibition of Nuclear Weapons in Latin America and the Caribbean (Treaty of Tlatelolco), Opanal, www.opanal.org/en/text-of-the-treaty-of-tlatelolco.

22

ENGAGING THE NUCLEAR-ARMED STATES IN THE TPNW DISARMAMENT PROCESS

Thomas E. Shea

The Treaty on the Prohibition of Nuclear Weapons (TPNW) has now entered into force. Yet, none of the nine states currently possessing nuclear weapons has expressed any positive interest in the treaty, continuing with impunity to reject every effort by the international community at beginning the process of nuclear disarmament. With the TPNW having entered into force, it for the first time presents the entire international community – including the nine nuclear-armed states (China, France, India, Israel, the Democratic People's Republic of Korea [North Korea], Pakistan, Russia, the UK and the USA) – with a *fait accompli*, a legal framework intended to encourage progress towards the elimination of all nuclear weapons, to verify every step taken, to detect cheating, and to celebrate advances towards peace and stability.

Perhaps the most consequential decisions facing the TPNW parties will be on establishing the TPNW verification system[1] by fixing its scope, its institutional assignments and the methods and procedures for eliminating each nuclear arsenal, eliminating each state's nuclear weapons support installations or irreversibly converting some of those facilities to peaceful use, and for assuring that each nuclear-armed state does not hide away existing weapons for later use or manufacture new weapons. As the parties make their choices and thereby define the operational modalities of the TPNW, the nuclear-armed states will reconsider whether they should continue to reject this treaty or perhaps offer an alternative easier for them to contend with, or consider whether participating in the TPNW might in fact, better serve their interests.

We should anticipate that the TPNW parties will bring relentless diplomatic pressure through every venue to make continuing rejection uncomfortable for the nuclear-armed states, via the United Nations General Assembly, the Nuclear Non-Proliferation Treaty (NPT), the International Atomic Energy Agency General Conference and through the Comprehensive Nuclear Test Ban Treaty Organization.

DOI: 10.4324/9781003227502-25

Depending on the nature of a nuclear incident and its proximity, every state would suffer as victims powerless to prevent the catastrophic consequences of nuclear war, unauthorised use of nuclear weapons, sabotage leading to the detonation of one or more nuclear weapons, theft of one or more nuclear weapons by terrorists or unauthorised sales to any state or subnational organisation, and the de facto encouragement represented by international tolerance of the world's nuclear arsenals for too long. How the TPNW addresses each of these risks will affect the success of the TPNW.

The parties need to help the nuclear-armed states appreciate that all states have a vested interest in the success of the TPNW and that all bear enormous moral, ethical and legal obligations to avoid nuclear catastrophe. The nuclear-armed states should, one by one, begin the steps called for in the TPNW and contribute their talents and resources to building the TPNW capabilities essential for success.

The TPNW will anchor the future international nuclear disarmament regime, just as the NPT is the cornerstone of the non-proliferation regime. Greater progress will be made under the TPNW if its verification system anticipates separate nuclear arms reduction agreements between nuclear adversaries and includes confidence-building measures aimed at managing the risks posed by their arsenals.

Recognising that the nine nuclear-armed states have in common the fact that each possesses nuclear weapons, they differ in fundamental ways. Tailoring the verification system to each nuclear-armed state will be necessary. Rather than nine separate approaches, however, forming two groupings of three each should be pursued. The first should include Russia, the United States and China; the second should include China, India and Pakistan. The remaining nuclear-armed states – France, Israel, North Korea and the UK – should be addressed separately, as these four do not hold sway over the others, and hence tying their progress to that of others would inevitably involve added complications and extended delays.

Special honours and distinctions should be afforded to whichever nuclear-armed state is first to come on board. As an American, an Irishman and an optimist, I hope that included in President Joe Biden's list of top priority actions will be a full review of US non-proliferation and disarmament-related policies in preparation for the NPT Review Conference, which was postponed from 2020 due to the Covid pandemic. Or Russia, perhaps.

Each nuclear-armed state should take steps when it is convinced that its national security will not be imperilled and its actions will serve to encourage similar actions by its nuclear adversaries – and by all nuclear-armed states.

To quote former US Senator Sam Nunn:

> To me, you have to ask, what is more naïve, a world without nuclear weapons or moving in that direction, step-by-step, with the ultimate goal of giving people hope, giving them a vision, and a chance to work together toward that long-range goal? What's naïve? Is that naïve? Or should we believe that we can stay mounted on the tail of this nuclear tiger with eight other countries joining us, and avoid absolute catastrophe? History will tell us.[2]

Notes

1 Thomas E. Shea, "On Creating the TPNW Verification System," Chapter 7 in this volume.
2 Sandia National Labs, "On Deterrence," documentary, 1 March 2017, www.youtube.com/watch?v=tQBLpJFi6f0.

23

DON'T MENTION THE BAN

Australia's evasion of the TPNW

Gem Romuld

The Treaty on the Prohibition of Nuclear Weapons (TPNW) is a game-changer. It puts all nuclear-armed states in breach of international law, along with any state that includes these weapons in its security doctrines. It coalesces regional nuclear weapon-free zones, builds upon other nuclear arms control agreements and in ten simple pages condemns any activity that condones nuclear weapons.

This agreement is not a vision statement, an aspirational manifesto or a watered-down outcome document from a conference. It is a comprehensive, United Nations-negotiated treaty that became permanent international law on 22 January 2021.

Besides the prohibitions, it sets out positive obligations that states parties must fulfil, and a framework for the negotiation of stockpile elimination with nuclear-possessor states. With entry into force, states parties are bound by their treaty obligations. They are obliged under Article 12 to seek universality, by encouraging states not party to ratify the treaty. This could take place during international fora or bilateral meetings. Any that do not already have a comprehensive safeguards agreement in place with the International Atomic Energy Agency will be obliged to complete one, and the treaty states that parties that have signed up to the Additional Protocol will be obliged to maintain it.

For the first time, states parties will be obliged under Articles 6 and 7 to co-operate on addressing the long-term harms inflicted on bodies and the environment by nuclear weapons use and testing. This assistance will be provided according to capacity, with an obligation upon states that have conducted nuclear testing programmes.

Australia did not participate in the negotiation of the TPNW and continues to avoid parliamentary efforts to debate the matter, including the denial of motions proposed by Greens and Labor members of parliament in November 2020. The website of the Department of Foreign Affairs[1] carries one paragraph on Australia's

DOI: 10.4324/9781003227502-26

view of the TPNW. This one paragraph is brief yet riddled with misrepresentations, all of which are countered in a new International Campaign to Abolish Nuclear Weapons publication, "For the record...[2]

Australia presents itself as a country committed to nuclear disarmament, while at the same time claiming the US nuclear arsenal is essential to its security. This is a contradictory position and our leaders know it. The TPNW exposes such hypocrisy by rejecting any legitimate role or purpose for nuclear weapons, which is what Australia's reluctance boils down to. Any nation that countenances the potential use of nuclear weapons in its name is delaying progress on disarmament. Efforts to compel the nuclear-armed states to disarm within existing agreements have clearly failed.

There are some who truly believe Australia's security stems from the US nuclear arsenal, despite no clear undertaking that the USA would indeed defend Australia with its nuclear weapons. For those people, closing the "nuclear umbrella" is an intolerable leap of faith. For the global majority, every day in a world armed to the brink with nuclear weapons is unacceptably risky, with prevention the only option, and elimination the only guarantee.

In July 2017 a total of 122 nations voted to adopt the TPNW, rejecting the minority rule of the nine nuclear weapons possessors. Since then, despite the best efforts of some within the industry-funded defence think tanks, Australian appetite for a nuclear-free foreign policy continues to grow. A July 2020 Ipsos opinion poll found 71% of Australians in favour of joining the TPNW, with only 9% opposed. All levels of government are engaging with the issue, from local councils to federal parliamentarians, 88 of whom have pledged to work for Australia to join the ban. The Australian Labor Party has committed to sign and ratify the treaty in government.[3] Dozens of unions, religious, medical, humanitarian and environmental organisations have joined the movement, including the Australian Medical Association, Australian Red Cross and Australian Council of Trade Unions.

In the days before the TPNW acquired its 50th ratification, the threshold for entry into force, the US Administration wrote to all states parties suggesting they had made a "strategic error" and urging them to withdraw.[4] This desperation is surprising but the intent is not. The nuclear-armed states will continue to oppose the ban in myriad ways.

Australia has disagreed with its major military ally on the prohibition of other unacceptable weapons and we must do so again. If our alliance requires allegiance to weapons of mass destruction, who does it really serve? The treaty was negotiated specifically to allow ongoing non-nuclear military co-operation between allies. Australia is under no legal obligation, under the ANZUS Treaty or otherwise, to maintain a policy of nuclear "deterrence." Far from protecting us, such a policy compounds the risks posed by cyberwarfare, technological failure or the whims of nuclear-armed leaders now and into the future.

The treaty has popular support, clarity of purpose and a coherent pathway forward. No, this is not another commission, talk-fest or vague "initiative." The ban provides Australia with the mechanism to make its most powerful contribution to nuclear disarmament in decades. Our best position to leverage pressure on the nuclear-armed states is from within the tent of the prohibition treaty.

The first meeting of states parties to the treaty must occur within one year from 22 January 2021, the date of its entry into force. Austria will host the first meeting and invite all states, with the option for non-states parties to attend as observers. Australia must join the ban, and a first step would be to accept Austria's invitation to engage. The tide is turning against nuclear weapons; we had better swim with it.

Notes

1 Australian Government Department of Foreign Affairs and Trade, "Australia and nuclear weapons," www.dfat.gov.au/international-relations/security/non-proliferation-disarmament-arms-control/nuclear-issues/australia-and-nuclear-weapons.
2 ICAN Australia, "For the record…," 2 December 2020, https://icanw.org.au/for-the-record.
3 Anthony Albanese, "Speech to the 48th Annual Conference of the Australian Labor Party," 18 December 2018, https://anthonyalbanese.com.au/speech-moving-support-for-the-nuclear-weapon-ban-treaty-tuesday-18-december-2018.
4 Edith M. Lederer, "US urges countries to withdraw from UN nuke ban treaty," AP News, 22 October 2020, https://apnews.com/article/nuclear-weapons-disarmament-latin-america-united-nations-gun-politics-4f109626a1cdd6db10560550aa1bb491.

PART III

Arms control, disarmament and world order

DOI: 10.4324/9781003227502-27

24

SETTING NEW PRIORITIES

The EU shifts from civil peace and development projects to military policies

Herbert Wulf

The European Union (EU)'s foreign and security policy is plagued by unclear concepts, contradictory interests and fierce controversies between its member states. At the moment, priorities are set for a stronger military and defence role. The EU as a "power of peace," a term popular ten years ago, has been pushed aside and geopolitical ambitions moved into the foreground. This is a retrograde step for international peace and security and especially unfortunate at a time when the UN's primacy is already under challenge.

In 2012 the EU was awarded the Nobel Peace Prize and was particularly praised for its role in bringing about not only an armistice but real peace to Europe, after centuries of being ravaged by bitter armed conflicts. This served as an inspiring example to many other conflict-riven regions. Today, French President Emmanuel Macron repeats his mantra that the EU needs "strategic autonomy," particularly in terms of military strategy and capability. A global strategy and solving conflicts in the neighbourhood sometimes calls for "hard power." Loosely interpreted: In the current confrontational world order should the US no longer do the cooking and the EU the dishes? And the EU Commission assists by calling for a more assertive foreign, security and defence policy. This is often underpinned by geopolitical considerations, assuming that US withdrawal creates a vacuum that must be filled by the EU. On the one hand, there are frequent complaints about the EU's lack of political and military capacity to act in any international crisis. On the other hand, national sovereignty in defence policy is carefully guarded in the various capitals and not transferred to Brussels.

The emphasis on a stronger military role of the EU is faced with two problems: first, not all member states agree to this course and second, given the shortage of resources, this policy will in the long term be at the expense of the so-called "European Peace Facility." Before Brexit was completed, the UK objected to a strong EU defence role. Now, defence policies are largely promoted in the core

DOI: 10.4324/9781003227502-28

countries of the EU, or more precisely, pushed by the French and complemented by the German governments. But many other governments in the EU are not happy to be sidelined. With the EU enlargements, members were added, particularly the Baltic countries, who actually put more trust in North Atlantic Treaty Organization (NATO) for their defence than in the EU. The 27 EU members voice and pursue different policies on such issues as conflict resolution in Syria, Libya and Ukraine. There is disagreement on how to react to China's silk road project, on the use of autonomous weapons and most countries in Europe oppose the Treaty on the Prohibition of Nuclear Weapons, although Austria was a driving force behind the treaty and Ireland has signed and ratified it. And the role of French nuclear weapons in an EU security policy remains a taboo issue. Thus, the road to an EU policy is far from being clear.

Even the promoters of a stronger military role disagree on its implementation. When the French government talks about the "rediscovery of realpolitik" it has primarily military interventions in mind. And interventions are predominantly intended in Paris to counter terrorism. The German position is different. The German public – with an overwhelming majority opposed to military interventions abroad by the Bundeswehr – is always 'lectured' that engagement is necessary in the name of 'stability' in the intervened countries. Thus, French troops are engaged in battles, overtly and covertly, for example, in Mali and through military assistance to the militia of Khalifa Haftar in Libya, while German troops concentrate on training and equipping the security forces in Mali, Iraq, the Horn of Africa, South Sudan, Kosovo and until recently in Afghanistan. Inconsistency in these approaches is the result. Wolfram Lacher, an adviser to the German government, concludes: "The record of German and French policies in the crisis states of Mali and Libya is disappointing. While German engagement has remained largely ineffective, France's policies have often contributed to further destabilization."[1] And the EU Battlegroup, a military unit adhering to the Common Security and Defence Policy and in existence since 2007, has never been deployed.

A review of the past European military interventions shows that the EU has been slow and rather restrained in its self-defined responsibilities since the first Operation Artemis in eastern Congo in 2003. Overall, the record of Western military interventions is at best mixed. From Afghanistan (2001) to Iraq (2003) and Libya (2011) to Mali (2013), military successes have been followed by long-lasting instability. All these military engagements are now searching for face-saving exit strategies. The interventions in the Balkan countries (under NATO command) – although also highly controversial – produced better results and some of the countries of former Yugoslavia are now members of the EU.

The EU's practices in civilian crises prevention and peace promotion are much more positive. Its capacity and potential are enormous. Interestingly, the EU spends much more money on its development programs, civilian peace missions and democracy policies, mainly in African countries and the Balkans, than on military interventions. EU documentation lists 18 current and almost two dozen completed foreign missions.[2] About two-thirds of EU missions abroad are civilian, but only about 20 percent of the personnel. The EU budget for 2021–27 allocates almost €100 billion for neighbourhood and development policy, humanitarian aid, human rights, international co-operation and stability. These programs are much more popular among EU citizens than military interventions. A combination of anti-militarist currents and fear of costly military operations, of dire experiences in the past and the long-lasting or seemingly never-ending military engagements abroad, make the EU's military ambitions unpopular.

Notwithstanding such past experiences, the primary concern and focus of security debates among the EU elite is now on military interventions, all in the name of a global role for the EU. While defence matters were for many decades a "no-go" for the EU Commission, a change was introduced with the Treaty of Lisbon in 2009 that encourages member countries to cooperate in defence. Since then, the EU Commission assumes an expanded role and financial resources are allocated for that purpose in the present EU budget. Lobbying for defence has recently even successfully encroached into the peace facility. Despite its name, the "European Peace Facility" can also be used to fund military intervention.

Despite an overall positive impact, the "European Peace Facility" could be further strengthened by better coordinated United Nations-EU efforts and not getting mixed up with geopolitical and military ambitions. Instead of holding on to the pledge of spending 2% of GDP on defence, the EU should strive for meeting the long-promised goal of allocating 0.7 % of GDP on development.

Notes

1 Author's translation from Wolfram Lacher, *Unser schwieriger Partner: Deutschlands und Frankreichs erfolgloses Engagement in Libyen und Mali* (Berlin: SWP-Study 2021/S 03, February 2021), www.swp-berlin.org/publikation/deutschlands-und-frankreichs-erfolgloses-engagement-in-libyen-und-mali.

2 European External Action Service. https://eeas.europa.eu/headquarters/headquarters-homepage/area/geo_en.

25

ADVANCING THE TPNW

Tilman Ruff

The Treaty on the Prohibition of Nuclear Weapons (TPNW) entered into legal force on 22 January 2021. It is the first multilateral nuclear disarmament treaty to be negotiated in 25 years (since the Comprehensive Nuclear-Test-Ban Treaty, CTBT) and the first such treaty to enter into force in 49 years (since the Seabed Treaty which prohibits weapons of mass destruction including nuclear weapons being placed on the seabed).

The TPNW is here to stay and is a game-changer. It provides the first comprehensive and categorical prohibition of the worst weapons of mass destruction, the only weapons which pose an acute existential threat to humans and planetary health. The treaty now becomes the standard against which actions and inaction relating to nuclear weapons are measured. It includes the only internationally agreed and treaty-codified framework for the elimination of nuclear weapons and programs – time-bound and verified. And it is the first treaty obligating all states parties to assist the victims of nuclear use and testing and, where feasible, help remediate environments contaminated by nuclear use and testing.

There are many things to be done to build the legal, political and moral force of this historic treaty; grow its membership and implementation; and use it as effectively as possible to advance the eradication of nuclear weapons and reduce the likelihood and scale of their use in the meantime. With the hands of the Doomsday Clock this year still perilously further forward than they have ever been, at 100 seconds to midnight, implementation and impact from this one bright light of progress in a darkening nuclear landscape is both vital and urgent. We do not have the luxury of time, of tolerating and pussy-footing around the continued nuclear modernisation and refusal of nine states to fulfil their obligation to dismantle their global suicide bombs.

Not later than 30 days after the treaty enters into force for each state party (21 February 2021 for the first 50 ratifying states), each state party must lodge a

DOI: 10.4324/9781003227502-29

declaration with the United Nations (UN) Secretary-General delineating its nuclear weapons status.

Within 18 months of entry into force, each state party must have in force a comprehensive safeguards agreement with the International Atomic Energy Agency. Currently, the only state party not yet to have done so is Palestine, which signed a safeguards agreement in 2019 but still needs to bring it into force.

The treaty specifies a number of things to be decided by the first meeting of states parties, which is to be convened by 22 January 2022, and will be hosted by the Austrian government in Vienna:

- rules of procedure for such meetings;
- nuclear-armed states that join the treaty can "destroy [their nuclear weapons] then join" or "join then destroy." The time allowed for destruction of a state's nuclear weapons under the latter pathway needs to be decided by the first meeting.[1]

More broadly, the more progress that can be made in promoting and implementing the treaty at the first meeting of states parties, the better. While a lot can be accomplished in a well-prepared and well-led meeting of determined and like-minded states, it will be important, especially in the absence of a dedicated secretariat for the TPNW, that the first meeting sets up bodies and processes that can continue the work of treaty implementation and promotion in the two years before the next meeting, and beyond. The TPNW was negotiated through a UN process under a mandate from the UN General Assembly. Its depositary is the UN Secretary-General. Thus, advancing the treaty is UN business, including for the Secretary-General, and the UN Offices of Disarmament Affairs and Legal Affairs.

The first meeting of states parties could usefully augment these by:

- Defining an intersessional work programme with clear goals and timelines, potentially with working groups taking the lead in different areas.
- Holding preparatory and/or intersessional meetings.
- Establishing on-going or defined-term expert advisory bodies addressing key topics such as:

  a the competent international authorities required under the treaty to negotiate and verify the irreversible elimination of nuclear weapons programmes;[2]
  b regularly updating states parties on new evidence and developments on the humanitarian impacts of nuclear weapons and the risks of their use;
  c providing technical advice on the evidence base for action on the victim assistance and environmental remediation obligations;
  d providing legal and technical support and advice to states parties to assist the development of strong national implementation measures (and share good practice).

- Continuing the fertile co-operation and synergistic partnerships between governments, international organisations and civil society developed during the Humanitarian Initiative which gave rise to the treaty. This includes the world's largest humanitarian organisation, the Red Cross/Red Crescent movement, which played such a constructive role in the treaty negotiations and is prominently written into the treaty; the International Campaign to Abolish Nuclear Weapons, the lead civil society advocacy partner for governments on the TPNW; and global *hibakusha* – those directly affected by nuclear use and testing.

All this will require resources – both in-kind and financial. Treaty parties should come to the first meeting of states parties having done some homework on committing funds.

Prohibiting nuclear weapons "was the only potentially transformational step achievable without the engagement of the nuclear-armed states."[3] The power and value of this achievement now needs to be progressively enhanced. Important work for all treaty supporters is increasing the number of states signing the treaty and converting those signatures to ratifications. With 159 states supporting the Humanitarian Pledge and 122 states voting for the treaty's adoption, despite the reprehensible negative pressure from some nuclear-armed states and their accomplices, it should be possible to reach 100 ratifications over the next year or two. A key moment will come when the first nuclear-armed or accomplice state chooses to get on the right of history and become part of the solution rather than the problem.

States parties should implement their obligations in timely and effective ways, and report regularly on how they are doing so. Perhaps the greatest potential to broaden the treaty's impact before any nuclear-armed or accomplice states join is in strong implementation of the prohibition on assistance, encouragement or inducement of prohibited activities, for example mandating or incentivising divestment from companies building nuclear weapons; and through the potential to amend the treaty to enlarge its scope. For example, the treaty could be amended to require ratifying states to also ratify the CTBT. Of greater impact could be using the TPNW to advance the control and elimination of fissile materials, by requiring states parties to cease any production of highly-enriched uranium, end any reprocessing of spent nuclear fuel to extract plutonium, and eliminate or submit to secure international custody any stockpiles of separated plutonium.

The treaty is the best tool we now have against our worst weapons; let's use it well.

Notes

1 Moritz Kütt and Zia Mian, "Setting the Deadline for Nuclear Weapon Destruction under the Treaty on the Prohibition of Nuclear Weapons," *Journal for Peace and Nuclear Disarmament*, 2:2 (2019): 410–30, www.tandfonline.com/doi/full/10.1080/25751654.2019.1674471.

2 Tamara Patton and Sébastien Philippe, "Fit for Purpose: An Evolutionary Strategy for the Implementation and Verification of the Treaty on the Prohibition of Nuclear Weapons," *Journal for Peace and Nuclear Disarmament*, 2:2 (2019): 287–409, www.tandfonline.com/doi/full/10.1080/25751654.2019.1666699.

3 Alexander Kmentt, "The Humanitarian Initiative and the TPNW," Chapter 1 in this volume.

26

WILL NUCLEAR STATES ACCEPT POST-USE RESPONSIBILITY? IF NOT, WHY NOT?

George Perkovich

Critics and proponents of the Treaty on the Prohibition of Nuclear Weapons (TPNW) alike pay too little attention to its provisions on legal accountability for past and possible future detonations of these weapons. Among other things, the treaty calls on each state party to "provide technical, material and financial assistance to States Parties affected by nuclear-weapon use or testing" and to "provide assistance for the victims of the use or testing of nuclear weapons or other nuclear explosive devices" (Article 7). Such victims could be non-belligerent nations who had no say or benefit in the decisions of nuclear-possessor states.

Neglecting redress for the consequences of nuclear use makes it easy for governments to continue avoiding the dangers posed by these weapons altogether. This avoidance affirms many governments' sense that those who rely on nuclear deterrence have no empathy for those who do not – no feeling for what it is like to live as an innocent hostage to other peoples' leaders. Such non-empathy adds insult to the underlying injustice in the global nuclear order: under the 1970 Nuclear Non-Proliferation Treaty, five countries are permitted to have nuclear weapons, while the rest are not.

Nuclear disarmament is one way to solve these problems. But nuclear disarmament will take many years to implement even after all nine nuclear-armed states agree to relinquish their weapons (which they are nowhere close to doing now). In the meantime, until these weapons are dismantled, some form of nuclear deterrence will need to be maintained to help avoid the catastrophe of escalatory warfare up to and through mass casualty nuclear war. Greater attention to issues of legal accountability can strengthen self-restraint and deterrence among nuclear-armed states in ways that advocates and critics of the TPNW should appreciate.[1]

Critics of focusing on post-use accountability might argue that nuclear-armed states are not going to sign and ratify the TPNW, so there will be no obligations. Yet, rather than a flaw, this is a feature of the idea. If nuclear-armed states are

DOI: 10.4324/9781003227502-30

unwilling to get rid of these weapons, they at least should declare whether they will assist nations whose population and/or environment they could harm. Nuclear-armed states say that they are responsible, defensive actors and at least some of them insist that nuclear use could be limited. Why, then, should they object to rectifying harm to non-belligerents?

Those states that reject responsibility for providing technical, material and financial assistance to victims of their use of nuclear weapons would strengthen international demands for nuclear disarmament. They also would undercut any claims they have made to their own citizens and others that nuclear use can be kept limited: if it won't necessarily be so bad, then why will you not pay the consequences?

Those states that would accept responsibility could then be asked (repeatedly) to detail how they would deliver on the pledged assistance, and to demonstrate that they have prepared human and financial resources to do so. The scale of potential damages and therefore required assistance presumably would depend on the imagined number, explosive yield, and targets of weapons used. International discussion of the risks associated with various types and numbers of weapons and targeting plans, too, could help channel efforts to reduce the riskiest.

An alternative response to the notion of post-use responsibility is to say that it is bonkers – everyone will be dead. Nuclear disarmers and deterrers alike have said this. Disarmers because they do not believe or cannot admit that some number and type of nuclear weapons could be used against some targets in ways that do not produce humanitarian and environmental catastrophe. Deterrers because some think that positing limited nuclear war weakens deterrence by lowering self-inhibitions on nuclear use, and/or puts one's state on the extremely expensive and unstable path of nuclear counterforce warfighting. Others generally do not like the idea of international accountability, assistance to foreigners and paying for environmental remediation.

Focusing on the potentially catastrophic consequences of nuclear detonations has captured the attention of many non-nuclear-weapon states and civil societies in some states allied with nuclear-weapon states. However, it is too easy for nuclear-armed states to deflect pressure for disarmament (and the TPNW) by reminding their citizens that the point of these weapons is to deter war so that they will not have to be used. Rather than unwinnable debates on whether deterrence works and whether any and all use of nuclear weapons would produce humanitarian catastrophe, international society would gain clarity from knowing whether possessor states will take responsibility for remedying the consequences of their nuclear conduct if they survive.

Discussion of this question – domestically in states that allow it and internationally for all – would be more comprehensible and interesting to many people than debate over nuclear weapons themselves. Fixating on responsibility for consequences of nuclear use also will do more to compel leaders to demonstrate sobriety and restraint than debating whether they or their adversaries are more responsible for the lack of progress in nuclear disarmament. Even if the disarmament aims of the TPNW are not achieved, its accountability provisions could do much good if they receive the greater attention they deserve.

Note

1 For a fuller exploration of these issues, see George Perkovich, "Accountability after Nuclear War: Why Not Plan Ahead?," *Journal for Peace and Nuclear Disarmament*, 3:1 (2020), 115–22, www.tandfonline.com/doi/full/10.1080/25751654.2020.1751550.

27

MOBILISING THE WORLD BEHIND THE NUCLEAR WEAPONS BAN TREATY[1]

Ramesh Thakur

Setsuko Thurlow is an atomic bombing survivor who lives in Canada. She has been a highly visible public face of the hibakusha around the world, campaigning tirelessly for nuclear abolition and was included in the small delegation from the International Campaign to Abolish Nuclear Weapons (ICAN) to receive the Nobel Peace Prize in 2017. When she showed up in the audience at a lecture I delivered in Toronto a couple of years ago, the atmosphere in the room turned electric and I felt the full emotional weight of history settle on my shoulders. On 7 July 2017 she was given the signal honour to deliver the closing remarks after the historic adoption of the Treaty on the Prohibition of Nuclear Weapons at the United Nations (UN) in New York. On that occasion, she memorably declared: "Nuclear weapons have always been immoral. Now they are also illegal."[2] Her declaration was three years premature, but we knew the significance of her pronouncement.

On 24 October 2020, 75 years after the atomic bombings of Hiroshima and Nagasaki, on the 75th anniversary of UN Day, Honduras became the 50th country to ratify the ban treaty and it entered into force on 22 January 2021. From that date nuclear weapons will indeed become illegal according to international law. The postponed 50th anniversary of the Review Conference of the Parties to the Treaty on the Non-Proliferation of Nuclear Weapons (NPT) will be held in the shadow of this new institutional reality. The treaty cannot impose legal obligations on non-parties like China, the Democratic People's Republic of Korea (North Korea) and the US as bomb-possessing states; nor on Japan and Australia as allies sheltering under the nuclear umbrella. But it will reorder the envelope of humanitarian laws, norms, practices and discourse on nuclear weapons.

From our geographical-cum-geopolitical vantage point, the ban treaty has the great advantage of being non-discriminatory and universal. Three of the four Indo-Pacific possessor countries are outside the NPT. Only China is party to the NPT. India and Pakistan never signed, with the former being a passionate critic of the

DOI: 10.4324/9781003227502-31

nuclear apartheid that the NPT supposedly created between the five haves and all the rest of the have-nots. North Korea was a party but pulled out in 2003 and has built up a nuclear arsenal and an intercontinental delivery capability since then. This makes the NPT mostly irrelevant as the legal governance construct for the Indo-Pacific and for the Korean Peninsula, Indian–Pakistani and Chinese–Indian theatres, all potential nuclear flashpoints.

Uniquely in the family of arms control treaties, the Comprehensive Nuclear-Test-Ban Treaty (CTBT), adopted in September 1996, is fully operational in practice without having entered into force legally. It identified 44 countries with critical nuclear facilities and activities whose ratification was required for its entry into force. This looks unlikely in my lifetime, if not in God's lifetime. Among the eight holdouts, China and the US have signed but not ratified, while India, North Korea and Pakistan have not signed. Some suspect the formula was intentionally designed to sabotage the legal status of the CTBT. All nuclear tests since the CTBT's adoption have been in the Indo-Pacific between 1998 and 2017.

The Treaty on the Prohibition of Nuclear Weapons, it is alleged, has fallen into the opposite trap. All nine countries that possess the bomb have opposed the treaty, which does not require any of them being party before it enters into force. This makes the ban unimplementable in practice. Worse, say critics, it will damage the NPT and hamper its efforts to promote nuclear disarmament. In a condescending letter, a clearly rattled US told treaty signatories they've made "a strategic error" in adopting a treaty that "is and will remain divisive in the international community and risk further entrenching divisions in existing non-proliferation and disarmament fora."[3]

The NPT seems wearied with age, its normative potential exhausted. It's been remarkably successful but it was crafted to be the premier global framework for managing nuclear affairs in a fundamentally different geopolitical order. It did oversee a transfer of nuclear energy for peaceful purposes, with a couple of qualifications. The non-proliferation goal has been pretty much universalised to all countries without the bomb. This means in practice the only remaining part of the original three-part bargain yet to be implemented is the disarmament obligation set out in Article 6.

Tellingly, the substantial culling of US and Soviet/Russian nuclear warheads that began with Ronald Reagan and Mikhail Gorbachev and continued with their successors, was a bilateral process outside the NPT that has ground to a halt and is reversing course. Existing agreements are becoming roadkills on the highway of renewed geopolitical rivalry. China has rejected all efforts on trilateralism of the Intermediate Range Nuclear Forces Treaty. The US exit from the 2015 Iran deal and hesitations on extension of New START Treaty complete the bleak picture of the crumbling pillars of the nuclear order.

Worse, the refusal to operationalise Article 6 was accompanied by a creeping corruption of the original NPT bargain. The five NPT nuclear powers transitioned by stealth from claiming that the NPT permitted them to possess and deploy nuclear weapons, "to the language of entitlement, legal rights and enduring legitimacy," as Nick Ritchie put it.[4] There can be no better illustration of this than the Trump administration's top arms control official, Chris Ford, who gave a belittling dismissal of the arms control community in a speech in London in February 2020, suggesting they were virtue-signalling nuclear identitarians.[5]

The majority shareholders in the NPT society of states are non-nuclear. Exasperated by the arms control reversals and motivated by humanitarian concerns, they reclaimed agency to take back nuclear legitimacy. The deepening crisis of legitimacy for the deployments and doctrines of deterrence around the possession of nuclear weapons, that became illegal as well as immoral from 22 January 2021, will add to the domestic difficulties for umbrella states. A poll by the public broadcaster NHK in December 2019 showed 66 percent support among Japanese people for signing the treaty and only 17 percent opposition.[6]

The ban treaty will spur civil society and states to mobilise behind the new normative framework to achieve concrete progress toward the total elimination of nuclear weapons. As UN Secretary-General António Guterres said in acknowledgment of the historic occasion, abolition "remains the highest disarmament priority of the United Nations."[7] In 2017, for the first time, the General Assembly bestirred itself to assert normative primacy over the combined geopolitical weight of the five permanent members of the Security Council, who are also the five NPT nuclear powers. Beatrice Fihn, executive director of ICAN, is right: "This treaty is the U.N. at its best – working closely with civil society to bring democracy to disarmament."[8]

Notes

1 This article first appeared in *The Japan Times* on 30 October 2020 and was reprinted by the Toda Peace Institute with permission.
2 "Setsuko Thurlow Gives Final Remarks at Ban Treaty Adoption," Hibakusha Stories, https://hibakushastories.org/setsuko-thurlow-gives-final-remarks-at-ban-treaty-adoption.
3 Edith M. Lederer, "Nuclear weapons ban treaty to enter into force, United Nations says," *The Sydney Morning Herald*, 25 October 2020, www.smh.com.au/world/north-america/nuclear-weapons-ban-treaty-to-enter-into-force-united-nations-says-20201025-p568du.html.
4 Paul Meyer and Nick Ritchie, "The NPT and Prohibition Negotiation: Scope for Bridge-building", UNIDIR, 11 May 2017, www.unidir.org/publication/npt-and-prohibition-negotiation-scope-bridge-building.
5 US Assistant Secretary of State Christopher A. Ford, "Issues to Watch in Arms Control, Nonproliferation, and Disarmament" (text of a speech to the Institute for International Strategic Studies, London, 11 February 2020, that was originally titled "The psychopolitics of arms control"), *Arms Control and International Security Papers*, 1:24 (29 December 2020), www.state.gov/wp-content/uploads/2020/12/T-Paper-series-24-Issues-to-Watch-in-Arms-Control-Dec-2020-plain-text.pdf. The video of the speech is available at the IISS website: www.iiss.org/events/2020/02/the-politics-of-arms-control.
6 Reported by Eric Johnston, "U.N. nuke ban treaty to enter effect Jan. 22, heaping pressure on Japan to join," *Japan Times*, 25 October 2020, www.japantimes.co.jp/news/2020/10/25/national/un-nuclear-ban-treaty-japan.

7 Statement from the United Nations Secretary General, "Commending Ratification of Treaty Banning Nuclear Weapons, Secretary-General Says Entry into Force is Tribute to Test-Blast Survivors," United Nations, 24 October 2020, www.un.org/press/en/2020/sgsm20363.doc.htm.
8 Lederer, "Nuclear weapons ban treaty to enter into force, United Nations says."

28

VERIFYING THE ELIMINATION OF NUCLEAR WEAPONS AND PROVIDING ASSURANCE AGAINST BREAKOUT

John Carlson

The elimination of nuclear weapons is probably the single most important challenge facing the world today. Since the end of the Cold War political leaders and the public have lost sight of the dangers presented by nuclear weapons. The avoidance of nuclear war to date has been due in no small measure to good luck, but this cannot be expected to last indefinitely. As long as nuclear weapons exist, there is the risk they will be used, if not intentionally then by mistake, miscalculation or rogue action. And while these weapons exist additional states are motivated to acquire them, increasing the risk they will be used.

Nuclear weapons are not simply a bigger, better weapon: even a "limited" nuclear war will have global consequences, well beyond the protagonists, and a major nuclear war could result in human extinction. The International Court of Justice (ICJ), when asked to rule on the legality of nuclear weapons, concluded that the indiscriminatory nature, destructive force and environmental consequences of nuclear weapons are such that their use would generally be contrary to the rules of international law, particularly humanitarian law.[1]

Article 6 of the 1968 Nuclear Non-Proliferation Treaty (NPT) obliges all NPT parties to pursue negotiations on effective measures for cessation of the nuclear arms race and for nuclear disarmament. The ICJ found unanimously that this is an obligation not only to negotiate but to achieve nuclear disarmament. There are thus moral, legal and existential imperatives to find a way to reduce and eventually eliminate nuclear weapons. The challenge is how to do this in a way that does not lead to instability and increased risk – but the nuclear-armed states cannot keep saying disarmament is too difficult or unrealistic, time is not on our side.

DOI: 10.4324/9781003227502-32

Trust but verify

Effective verification will be absolutely essential to any disarmament process. No state will commit to deep reductions in nuclear weapons and to eventual elimination, without sufficient confidence that other states are meeting the same commitments. Each state will need confidence that others have not cheated or will not cheat in the future. Specifically, confidence is needed that no state has concealed significant numbers of nuclear weapons from the disarmament process and that any attempt to produce new nuclear weapons will be detected in time for effective action to be taken against the state concerned.

What is considered sufficient confidence is a judgment each state will have to make for itself. This is likely to be based on the state's assessment of a mix of factors – the verification system that applies, the state's analysis of national intelligence and other information, the level of transparency other states provide and the level of trust between states. Verification is central – it is essential in its own right and it contributes to transparency and trust. Also essential, but outside the scope of this paper, will be credible enforcement arrangements, that is, mechanisms for enforcing compliance with treaty commitments.

Verification can be described as the confirmation of facts through technical measures performed by personnel independent of the state being verified. The subject matter – objects (items), materials, facilities, activities – needs to be defined so as to be effectively and meaningfully verifiable, that is, verification will lead to valid conclusions. The technical measures can include: on-site inspections and observations; sample-taking and measurements; installation of cameras, instruments and seals; confirmation of building and container designs (for example, number of entry and exit points); and so on. Verification personnel can be bilateral/mutual (each party inspects the other), or multilateral (an international inspectorate, such as the International Atomic Energy Agency, IAEA).

Developing effective verification for nuclear arms control and disarmament might seem to be an impossible challenge, but there is substantial experience to build on, including: IAEA safeguards pursuant to the NPT; bilateral (USA/Russia) arms control inspections; CTBT (Comprehensive Nuclear-Test-Ban Treaty) monitoring; and collaborative projects on nuclear warhead and fissile material verification by the USA, Russia, the IAEA and the United Kingdom and Norway. IAEA safeguards and CTBT monitoring will be essential complementary regimes supporting disarmament verification.

Developing a framework for disarmament verification

The disarmament verification challenge is too diverse and complex to be addressed usefully in the abstract, instead it must be broken down into discrete and manageable tasks or missions. In broad terms a framework for developing disarmament verification needs to take into account both the formal structure and the subject matter. The former defines the verification objectives, commitments, institutions and mechanisms; the latter specifies exactly what is to be verified. This would include developing the specific steps required to achieve the goal of eliminating nuclear weapons.

A step-wise approach is anticipated by the NPT, which requires negotiations on cessation of the nuclear arms race, nuclear disarmament and a treaty on general and complete disarmament. Clearly these diverse objectives cannot be addressed in a single treaty, there will need to be a series of treaties. The NPT is not prescriptive and leaves it to the parties to decide on the specific treaties required.

On structure, IAEA safeguards and other existing treaty verification systems operate on a model involving a treaty, declarations and inspections. Future disarmament verification arrangements are expected to take a similar approach:

1. a treaty, stating the fundamental legal commitment – for example, that the parties will not use subject materials to produce nuclear weapons;
2. an obligation for parties to accept verification measures, to verify they are meeting treaty commitments;
3. definition of materials, items, facilities and activities subject to the treaty;
4. establishment of a treaty inspectorate (likely to be multilateral, but some aspects could be bilateral);
5. declarations – an obligation for parties to declare to the inspectorate relevant materials, items, facilities and activities, and to make available supporting documentation (records, etc.);
6. inspections – application by the inspectorate of verification measures, including regular on-site inspections and monitoring, to confirm parties' declarations;
7. inspection procedures in case of suspected undeclared materials, facilities and activities (investigations and challenge inspections);
8. procedures to deal with treaty breaches and non-compliance.

With several decades of experience, the IAEA safeguards system has been developed to address two fundamental concepts, correctness and completeness, and disarmament verification can be expected to build on this experience. Correctness refers to confirmation that declarations are consistent with the facts – that declared quantities of nuclear items and materials are as described. Completeness refers to confirmation that declarations include everything that is required to be declared – that there are no undeclared (concealed) items or materials. Since it is not possible to prove a negative – the absence of something – confirming completeness involves determining the indicators or observables expected to be present if there are undeclared items or materials, and conducting verification activities that have a high probability of detecting any such indicators.

On subject matter, there are three broad areas to be covered. First, all relevant *material and facilities* will need to be declared and verified, with ongoing verification that declared materials and facilities are not used to produce nuclear weapons. Second, there must be a declaration of all *nuclear weapons* in accordance with agreements (number and type of weapons allowable to be deployed, number to be retired and dismantled, and so on), monitoring of dismantlement and transfer of ex-weapons material to verified stocks. These transfers should be irreversible. That is, nuclear material recovered from weapons and transferred to verified stocks cannot be transferred back to weapons. There could also be verified limits on delivery systems and weapon-related materials. And third, *activities* to provide assurance there are no undeclared materials or weapons (weapons concealed from declaration, and production of new weapons either from materials concealed from declaration or from production of new materials) – including monitoring, challenge inspections, transparency measures, information analysis and so on.

Dimensions of fissile material verification: Some figures

Although the NPT and safeguards agreements are expressed in terms of nuclear materials, the term commonly used in discussion of nuclear weapons is fissile materials. There is no standard definition of fissile materials, but generally the term applies to highly enriched uranium (HEU) and separated plutonium (that is, plutonium separated from irradiated fuel through reprocessing). Fissile materials are not necessarily weapon-grade, but fissile materials are considered weapons-usable or, in the case of HEU at lower enrichment levels, easily re-enriched to higher enrichment levels.

Today most HEU is held in military programmes, there is relatively little in civilian programmes. For separated plutonium, however, over half is in civilian programmes, though not necessarily under IAEA safeguards. One of the issues for disarmament verification is going to be the need to extend IAEA safeguards coverage to civilian programmes in nuclear-armed states. Total global fissile material holdings are shown in Table 28.1. Only 17 percent of all fissile material is in civilian programmes. The process of disarmament will require that the 83 percent of fissile materials currently in military programmes will be progressively transferred to civilian programmes, or disposed of (placed in a waste form such as borosilicate glass or synroc and buried), or in the case of fissile materials in naval propulsion programmes, monitored to ensure they are not diverted to nuclear weapons.

Global fissile material holdings are broken down further in Figure 28.1:

TABLE 28.1 Global Holdings of Fissile Materials (2014)

	Separated plutonium (tonnes)	*HEU (tonnes)*	*Total fissile materials (tonnes)*
Military programmes	233 (46%)	1319 (96%)	1552 (83%)
Civilian programmes	271 (54%)	50 (4%)	321 (17%)
Total	504	1369	1873

Source: International Panel on Fissile Materials "Global Fissile Material Report 2015," http://fissilematerials.org/library/gfmr15.pdf.

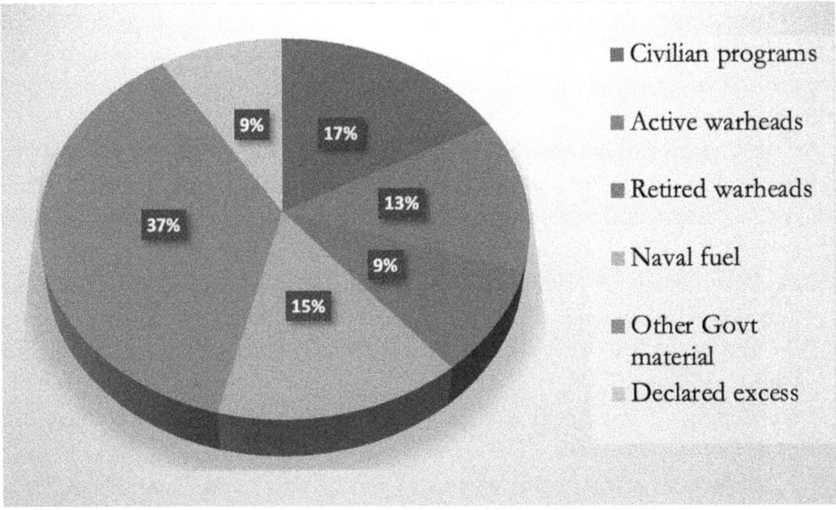

FIGURE 28.1 Global holdings of fissile materials (estimated percentages, 2013)
Source: NTI, Global Dialogue on Nuclear Security Priorities: Building an Effective Global Nuclear Security System,[2] 2016, based on IPFM data.

- Active warheads contain 13 percent of total fissile materials. This quantity will decrease with nuclear weapon reductions, as warheads are transferred progressively to retired status.
- Retired warheads contain 9 percent of fissile materials. This quantity will fluctuate, increasing with warheads transferring from the active category, and decreasing as weapons are dismantled and fissile materials are transferred to excess stocks.
- Stocks declared excess comprise 9 percent of total fissile holdings. This quantity will fluctuate, increasing as materials are transferred from dismantlement and decreasing as materials are transferred to civilian programmes or disposal.
- Naval programmes contain 15 percent of total fissile materials – these materials will require monitoring.
- The largest category – 37 percent – is other government material. Every effort should be made to declare these materials excess. Where this is not possible verification or monitoring will be required.

Step-wise approach to disarmament

A step-by-step approach to nuclear disarmament is implicit in the NPT and has been elaborated in successive NPT Review Conferences, notably in the "13 Steps" set out in the Final Document of the 2000 Review Conference.[3] It has become a subject of major political contention that currently no such steps are taking place. This was a key factor behind the majority of states supporting the negotiation of the Treaty on the Prohibition of Nuclear Weapons. Notwithstanding the level of support for this treaty, however, not a single nuclear-armed state participated in the negotiations and it is clear that a step-by-step approach is the only realistic way of achieving disarmament.

As yet there is no agreement on what these steps should be. In broad terms, something along the following lines can be expected (though not necessarily in this order). This list is not the same as the 13 Steps but has many elements in common:

- i Declarations on no first use (NFU), leading to a treaty on NFU. Nuclear-armed states would affirm that the sole purpose of nuclear weapons is to deter the use of nuclear weapons by others. NFU is already the stated policy of China and India.
- ii De-alerting – removing nuclear weapons from immediate readiness and launch-on-warning status.
- iii Agreement by the United States and Russia to extend New START and initiate negotiations on a successor (START IV?).
- iv Bringing the CTBT into force.
- v Establishing a multilateral negotiating process including all the NPT and non-NPT nuclear-armed states.
- vi Negotiating a Fissile Material Cut-off Treaty. The general view is this would apply to future production but not existing fissile material stocks. Fissile material production facilities (enrichment and reprocessing facilities) would be shut down or would operate under verification to ensure future production is not diverted to nuclear weapons.
- vii Reduction of deployed nuclear weapons, and progressive dismantlement of excess nuclear weapons. There would be a series of agreements on numbers and types of nuclear weapons in deployment, with excess weapons being progressively declared and transferred to dismantlement. Recovered fissile materials would be declared as excess materials and transferred or disposed of in accordance with step (ix).
- viii Ensuring nuclear materials in naval propulsion programmes are not diverted to nuclear weapons.
- ix Transfers of excess military fissile material to civilian use, or disposal, under irreversibility arrangements. There would be a series of agreements by the various parties, under which specified quantities of fissile material would be declared and transferred to monitored storage, then progressively transferred to civilian use or disposal.

This list is not intended to represent definitive and discrete steps. The steps actually agreed by states could be different and there could be further steps within the steps described here. For example, reduction and dismantlement of deployed weapons is likely to involve a series of separate agreements. At a broad level, the International Commission on Nuclear Non-Proliferation and Disarmament (ICNND), in its 2009 report,[4] recommended a two-phased approach, with minimisation as the immediate goal and elimination as the ultimate goal. A series of specific steps would be required within each phase. The minimisation point, considered to be achievable by 2025, would be characterised by low numbers of weapons (500 each for the USA and Russia, and no more than 1,000 in total held by the other nuclear-armed states), agreement on no first use, and force deployments and alert status reflecting a no first use posture.

Verification considerations

As discussed, the various steps outlined above do not constitute an agreed or definitive list, but the steps taken are likely to be along these lines. The verification requirements for the various steps can be summarised as follows.

No first use, de-alerting

Some steps either do not lend themselves to verification or do not require verification. For example, whether a state can be relied upon to honour a no first use commitment is not verifiable. The state's commitment is reinforced by mutual deterrence, rather than verification. However, some transparency and confidence-building measures might be helpful: states could consider whether there are indicators that would provide confidence that others are acting consistently with a commitment to no first use, for example, the nature of weapon and delivery system deployments. Likewise, while de-alerting is not readily verifiable, some form of confidence-building might be helpful.

"START IV," deployment limits

For a START IV or similar agreement, the USA and Russia can be expected to apply bilateral verification arrangements similar to those implemented under New START and preceding agreements. Similar agreements negotiated by other states are expected to build on US and Russian experience.

Dismantlement of nuclear weapons

Because specific data on warheads – shape, mass, isotopic composition – is classified, there is a need to develop verification measures to provide the necessary assurance without revealing classified information. These special verification measures will apply until the fissile material from warheads has been altered in form and composition such that it is no longer classified, and more conventional verification, similar to IAEA safeguards, can apply.

Initially nuclear weapons retired from service pursuant to reduction agreements would be placed in storage pending dismantlement. Verification will have to show that an item declared to be a warhead meets certain parameters (attributes) consistent with the declaration – mass within a certain range, radiation signature, and so on. The

Trilateral Initiative[5] between the USA, Russia and the IAEA has demonstrated techniques for this kind of verification and provides a good basis for further development.

Once in storage, warheads would be monitored to ensure they remain in storage, and are not removed except under verification. In due course, each warhead would be moved into the dismantlement process. Here too verification will be required to provide assurance without revealing classified information. It is expected dismantlement will be carried out in specially constructed facilities, where an item entering the process can be authenticated (that it has expected attributes), there is assurance material cannot be removed from the process without the knowledge of the verifiers, and an appropriate material balance can be established – material leaving the process corresponds to the material that entered the process. This overall verification approach is described as ensuring chain of custody or continuity of knowledge. Verification procedures along these lines have been demonstrated in collaborative work by the United Kingdom and Norway.

After dismantlement, nuclear components would be processed (altering shape and composition) to remove classified attributes, and the recovered nuclear material would be transferred to excess stocks, where it would be monitored until it is transferred to civilian programmes or disposed of.

Nuclear materials declared excess to military requirements

Some of the disarmament steps will involve verification measures similar to established IAEA safeguards. Verification of excess materials is an example of this. The initial issue will be whether materials declared excess have classified form or composition. If so, they will have to be authenticated and quantified without revealing classified attributes, as described above. When these materials have been declassified (for example, by blending), or for materials that are not classified when transferred to excess stocks, standard IAEA safeguards or something like them can be applied. Subsequently the materials would be transferred into civilian programmes with safeguards to ensure irreversibility, that is, that they are not returned to weapons use, or they would be conditioned and disposed of in a repository.

There is already experience with bilateral agreements on the disposition of excess fissile materials, notably the Megatons to Megawatts programme of 1993–2013 under which the USA purchased 500 tonnes of HEU from the Russian nuclear weapon programme and downblended it to fuel US power reactors. Another example is the 2000 Plutonium Management and Disposition Agreement under which the USA and Russia each agreed to the disposition of 34 tonnes of excess military plutonium (the latter agreement has yet to be implemented). Under the Megatons to Megawatts programme there were bilateral inspections to verify implementation.

Fissile Material Cut-off Treaty

This is another example where verification measures would be similar to established IAEA safeguards. Verification of a Fissile Material Cut-off Treaty would require safeguards measures on enrichment and reprocessing facilities and on fissile material produced after the treaty's entry into force. The treaty is expected to allow enrichment of HEU and reprocessing (separation of plutonium) for non-explosive purposes. There is limited civilian requirement for HEU, any further production is likely to be mainly for naval propulsion, raising verification issues as discussed below. As with IAEA safeguards, verification activities would also be required to provide assurance that there are no undeclared enrichment or reprocessing facilities.

Naval programmes

As Figure 28.1 indicates, there is more fissile material in naval programmes than in active warheads. This material is almost entirely HEU (though not all weapon-grade). Some is in the form of fuel loaded in reactors (submarines and other vessels), some is held in reserves for future fuel requirements. Clearly having such large quantities of HEU outside verification arrangements could present a risk to disarmament efforts. Accordingly, monitoring or confidence-building measures are required to provide assurance that naval programmes do not provide an opportunity for diversion of fissile material to nuclear weapons.

The complication here is that the details of naval fuel design are classified, so intrusive verification will not be accepted. Novel verification approaches will have to be developed. These might be complemented by transparency arrangements. For example, it is easy to check that a vessel is at sea (and therefore that its reactor contains fuel). A substantial portion of naval material however is in reserves where sensitivities should not apply and established monitoring measures could be used.

Nuclear archaeology

In principle it is possible to establish the nuclear materials flows and balances for a nuclear weapon programme, that is, to establish how much HEU and plutonium was produced historically, how much was lost in processing, how much was consumed in testing, how much is in weapons and reserves today, and an explanation for inventory differences. This information could be used to cross-check declarations and verification results as disarmament proceeds, to provide assurance that no fissile material, whether in weapons or as bulk material, is being concealed from the verification process.

In practice confirming historic nuclear material flows is not straightforward, particularly for the older and larger nuclear programmes (US and Soviet/Russian) where rigorous records were not always kept. As a consequence, nuclear archaeology – comprising technical methods for auditing and substantiating historical production, losses and consumption – has been developed. These methods include examining facility operating characteristics and records, analysing radiation effects on facility components and related materials and analysing radioactive wastes. Studies into the historic production of fissile materials in the USA and UK are encouraging and show that nuclear archaeology could have an important role in disarmament verification.

Verification problem areas

The greatest problem for verification will be addressing the possibility of undeclared nuclear weapons or materials, discussed below. Another practical problem will be delay in the opportunity to fully verify materials. For example, where classified items or materials enter monitored storage via attribute verification, it could take some years before dismantlement and conversion to unclassified form are completed and the quantity of material can be finally confirmed. Procedures will be needed to maximise confidence that a state could not use this delay to conceal incomplete declarations.

A further practical problem will be the resources – human, technical and financial – required for verification. In addition to verification of the various disarmament steps, resources will be required to extend IAEA safeguards into the nuclear-armed states, which will progressively become non-nuclear-weapon states. It will take time to train verification personnel, whether national or multilateral. Currently nuclear weapon programmes require very substantial resources. As disarmament progresses these will be available for reallocation to other purposes – the highest priority should be supporting the disarmament effort.

Breakout risks

Assurance against the possibility of breakout – a state unexpectedly producing nuclear weapons – is by far the greatest challenge facing disarmament verification. In any agreement on deep nuclear reductions – particularly reductions to zero – states will require a high degree of confidence that no other state has undeclared nuclear weapons or fissile material.

Of course, the risk of breakout is not confined to states that had nuclear weapons. Paradoxically, in a nuclear weapon-free world a rogue state might feel more motivated to pursue nuclear weapons – a minor state might hope to become a superpower. A robust non-proliferation regime, applying to all states, is absolutely essential to achieving and maintaining disarmament.[6] This not only involves IAEA safeguards. Also important, but outside the scope of this paper, will be institutional and technical measures to reduce breakout potential, such as proliferation-resistant fuel cycle technologies and multilateral control over proliferation-sensitive stages of the fuel cycle.

Breakout could take two forms: a state concealing existing nuclear weapons from the disarmament process; or alternatively, a state could produce new nuclear weapons. Fissile material for this purpose could have three sources: existing material concealed from the disarmament process; material diverted from safeguarded or monitored activities (civilian programmes or naval programmes) in the future; or material produced with secret facilities in the future. In all three cases, in addition to fissile material the state will require a secret nuclear weapon fabrication facility. The state will also require related materials – electronics, high explosives, tritium – and also nuclear-capable delivery systems. None of these would present insurmountable problems to a state that had a nuclear weapon programme (or still has nuclear weapons – breakout could occur not only after nuclear weapons have supposedly been eliminated, but during progress towards elimination).

To counter these different pathways, it will be necessary to analyse the indicators for each – what are the observables that verifiers and national intelligence agencies should be looking for? It is not simply a question of whether a state could conceal nuclear weapons; the state will also need delivery systems (missiles or nuclear-capable aircraft), personnel for guarding, maintaining and launching nuclear weapons, a command and control structure, and so on – a whole range of things that would have to be hidden and for which there will be indicators or observables. The key will be establishing procedures that will detect these.

It is important to remember this is not a new problem, we are not starting with a blank page. The IAEA safeguards system has long faced the same problem of how to detect undeclared nuclear facilities, items or materials. The IAEA's efforts are a work in progress, but they present a substantial body of experience to build on. It is also important to appreciate that detection is not solely reliant on the verification system. National intelligence programmes will also be important. So too will be complementary regimes and arrangements – IAEA safeguards, the CTBT, nuclear-weapon-free zones, transparency and confidence-building measures such as information exchanges, communication hotlines, Open Skies-type overflights, exchange of observers, open-source information and so on.

Ultimately, verification will never be able to absolutely prove the negative – that there is nothing hidden away. But by combining a broad range of information from many sources (what has been termed a web of confidence), over time the verification system, complementary measures and states' own efforts can build greater and greater confidence that the overall picture presented in declarations is complete and that the risk that anything substantial is hidden is small.

International collaboration

There have been several collaborative projects on verification, particularly between the US and Russia and the UK and Norway. The Nuclear Threat Initiative's (NTI) 2014 report *Verifying Baseline Declarations of Nuclear Warheads and Materials* [7] recommended, amongst other things, the establishment of new programmes for international technical collaboration on developing disarmament verification. This recommendation has been taken up by the International Partnership for Nuclear Disarmament Verification, a group of over 25 states, with and without nuclear weapons. Currently the International Partnership has working groups on Verification of Nuclear Weapon Declarations, Verification of Reductions, and Technologies for Verification. This collaboration is important both to demonstrate that effective verification in support of nuclear reductions and elimination is available or can be developed, and to build expert-level networks that will contribute to the confidence and trust needed to proceed down the path to elimination.

Conclusion

Nuclear-armed states will not be expected to disarm immediately, as proposed by the nuclear weapons prohibition treaty. Clearly this is unrealistic – moving to zero will require high levels of confidence and trust that will take time to develop. This will require a step-by-step approach to disarmament, accompanied by the progressive development and implementation of verification systems.

As outlined above, a number of the required verification methods and capabilities are already established, but others need substantial research and development. Today the robust verification required for progressing to zero has yet to be demonstrated. The step-by-step approach takes this into account. If the two-phased approach recommended by ICNND is adopted, the minimisation phase is not critically dependent on the performance of the verification system (numbers of weapons, while low, would be above a minimum credible deterrent) and this phase can proceed while the verification system is developing. The minimisation phase provides a period for building systems and networks, developing procedures and so on. It is in the elimination phase that verification will become increasingly critical as reductions progress. By then there will be years of experience with verification, transparency and confidence-building, all contributing to the high levels of confidence and trust required.

It is a mistake to think of a future world where nuclear weapons have been eliminated as being like today's world minus nuclear weapons. Thinking in these terms could reinforce a sense of pessimism whether elimination can ever be achieved. Rather, we must work to achieve a new world, where states are committed to collective security and the peaceful settlement of disputes and international institutions are strengthened accordingly. The collaborative effort required to achieve substantial reductions will help to build the institutions, trust and confidence needed to take reductions all the way to zero. Verification will make an essential contribution to these efforts.

Notes

1 1996 Advisory Opinion on the legality of nuclear weapons, www.icj-cij.org/public/files/case-related/95/095-19960708-ADV-01-00-EN.pdf. The ICJ was unable to conclude definitively whether use of nuclear weapons could be lawful (only) in an extreme circumstance of self-defence, but emphasised the obligation to comply with humanitarian law.
2 Joan Rohlfing, Samantha Pitts-Kiefer and Andrew J. Bieniawski, "Global Dialogue on Nuclear Security Priorities:Building an Effective Global Nuclear Security System," NTI, 2016, www.nti.org/media/pdfs/Global_Dialogue_Report_final.pdf?_=1458780838.
3 Arms Control Association, "U.S. Implementation of the '13 Practical Steps on Non-proliferation and Disarmament' Agreed to at the 2000 NPT Review Conference," 4 April 2002, www.armscontrol.org/pressroom/2002-04/us-implementation-13-practical-steps-nonproliferation-disarmament-agreed-2000-npt.
4 ICNND, *Eliminating Nuclear Threats: A Practical Agenda for Global Policymakers*, www.icnnd.org/reference/reports/ent/contents.html.
5 Thomas E. Shea, "The Trilateral Initiative: A Model for the Future?" *Arms Control Today*, May 2008, www.armscontrol.org/act/2008-06/features/trilateral-initiative-model-future.

6 One major problem with the nuclear weapon prohibition treaty is that it compromises safeguards standards. See John Carlson, "The nuclear weapon prohibition treaty – a safeguards debacle," *Trust & Verify*, 158 (2018), www.vertic.org/media/assets/TV/TV158.pdf.

7 John Carlson et al., "Innovating Verification: Verifying Baseline Declarations of Nuclear Warheads and Materials," NTI, 16 July 2014, www.nti.org/analysis/reports/innovating-verification-verifying-baseline-declarations-nuclear-warheads-and-materials. This is part of NTI's set of reports Innovating Verification: New Tools and New Actors to Reduce Nuclear Risks, www.nti.org/analysis/reports/innovating-verification-new-tools-new-actors-reduce-nuclear-risks.

29

EXPLORING NEW APPROACHES TO ARMS CONTROL IN THE 21ST CENTURY

Lessons from the INF Treaty and Presidential Nuclear Initiatives[1]

Hugh Miall

The state of arms control and disarmament today

The international arms control regime is in peril. The 20th century arms control regime reached its highpoint in the late 1980s and early 1990s with the Intermediate-Range Nuclear Forces (INF) Treaty, START (Strategic Arms Reduction Treaty), the Conventional Forces in Europe (CFE) Treaty and the Presidential Nuclear Initiatives (PNIs) along with the indefinite extension of the Non-Proliferation Treaty (NPT), the negotiation of the Chemical Weapons Convention (CWC) and the adoption of the Comprehensive Nuclear-Test-Ban Treaty (CTBT). In the INF Treaty, the USA and the Soviet Union agreed to remove from Europe ground-launched missiles of intermediate range (between 500 to 5,500 km), including cruise and ballistic missiles. START cut the number of strategic weapons on both sides and this was extended in the New START agreement of 2010. The PNIs of 1991 brought about unilateral, reciprocal measures to mitigate the uncertainties and destabilising effects associated with non-strategic or tactical nuclear weapons. All together, these measures reduced nuclear warhead stockpiles to about a fifth of their peak numbers by 2015. The CFE Treaty of 1990 capped heavy conventional weapons between the Atlantic and the Urals. The 1972 Anti-Ballistic Missile (ABM) Treaty banned strategic missile defence.

The NPT, which came into force in 1970, remains the lynchpin of the global arms control, non-proliferation and disarmament system. Under the NPT, non-nuclear-weapon states have agreed never to acquire nuclear weapons and all states have agreed to share peaceful nuclear technology and to pursue nuclear disarmament, with a view to the elimination of all nuclear weapons. Measures to assure the global community of progress towards these requirements of the NPT are important for renewing confidence in its principles.

This arms control regime has been under pressure for some time. The USA decided to withdraw from the ABM Treaty in 2002. The presidency of George W.

DOI: 10.4324/9781003227502-33

Bush brought critics of arms control into the White House and with President Donald Trump's election and the 2018 Nuclear Posture Review, US criticisms of arms control agreements have intensified. On the Russian side, too, there are those who question the value of the INF Treaty and discuss the benefits of abandoning New START and the CTBT. In 2014 the USA accused Russia of violating the INF by testing an extended-range missile. Russia denied the accusation and countered that the USA was violating the treaty by using missiles banned under its terms as test targets, developing drones and deploying missile launchers as part of theatre missile defences that are capable of firing intermediate-range nuclear missiles.

The deterioration of relations between the USA and Russia in recent years has made conditions worse for promoting arms control and confidence-building measures. Russia's fears of the expansion of the North Atlantic Treaty Organization (NATO) and US and European reactions to Russia's military actions in Ukraine and annexation of Crimea have played a major part. From a European point of view, the breach in the principle of territorial integrity marks a sharp distinction between the present era and the one that came before. Trust has been broken and it will not be easy to rebuild.

Meanwhile, both the USA and Russia are embarking on programmes to modernise their nuclear forces. China's national security posture is developing rapidly. The USA under Trump abandoned its leadership of the liberal international order, preparing itself for a new era of national competition instead, while Russia and China are seen to be challenging the legitimacy of the international rules-based system. States are becoming acutely conscious that they are in a security dilemma.

Two important developments affect the prospects for arms control. The first is the increase in the number of nuclear-armed states. Apart from the USA and Russia, all of the other nuclear-armed states have missiles of intermediate range. Approximately half of these missiles are ground-based. Over 90 percent of China's missiles are of intermediate range and Pakistani, Indian and North Korean weapons would also be banned if those states were parties to the INF.

The second is the rapid developments in military technologies, including the development of hypersonic missiles and new conventional weapons of such accuracy and destructive power that they could substitute for the missions designated for nuclear weapons alone in the past. To adapt the 20th-century arms control regime to 21st-century conditions, it has to cover more actors and more types of weapons systems.

Preserving the NPT is a shared security imperative for all. The NPT is the backbone of a comprehensive non-proliferation regime including international safeguards, restrictions on technology transfers, export controls and nuclear-weapon-free zones. The regime has been exposed to a variety of challenges over the years but has turned out to be resilient against external and internal shocks. Today, however, it is under stronger pressure than ever before, in particular because the nuclear-weapon states behave as if Article 6 of the NPT (the disarmament article) does not have the same legal force as the rest of the treaty.

The US threat to withdraw from the INF Treaty suggests to some that it is incapable of making lasting treaties. The USA has left the ABM, refused to ratify the CTBT, would not agree to the new CFE, left the Iran nuclear deal and declared its intent to walk back on its Paris climate change commitments. If the USA were to site new ballistic or cruise missiles in Germany or eastern and central Europe, the Russians would see this as a highly provocative and would take steps either to prevent or respond to it. It would be seen as a Cuba crisis in reverse.

From the perspective of European governments, the new developments in weapons and the threats to the arms control regime pose a real security risk. European and Japanese experts were disturbed that their governments had not been forewarned by the USA about the announcement of the INF decision. Germany and Japan – along with other European countries – would likely not be willing to host new INF weapons should that be in US plans; several have already declared publicly that this is the case.

The failure of the INF Treaty

The USA gave the formal intention to withdraw from the INF on 20 October 2018, suspended its compliance with the treaty on 2 February 2019 and Russia reciprocated. The USA withdrew from the treaty six months later, on 2 August. Before that occurred, there were different views as to whether it could be saved or whether it was desirable to do so. Several analysts concluded that we are already at the treaty's post-mortem. Others viewed the INF Treaty as salvageable if technical issues were addressed but admitted that the political will to do so was lacking. The Putin-Trump summit at Helsinki suggested that progress on INF and other arms control issues was possible, but subsequent political developments suggested that this assessment might have been overly optimistic. Both the USA and Russia seemed reluctant to make use of the Special Verification Commission under the INF as a means of fully settling compliance issues. Moreover, the treaty could be amended and efforts could be made to extend its geographical scope. Many countries and experts believe that it is desirable to preserve the treaty and that measures to explore complaints and return to compliance have not been exhausted. Flight tests might help to determine the range of disputed missiles. Multilateral verification could be conducted based on the Open Skies framework. On-site challenge inspections could be adopted. There was scope for exchanges of data, telemetry and technical information. The response to compliance issues in the 1970s to 1990s was to develop and strengthen verification measures, rather than abandon arms control.

However, officials and analysts from many countries in Europe took the view that Russia was in violation and were not hopeful that the treaty could be saved. Instead, they urged measures to preserve and uphold New START as a matter of urgency, with follow-on arms control measures to be considered as well. Some analysts suggested that it would be helpful if European governments declared that they would not accept new US nuclear weapons on their territory. With the gulf widening between the USA and Europe, it might be necessary to think in terms of European strategic autonomy. The NATO–Russia Founding Act stipulates that there should be no permanent additional combat forces in Europe and up to now this has been complied with. It could be taken as a basis for further constructive ideas, limiting exercises, exchanging data, and similar steps.

Experts differ on the extent to which US commitments to East Asian security considering China's capabilities are an important factor in the US decision to withdraw from the INF Treaty. Some US security analysts view concerns with the broad Chinese military build-up as the real reason for the USA to consider withdrawal from the INF Treaty. Others view the issue as entirely one of compliance. If the USA and Russia were to decide they wanted to keep the treaty, ways could be explored to adjust it to take account of relevant Chinese capabilities. It should be in US and Russian interests to bring China into arms control agreements as a significant international actor. It has to be recognised that this would be an ambitious task, since medium-range ground-based missiles account for a significant proportion of China's nuclear forces, but it can be argued that similar ambitions in arms control have been achieved in the past, for example in Russia's acceptance of intrusive verification measures in the 1980s.

From a civil society perspective, trust depends on enlightened cosmopolitanism and humanity. The world cannot afford a retreat into national boundaries. We need to reassert multilateral institutions and the rule of law. Violation or abrogation of international agreements damages the multilateral order. If the USA and Russia were to mutually agree to renegotiate the treaty or to develop a subsequent treaty that incorporates the same measures of mutual security and restraint, the impact on the world order would be mitigated.

If the arms control regime could be expanded to take in China, then India and Pakistan could be invited to join in too. It is critical to begin exploring options for more global approaches. The INF crisis is a reminder that the international arms control community needs to develop new concepts and bring in new partners in order to manage the proliferation of intermediate-range nuclear-armed ballistic and cruise missiles around the world.

Returning to the short-term consequences of the US withdrawal, another concern is that if the US were to choose to deploy new INF weapons on the territory of its European allies, Russia would be provoked to take military measures to stop it. However, NATO is an alliance of 29 sovereign states and a decision to deploy is considered highly unlikely since it would need a positive consensus for a deployment decision, as well as the willingness of a host state.

New frameworks for arms control

Three substantive proposals are proposed below as steps towards a new and more comprehensive approach to arms control and disarmament:

A ban on nuclear-armed cruise missiles

The first is a proposal for a ban on all nuclear-armed cruise missiles. It has been observed that if a missile were coming towards any country (e.g., Russia or the

USA) that could carry a nuclear warhead, that country would assume that it carried one and react in accordance with that assumption. Yet both countries have nuclear-armed cruise missiles and are likely to develop new capabilities for this type of weapon in their arsenals. The UK has conventional Tomahawk cruise missiles but made a transparent decision not to develop new nuclear-tipped cruise missiles, owing to their inherent ambiguity and other strategic stability concerns. France has only air-launched nuclear cruise missiles. China, India and Pakistan have thus far refrained from developing them but there are grave concerns that the Asia-Pacific is about to see a dangerous proliferation of this type of nuclear weapon.[2] US, Russian and international analysts have developed multiple concepts for verifying that any country's cruise missiles are non-nuclear, indicating that eliminating this class of weapons could be a focal point for multilateral arms control.

Whatever the outcome of the INF Treaty, a better framework is needed as we move forward. The crisis over the treaty could be an opportunity for reinvigorating arms control. It is necessary first to focus on types of nuclear weapons that are most destabilising. More usable, lower-yield weapons muddy the line between the strategic and the non-strategic. Creating a clear boundary between nuclear and conventional weapons is important to many countries.

Eliminating an entire class of nuclear weapons might be easier than regulating numbers or missile ranges. Moreover, it can apply globally. Bringing China into new arms control arrangements to end nuclear cruise missiles would only require them not to develop such weapons systems, since China does not yet have an arsenal of these types of nuclear weapons. The International Partnership for Nuclear Disarmament Verification and others could undertake case studies on how countries could collaborate to verify that cruise missile stocks are solely conventional.

A new framework for strategic nuclear arms control

Another proposal is for a framework for reducing strategic nuclear weapons to lower levels. Going beyond the New START framework, this would aim to regain strategic stability and eliminate the consideration of nuclear weapons either for war-fighting or as a tool of international statecraft other than deterrence purposes. The framework seeks to reduce miscalculation by avoiding the resurgence of dual-capable and non-strategic weapons; this would help to contribute to NPT disarmament obligations by eliminating many tactical and delegated-control systems. Under such a concept, nuclear weapons possessing states would progressively move towards holding only a single survivable strategic system each, pending further reductions to zero. They would agree on a Code of Nuclear Responsibility, and arms control agreements and confidence-building measures would be adopted to contribute towards this goal. Under a Code of Nuclear Responsibility, nuclear-armed states would exercise restraint in posture, rhetoric and readiness, ensure unambiguous communications, refrain from using nuclear weapons for any purpose other than deterrence of other nuclear states, pursue reciprocity, avoid attacking strategic command and control systems and take steps to reduce the salience of nuclear weapons. This framework seeks to adhere to the NPT Article 6 commitments while maintaining minimum credible strategic deterrence.

A new framework for confidence-building and risk reduction

The third proposal is for a new approach to confidence-building and risk reduction. The European arms control architecture is collapsing, and a more globalised approach is needed. But the trust that has existed between the USA, Europe and Russia has eroded and this makes Europe in need of a new risk reduction architecture. This is a top priority. Leaders need to reaffirm that nuclear war cannot be won and must never be fought. There is widespread support for seeking a restatement of the original 1987 Reagan-Gorbachev declaration. Leaders of other nuclear-armed states and allied states should endorse it too. The UN Under-Secretary-General for Disarmament has called for such a declaration. A global declaration along these lines could help to bolster confidence that nuclear doctrines and deployments are not aimed at war-fighting.

At a time when the security environment is deteriorating, negative security assurances can help. The principles of the NATO–Russia Founding Act could be reaffirmed. In order to build confidence, NATO could declare that there is no need, no plan and no intention to deploy nuclear weapons further east than they are now; and Russia could declare that there is no need, plan or intention to move nuclear weapons to Kaliningrad. It would be helpful to publicly confirm that there is no intention to bring back Cold War-era nuclear postures in Europe. It would also help if the five NPT nuclear weapon states would reaffirm the negative security assurances of 1995. Even more important, adoption of no first use doctrines should remain a high priority objective. Other declarations could include a resolution not to interfere in each other's internal affairs and a common area of equal security, in which no side would seek security gains at the expense of others. It would be helpful for Russia to declare it does not have an "escalate to de-escalate" policy, as Western defence planners are assuming that it has.

Crisis communications are essential, and measures should be developed and extended to give states better capacities for managing nuclear crises. At the moment, nuclear states are incapable of a point-to-point dialogue between key policy-makers in times of crisis. Military-to-military contacts could be improved. Cooperation in Syria has shown this is possible. The practice of 'buzzing' the aircraft and airspace of states can be dangerous in a crisis and incident prevention mechanisms should be implemented and developed. Existing bilateral and multilateral mechanisms could be extended to other areas. For instance, satellite buzzing could also be stopped. Russia has made proposals to extend the Open Skies agreement and has suggested an addendum.

The International Code of Conduct against Ballistic Missile Proliferation, which requires states to give notice of ballistic missiles launches, could be extended to cover information exchange on dual-capable missiles.

A Vienna Document for missiles might be one useful concept to explore. The Vienna Document of the Organization for Security and Co-operation in Europe (OSCE) provides for exchange of military information and notifications to reduce risk from the Atlantic to the Urals. This process could be made stronger and its scope could be extended to include modern weapons systems and other forces. It was helpful when the US declared its nuclear stockpile numbers under the Obama administration; others could be encouraged to reciprocate. Notifications and data exchange could be supplemented by track 1.5 meetings to improve communications on threat assessment and confidence building. A serious discussion of force postures and threat assessments goes on within the OSCE, but this does not take place directly between Russia and the USA. States could fortify their efforts in this structured dialogue to achieve tangible results.

There is a need for new crisis machinery between new nuclear weapons possessing states. In particular, measures to avoid incidents between India and Pakistan are crucial.

Verification also remains vital. It is worthwhile to put in place the systems required to make treaties verifiable. All such risk reduction and crisis management measures contribute to the important goal of building trust.

Arms control benefits from a stable multilateral order and contributes to stability and multilateralism. The biggest low-hanging fruit at present is the extension of New START. This is of great importance, in its own right and as a signal of intent to continue arms control. It could give the two nuclear weapons states party to the treaty a basis for going in to the delayed 2020 NPT Review Conference. New START is in the interests of both the United States and Russia, and President Joe Biden and President Vladimir Putin agreed in principle to move forward with the Treaty in 2021.

However, the institutional support for arms control is not as strong now as it has been in the past. In the USA, a current of hostility towards arms control is running among many politicians. Defence planners are developing nuclear strategy in war-fighting (rather than solely deterrence) terms. The institutional memory of the security benefits of arms control is limited. In Russia, while the official attitude towards arms control remains supportive in principle, the approach is to invest in military modernisation first and then approach arms control from a position of strength. However, Russia still seeks to return to the club of respectable international actors and arms control might be one way to achieve that aim.

Unilateral reciprocated measures: Building on the Presidential Nuclear Initiatives

In the 1990s, the Presidential Nuclear Initiatives (PNIs) undertaken by President George H. W. Bush and reciprocated by Presidents Mikhail Gorbachev and Boris Yeltsin were important steps in reducing the numbers and tactical capabilities of nuclear weapons stockpiles. A confluence of factors made this possible. Geopolitical changes in Europe and the Soviet Union made rapid action necessary. US and

Soviet leaders seized the opportunity. The US withdrew all of its tactical nuclear weapons from European soil and from ships and submarines, except a few hundred gravity bombs for delivery by aircraft. At the same time, strategic bombers were taken off alert, and mobile nuclear missile programmes were cancelled. The Soviet response was faster and more sweeping than the USA expected. The Soviet Union declared that it would eliminate its nuclear artillery, short-range nuclear warheads and nuclear mines. Nuclear weapons outside Russia were returned to Russian territory. Some of these weapons were put in central storage, though Russia defined this concept in a different way than the USA, which has given rise to accusations of non-compliance. Gorbachev also cancelled several new missile programmes, removed several nuclear submarines from duty and announced a one-year moratorium on nuclear tests.

Are there lessons from this remarkable episode in arms control for the present day? Some experts believe that today's geopolitical context is so different that lessons cannot be drawn. They observe that Russia's fulfilment of its PNI declarations had been disappointing and consider the prospects poor for using PNIs again in the light of events in Crimea, Russian threats to its neighbours and the Trump administration's scepticism about arms control. The PNIs were seen as a product of a time when arms control was on the rise, and when Russia hoped to be welcomed into a new political order. How conceivable is it that Russia would undertake unilateral measures while it faces sanctions and US withdrawal from the INF Treaty? However, President Putin has declared that Russia does not have a policy of planning a first strike. Moreover, Russia has declared that it will not use nuclear weapons first unless there is an incursion into Russian territory putting the very existence of the state at risk.

The principle of unilateral actions leading to reciprocation still holds potential. The case of the PNIs indicated that in the right circumstances, strong national leaders can see their way through the nuclear bureaucracies to take measures that are clearly in their countries' security interests. Possible unilateral measures include refraining from developing new technological capacities in destabilising domains. States could declare they would not make cyber-attacks on critical infrastructure, that they would respect assets in space which are critical for early-warning and communications and that they would commit to keeping command, control and intelligence systems under human control rather than allowing algorithms to determine judgements. Nuclear command and control systems should not be subject to cyber-attacks. Declarations could be made that tactical nuclear weapons in Europe would not be mated with delivery vehicles. Unilateral declarations on these measures could lead to reciprocated agreements. Verification measures for such commitments should be elaborated further.

Follow-up measures

There is a need to develop new concepts of arms control and strategic stability for the 21st century that governments might adopt. This should take account of the wider range of actors in the current multilateral nuclear order and of the rapid and transformative developments in technology.

Further studies building on the concept of a new framework for strategic stability are needed. They should consider the security implications of the proposed measures for 'umbrella' countries, and how to convince countries to reduce nuclear weapons step by step if they fear their security is diminished by the removal of the umbrella over time. Following the failure of the INF Treaty, a report on how to build on its ruins would be helpful. The priority is how to limit the fallout. It is important to find ways to re-engage civil society, which was crucial in the genesis of the INF Treaty.

There is scope for academic work in this area, since new concepts, visions and paradigms of arms control and disarmament are needed. What does the concept of strategic stability mean in the 21st-century context and how does it apply in different regions? There is a poor understanding of the potential escalation of crises in the Twitter age and it might be helpful to review Cold War reports on crisis behaviour and crisis management.

There is also the important dimension of discussion between the nuclear-armed states and non-nuclear weapons states. For some, the threat to the arms control regime serves to reinforce the importance of the Treaty on the Prohibition of Nuclear Weapons (also known as the Ban Treaty); others considered that the significance of this treaty remains to be seen. It was suggested that a new dialogue on prevention of nuclear war and on the risks of nuclear war would be timely, in the light of new research on the humanitarian and environmental consequences of even a limited nuclear exchange.

The concept of common and co-operative security is worth re-examining. This was formulated by the Palme Commission, taken up by Gorbachev and European leaders and recently recapitulated as a declaratory policy by Xi Jinping. This remains a potential lynchpin of a 21st-century approach to arms control and disarmament.

Notes

1 This chapter is based on a report of a track 1.5 workshop organised by the Toda Peace Institute and the Norwegian Institute of International Affairs and including Chatham House, Clingendael and the Council on Strategic Risks in Oslo in October 2018. The meeting brought together leading arms control officials, scholars and policy advisers from the USA, Europe and Russia.

2 Indeed North Korea developed a strategic cruise missile capable of carrying nuclear weapons in 2021.

30

WORLD ORDER AND ARMS CONTROL

David Holloway

Our current discussions about world order reflect a widespread sense that the present order is in decline. Whether it will collapse completely is unclear and so too is what will replace it. But the trends to which analysts point – the rollback of democracy, the rise of populism, growing trade protectionism, the weakening of international organisations – suggest that something fundamental may be under way. The renewed interest in world order predates the Trump Administration, but US policies since 2017 have deepened the concern.

There is more to it than that. The consciousness that the world is undergoing profound and rapid transformation at several levels also shapes our discussion of world order. We are witnessing dramatic technological change, with far-reaching social and political consequences that we are still trying to come to grips with. Three examples will suffice: the popularity of social media has raised questions about our ability to keep elections free from outside interference; our debates about Artificial Intelligence (AI) demonstrate how conscious we are of new possibilities that inspire both great hope and great fear; gene-editing poses profound ethical issues. To add to that, we confront demographic shifts and climate change which are acquiring growing significance. The processes of change – technological, demographic, and climatic – present enormous challenges for governance at all levels, from the local to the global. These challenges give a new urgency to the question of world order.

We can think about world order historically, as a succession of different phases of the international system: post-Westphalia, for example, or after the Congress of Vienna. Our current debate is commonly framed in terms of the decline of the West or the rise of the East. A second approach is conceptual: we can describe a particular order as a concert, as an empire, as a bipolar system, as globalisation and so on. We use these terms when we are trying to characterise the order, not merely describe its temporal parameters. The world created at the end of World War II is

DOI: 10.4324/9781003227502-34

now often described as "rules-based." It is sometimes argued that this is now being replaced by a world order of great power politics. In other words, American predominance is weakening and the power and influence of other powers is growing.

Whether or not we accept these characterisations of the world order, there is a sense that we are at a point of transition but do not know what we are transitioning to. How can we ensure that these processes do not threaten international peace and security? How can we direct the processes of change and transformation to our advantage while avoiding the dangers that they create? What adjustments do we have to make to ensure that the basis exists for co-operative security in the emerging world order? This paper will focus on nuclear weapons.

The rules-based order

The origins of the "rules-based" world order are commonly traced to World War II and in particular to the Roosevelt administration's ideas for avoiding a repetition of the economic and political disasters of the interwar period. The Atlantic Charter, the United Nations (UN) Charter, and the Bretton Woods agreements were among the most important products of this endeavour. It did not take long, however, for this vision of a universal world order to be complemented, and partially supplanted, by the two competing models of the Cold War.

The world order was bipolar, dominated by the two superpowers and their respective allies. Each alliance shared, to a greater or lesser degree, a commitment to economic and political principles that it wanted to extend to the whole world, along with a common hostility to the principles espoused by the other alliance. When we speak of a rules-based world order after 1945, we have to bear in mind that there were competing orders as well as a shared order. Moreover, there were clashes of principle not only between the competing orders, but also between those orders and the universal order. That was the case when one or other of the superpowers infringed on the "sovereign equality" enshrined in Article 2 of the UN Charter by intervening in one of its own allied states. A notable example is the Brezhnev doctrine of limited sovereignty, formulated in late 1968 to justify the Warsaw Pact invasion of Czechoslovakia: "the sovereignty of individual socialist countries cannot be set against the interests of world socialism and the world revolutionary movement."[1]

The collapse of the Soviet Union and the Soviet bloc marked the end of the Cold War. Communist parties continue to rule in several countries but with significant differences from the Soviet model, notably in their economic policies. The UN, which had played an important role in decolonisation, now had new opportunities, for example in peacekeeping, which had been stymied by the tensions and rivalries of the Cold War.

It was widely assumed in the West that the collapse of the Soviet Union marked the end of communism: instead of competing orders there would now be just one order, which would eventually extend to the world. Barriers to globalisation would diminish. Market economies and democratic politics would become the norm. The "democratic peace" argument gained popularity in the USA: a democratic world would be a peaceful world. Programs to foster democracy and even, in certain circumstances, to impose democratic rule, would lead to peace.

These hopes have not (yet) been realised: the third wave of democratisation has stalled and gone into reverse; globalisation has elicited strong political reactions; trade wars have overtaken efforts to liberalise trade; and attempts to spread democracy by force have proved unsuccessful, not to say disastrous.

The end of the Cold War has not removed tensions among the rules to be applied in the "rules-based" order. Sovereignty has been one of the focal points of tension. In 1999 the North Atlantic Treaty Organization (NATO) decided that it could not stand by in the face of a possible humanitarian disaster in Kosovo and launched a military attack on Serbia in defence of the Kosovar Albanians. The UN Security Council did not authorise NATO action, and would not have done so if asked. The Kosovo intervention sparked widespread discussion about the circumstances under which the international community (however defined) would be justified in intervening forcibly in a sovereign state.

This discussion pushed toward a redefinition of sovereignty from control over territory to state responsibility: states enjoy sovereignty only to the extent to which they conduct themselves responsibly in their relations with other states as well as towards their own citizens. The idea of The Responsibility to Protect implies that states are liable to intervention if, for example, they violate in an egregious manner the human rights of their citizens. That raises serious questions: who besides the UN Security Council can authorise such intervention? And is the system not inherently inequitable, given the disparities in power among states and the weakness of enforcement and adjudication mechanisms in international relations?

The point here is not to offer a judgment on Kosovo or on the principle of the Responsibility to Protect, but to note that the rules in the rules-based order are not always unambiguous and consistent. They may be open to different interpretations. The fact that rules can be contentious is perhaps a tribute to their importance. Otherwise, why have arguments about them?

Co-operative security in the rules-based world order

The first attempt to regulate atomic energy took place under the auspices of the UN. Negotiations to bring atomic energy under international control began in the UN Atomic Energy Commission in June 1946. The advocates of international control regarded it as the best way to head off a dangerous arms race. But even in a period of great institutional innovation, international control proved too ambitious. Nor did agreements result from negotiations in the late 1940s and 1950s on general and complete disarmament. Change began in the mid to late 1950s, with negotiations on partial issues – the comprehensive test ban treaty, surprise attack. The first formal nuclear agreement in which the USA and the Soviet Union both took part was the Statute for the International Atomic Energy Agency, which was set up in 1957 and has been a vital institution in the nuclear non-proliferation regime.

In the 1960s, arms control replaced disarmament as the guiding concept for negotiations. Rather than aiming for the elimination of nuclear weapons, arms control sought to make the US–Soviet nuclear rivalry less dangerous by enhancing strategic stability (defined as the situation in which neither side, in striking first, could destroy the other's ability to strike back). Preliminary discussions about strategic arms control began in the 1960s, with formal talks starting in the fall of 1969. These resulted in the Strategic Arms Limitation Treaty (SALT) agreements of 1972: the Anti-Ballistic Missile (ABM) Treaty and the Interim Agreement on Offensive Missiles. From then until 2010, more or less continuous negotiations led to a series of agreements (in 1979, 1987, 1991, 1993, 2003 and 2010) regulating the strategic nuclear balance of forces between the USA and the Soviet Union/Russia. These agreements changed in character over time: from limits to reductions; from launchers to launchers and warheads; from monitoring and verification by "national technical means" to on-site inspections. In both Washington and Moscow, these negotiations were often highly contentious, but their net effect was to see a reduction to 1,550 in the number of deployed strategic warheads on each side from totals of over 10,000 in the early 1980s.

Not everything went smoothly: the SALT II Treaty was not ratified, for example, but the two sides did agree not to undermine its provisions. The USA withdrew from the ABM Treaty in 2002, over strong Russian objections and continuing unhappiness. Nonetheless, the almost 50 years of strategic arms control was one of the most important security innovations of the post-World War II world order. Apart from limiting and reducing strategic nuclear forces, arms control helped in the management of the US–Soviet/Russian strategic nuclear relationship by providing an element of predictability and reassurance. The agreements also created institutional mechanisms for the resolution of disputes over the implementation of the agreements.

Following William Walker, we can think of the global nuclear order as consisting broadly of two main elements.[2] The first is the "managed system of military engagement with nuclear technology." US–Soviet/Russian arms control, which seeks to ensure that deterrence is stable, is a prime example of that element. Management of the US–Soviet/Russian nuclear relationship has been one of the key examples of co-operative security in the post-World War II period. Two intense rivals, armed with enormous destructive power, have so far managed their relationship in such a way as to prevent a nuclear war, which they understand would be catastrophic for both and for the world as a whole.

The second element in the nuclear order, in Walker's words, is the "managed system of military abstinence from, and civil engagement with, nuclear technology." This refers to the Nuclear Non-Proliferation Treaty (NPT) and the associated agreements, which seek to stop the spread of nuclear weapons even while encouraging the development of nuclear power. This too is closely linked to the idea of world order. The literature on the "rules-based order" ascribes to the USA the dominant role in the formation and maintenance of that order. There is a key paragraph in the 1965 Gilpatric Report on nuclear non-proliferation that connects the

American role in world order with nuclear non-proliferation. The report, which was commissioned by President Lyndon B. Johnson after the Chinese nuclear test in October 1964, states: "as additional nations obtained nuclear weapons, our diplomatic and military influence would wane, and strong pressures would arise to retreat to isolation to avoid the risk of involvement in nuclear war."[3] A proliferated world might make it impossible for the USA to retain its central position in world politics.

These two elements in the nuclear order are the result of co-operation between the USA and the Soviet Union, the leading protagonists in the Cold War. They are also based on divergent premises. Strategic arms control aims to stabilise nuclear deterrence. (But the danger remains of accidents, miscalculation, and terrorism.) The non-proliferation regime aims to stop the spread of nuclear weapons, on the grounds that the world would be more dangerous if more states had nuclear weapons; that is, it does not see nuclear deterrence as a guarantee of peace. Kenneth Waltz made the argument that if deterrence worked, then more nuclear-armed states would lead to a more peaceful world because nuclear deterrence would spread its beneficent effects more widely. That argument shocked many people and is not widely accepted by governments. Article 6 of the NPT suggests the opposite by committing parties to the treaty "to pursue negotiations in good faith on effective measures relating to cessation of the nuclear arms race at an early date and to nuclear disarmament."

The decline of the rules-based order

Sometimes the transition from one world order to another is marked by a clean break, like the final defeat of Napoleon, for example, or the end of World War I. But our transition seems more gradual and ambiguous: one state of world order is fraying, and another is beginning to emerge. How clean the break will be is not clear; nor is it clear what will follow it. When we look back, what will we identify as the key date – the end of the Cold War or the financial crash of 2008 perhaps? One thing is clear: we do not have a Congress of Vienna or a Paris Peace Conference to map out the new world order. That may – or may not – be a bad thing.

Nuclear weapons have not been used in war since 1945 and fewer states than anticipated have acquired them. The nuclear order outlined above has made its contribution to these outcomes; so too has a fair measure of luck. That order is now facing serious problems. We appear to be coming to the end of one particular way of dealing with nuclear weapons – arms control treaties between the USA and Russia. The Intermediate-Range Nuclear Forces (INF) Treaty is no longer in force since August 2019. Since the signing of New START in 2010 there have been no negotiations between the USA and Russia on a new strategic arms treaty. New START could be extended for five years until 2026 by agreement of the US and Russian governments; no ratification by the Congress or the Duma would be needed. It is, however, not clear that that will happen.

There appears to be little interest on either side in a resumption of arms control negotiations. One reason seems to be that strategic stability (in the sense defined above) has lost its salience in the discussion of arms control. That concept offered a way of quantifying deterrence by making it possible to calculate the destruction a retaliatory strike needed to be able to inflict on an aggressor in order to deter him. Calculations of the capacity to inflict assured destruction could be made for different scenarios, thus providing criteria for decisions about force levels and force structure.

Now, however, many experts believe that strategic stability can no longer be defined in that way. Ballistic missile defences, precision-guided munitions, non-nuclear strategic ballistic and cruise missiles, hypersonic missiles, anti-satellite weapons and space-based weapons, and cyber weapons all have to be factored in, not to mention underwater drones and nuclear-powered cruise missiles, as well as the technological potential of AI. If we redefine strategic stability in this way, it loses the clarity that the earlier conception had. It makes arms reductions more difficult because it introduces elements of uncertainty and incalculability into the negotiations.[4] An additional complication is that the USA and Russia have called for a shift to multilateral negotiations so that the nuclear forces of other countries (especially China) can be taken into account.

Strategic arms control has played a useful role in the management of the US–Soviet/Russian nuclear relationship. It has provided a certain measure of predictability, but it is now in crisis. Arms control, as we have known it, may be at an end. A new period of technological competition, qualitative rather than quantitative, appears to be under way. The optimism of Obama's April 2009 Prague Speech is now far in the past.

Will this have an impact on the NPT, given the commitment to disarmament in Article 6 of the treaty? Will the nuclear non-proliferation regime lose its legitimacy if moves toward disarmament are postponed sine die? The Ban Treaty is an expression of the disillusionment and frustration that many feel at the slow progress towards a world free of nuclear weapons. The opposition of the nuclear-weapon states and the slow pace of ratification by states that have signed it suggest that the Ban Treaty will not lead quickly to the desired goal of the elimination of nuclear weapons. It is possible, however, that in a world without arms control of any kind, the Ban Treaty would gain more support in protest against the lack of efforts to deal with the dangers posed by nuclear weapons.

We will lose some transparency in the nuclear field if on-site inspections no longer take place, but other forms of intelligence will make up for some of that. Restraints and restrictions on nuclear weapons development and deployment will be weakened, as the aftermath of the ending of the INF Treaty already suggests. If arms control ends, do the assumptions that underpinned agreements also go, or do they remain in force? Will there be a continuing understanding of: the catastrophic nature of nuclear war; the dangers of crises; the interconnection between offence and defence at the strategic level?

Besides arms control, there are two other nuclear issues that should at least be noted here. The first is the safety and security of nuclear materials. Since the end of the Cold War, this has become an important focus of arms control efforts. The second is the apparent adoption (or at least accusations of the adoption) of military doctrines that may make the use of nuclear weapons more likely, creating the danger of escalation to nuclear war. US–Russian and Indo–Pakistani relations are marked by such claims and counterclaims. This can contribute to mutual misunderstanding and to miscalculations, thereby increasing the danger of an inadvertent war.

Thinking about the future

Some elements of the current world order are likely to persist: it will still be an international states system. Tariffs and trade wars may change the pattern of economic globalisation and additive manufacturing too may affect supply chains. But there are elements of globalisation – cyberspace for example – that will remain, even if national governments come to exercise greater control over social media. The global challenges we face provide another element of continuity. Climate change; demographic change; pandemics to name but three – cannot be dealt with only at the national level.

Notwithstanding these elements of continuity, the world order is in flux and it is not clear what will replace it. In such a situation, Henry Kissinger notes, "everything depends … on some conception of the future."[5]

To elaborate on this point, four questions may be useful.[6] The first qualifies Kissinger's statement. The question is not whether a shared vision of the future can be formulated and implemented. That might only encourage efforts to impose a particular conception of the future on the world. The more productive approach is to explore not a shared vision of the future but a vision of a shared future. This distinction is crucial. Are the relevant parties able and willing to articulate a future that other parties would find bearable?

What is important here is not so much the answer as the question. We should not assume that a new world order would embody a single conception of the future. There might be multiple orders, as in the Cold War, based perhaps on ideological or confessional identities or on regional orders dominated by great powers. What matters then to each party is some assurance that the shared future provides it with a place it can live with. As Lee Kwan Yew remarked some years ago, "the concern of America is what kind of world they will face when China is able to contest their predominance."[7]

This raises a second question: that of trustworthiness. Can the relevant parties trust one another to honour commitments and to take the steps necessary toward that shared future? Trust is an essential ingredient in co-operative relations. It may be based on the belief that those who are co-operating have shared interests. But there is a richer conception: "I trust you because I think it is in your interest to attend to my interests in the relevant manner. This is not merely to say that you and I have the same interests. Rather it is to say that you have an interest in attending to my interests because, typically, you want our relationship to continue."[8] If trust derives not merely from a coincidence of interests but from a commitment to a continuing relationship, then the enactment of a vision of a shared future might precede rather than follow the creation of trust.

The third question is that of loss acceptance. A new world order will mean that not every party can get what it wants. Are the relevant parties ready to make the necessary compromises in fashioning a new order? According to one account, the current transition in world order is a consequence of the decline of the dominant position of the USA. Would the USA be willing to accept the compromises necessary for a world order in which it enjoyed a less dominant role? Or would China be willing to accept restraints on its ambition to be a "nation with global influence" by 2050? Has Russia accepted the losses it suffered with the collapse of the Soviet Union?

The fourth question concerns justice. Can the parties accept an agreement that does not meet what they see as the requirements of justice; are they willing to work together to alleviate or rectify the most serious injustices that are apt to remain in a new world order? Order does not entail justice. One might want to argue that justice requires order, but the reverse is not true. Hitler's "New Order for Europe" was not a just order. Order can, in principle, just be enforced, but to be stable it will require legitimacy, either in line with some principle of legitimacy or in terms of its capacity to deliver certain public goods.

These are very broad and complex questions and they raise many issues. If we treat them in a very schematic way, we can make the following points about co-operative security. First, there is a commitment to a shared future, in the sense that the political leaders of the main nuclear weapon states understand that the consequences of a nuclear war would be catastrophic. Second, there has been an element of trust between the leaders of the major nuclear powers, who have shared a mutual understanding that a nuclear war would be a catastrophe and wanted their relationship to continue. Third, loss acceptance is very difficult, partly because international politics are fluid, allowing the hope that losses can be recouped. Fourth, the nuclear non-proliferation regime is a discriminatory regime. It creates two classes of states, but it has functioned now for almost 50 years because it does something almost all states want: it helps to set limits on the spread of nuclear weapons.

That does not mean that limited nuclear wars will not happen or that a major nuclear war might not happen even though no one wants it. Such a war could happen by accident or miscalculation, especially through escalation from limited use of nuclear weapons. The nuclear danger is in some ways greater than in the Cold War because power relations appear to be shifting, boundaries of influence are being contested, and mechanisms of consultation weakened.

What is to be done?

In light of this discussion, what recommendations can one make?

First, extend New START to 2026. This may seem perverse in view of the discussion above, but there is one very strong argument for it. Extension of the treaty would signal that the two major nuclear powers are willing to stay engaged in the effort to manage their nuclear relationship. Even though the world is no longer bipolar in the way it was during the Cold War, Russia and the USA are still by far the dominant nuclear powers, possessing between them over 90 percent of the world's nuclear weapons. During the period of the extension the USA and Russia should discuss other possible topics for bilateral and potentially multilateral talks: co-operation in space (dealing with space debris, or clarification of codes of conduct) or co-operation in early warning of ballistic missile attacks, for example. It would be good if other countries could be drawn into such discussions.

Second, the prospects for bilateral arms control may be limited, but there appears be a place for multilateral negotiations. The four Nuclear Security Summits between 2010 and 2016 offer a model that could be adapted to other security purposes. The aim of the summits was to lessen the threat from nuclear terrorism. Much was done (though much remains to be done) to secure weapons-usable civilian nuclear materials, enhance international co-operation and take steps to strengthen the global nuclear security system. More than 50 countries took part.

Third, a proposal for a multilateral approach to disarmament emerged from the 2007 call of the "Gang of Four" for a world free of nuclear weapons. The idea is to create a "joint enterprise" dedicated to nuclear disarmament. The initial impetus could come from a summit meeting of 20–25 states. Ultimately all nuclear-armed states would have to be included and significant work done over a protracted period to implement such a programme.[9]

Fourth, the Trump Administration has launched an initiative called Creating the Environment for Nuclear Disarmament. This is a response to the Ban Treaty and evidently designed to provide evidence of US good intentions with respect to Article 6 for the next NPT Review Conference. What it will ultimately amount to is unclear. Forty-two countries (including Russia and China) took part in a meeting in Washington, DC in July 2019 to discuss ways to improve the security environment and reduce the likelihood of war among nuclear-armed states. This overlaps somewhat with the preceding recommendation.

Fifth, moves in the direction of nuclear disarmament and efforts to improve the security environment would provide more favourable conditions for sustaining the nuclear non-proliferation regime. This is an issue in which the leading nuclear weapon states would seem to have a common interest. There are dangerous nuclear trends in the Middle East and it is perhaps not inconceivable that new states might enter into a nuclear arms race. Co-operation to maintain and strengthen the non-proliferation regime should be a high priority for the leading powers.

There is a paradox here. I am recommending that the way to keep the possibility of co-operative security alive when the rules-based order has fallen into disrepair is to adopt procedures that can be seen as characteristic of a liberal democratic conception of world order.

Notes

1 Quoted in Mark Kramer, ""Beyond the Brezhnev Doctrine: A New Era in Soviet-East European Relations?" *International Security*, 14:3 (1989–1990), 25.
2 William Walker, *A Perpetual Menace* (New York: Routledge, 2012), 23–24.
3 Report by the Committee on Nuclear Proliferation, January 1965, in *Foreign Relations of the United States, 1964–1968*, vol. XI, Arms Control and Disarmament, Document 64: 174.
4 Alexander Savelyev, "Russia-US: On the Brink of a New Nuclear Arms Race," Russian International Affairs Council, August 2019, https://russiancouncil.ru/en/analytics-and-comments/analytics/russia-us-on-the-brink-of-a-new-nuclear-arms-race.
5 Henry Kissinger, *World Order* (New York: Penguin, 2014), 371–72.
6 Colleagues at the Stanford Center for International Conflict and Negotiation have devised these questions to help in framing discussions about conflict. See Byron Bland, Brenna Powell and Lee Ross, "Barriers to dispute resolution: Reflections on peacemaking and relationships between adversaries," in *Understanding social action, promoting human rights*, edited by Ryan Goodman, Derek Jinks and Andrew K. Woods (New York: Oxford University Press, 2012): 265–91.
7 Lee Kuan Yew, *The Grand Master's insights on China, the United States, and the world* (Cambridge MA: MIT Press, 2013), 4.
8 Russell Hardin, *Trust and trustworthiness* (New York: Russell Sage Foundation, 2004), 4.
9 James E. Goodby and Steven Pifer, "Creating the Conditions for a World without Nuclear Weapons," in *The War that Must Never Be Fought*, edited by George P. Shultz and James E. Goodby (Stanford California: Hoover Institution, 2015).

31

THE FUTURE OF NUCLEAR ARMS CONTROL

Time for an update[1]

Angela Kane and Noah Mayhew

From the golden age of arms control to nuclear identity politics

It is useful to recall why arms control became an integral part of the global security architecture. Arms control was considered important because people understood that the alternative was unimaginable. The arms controllers of the past came from a generation that remembers the Cuban Missile Crisis and US President John F. Kennedy's declaration that the policy of the USA would be "to regard any nuclear missile launched from Cuba against any nation in the Western Hemisphere as an attack by the Soviet Union on the USA, requiring a full retaliatory response upon the Soviet Union."[5] This is not to negate the fundamentally dangerous practice of nuclear brinkmanship, but rather to say that arms control proceeded in spite of this practice.

Following the Cuban Missile Crisis, the USA, the Soviet Union and the United Kingdom ratified a treaty that banned nuclear testing in the atmosphere, outer space and underwater, as well as the foundational Treaty on the Non-Proliferation of Nuclear Weapons (NPT), which belayed fears of a proliferation chain that could result in 20 or 30 nuclear-armed nations. The USA and Soviet Union engaged in two rounds of Strategic Arms Limitation Talks (SALT I and II) to reduce the risks posed by nuclear war. One result of those talks was a 1972 ban on anti-ballistic missile defence (the ABM Treaty), based on the notion that one side might be able to resist a nuclear attack from the other, thus increasing the viability of a first strike.

When the now-famous Reagan-Gorbachev doctrine was coined in 1985, there were approximately 70,000 nuclear weapons in the world.[6] Since then, that number has come down to under 14,000 and the nations of the world have endeavoured to ban nuclear testing through the Comprehensive Nuclear-Test-Ban Treaty (CTBT).[7] The USA and Soviet Union agreed not to deploy short and medium range missiles in Europe (the Intermediate-Range Nuclear Forces Treaty,

DOI: 10.4324/9781003227502-35

INF Treaty), owing to their detrimental effect on strategic stability and European security. The US and newly minted Russian Federation engaged in Presidential Nuclear Initiatives in 1991, intended to unilaterally limit and reduce nuclear weaponry.[8] The two countries have been through three Strategic Arms Reduction Treaties (START I, START II and New START), with the aim to make meaningful reductions in deployed nuclear weapons and the risk of their use.

In the early 2000s, with new leaders in the White House and the Kremlin, bilateral arms control began to stagnate. The USA withdrew from the ABM Treaty, which resulted in the Russian withdrawal from the START II Treaty.[9] In a course correction, the two countries signed the Strategic Offensive Reductions Treaty in 2002. It was superseded by the New START Treaty that entered into force in 2011. Other arms control and non-proliferation initiatives decelerated dramatically during this period. For example, efforts to dispose of excess, weapons-usable plutonium slowed to a crawl, a growing number of countries vocally questioned the US and Russian commitment to further arms reductions and allegations of violation of the INF Treaty began to surface.

As relations between the US and Russia worsened, owing notably to eastward expansion by the North Atlantic Treaty Organization (NATO), the Ukraine Crisis and Russia's annexation of Crimea, arms control became a barb to throw *in the context* of other bilateral disagreements, rather than an important process to engage in despite those disagreements. The alleged violations of the INF Treaty, which might have been swiftly resolved under different political circumstances, became a narrative of confrontation even under President Barack Obama.

In 2017 Donald Trump became President of the USA. Since the beginning of his run in the White House, he and his administration have shown marked contempt for arms control and non-proliferation, including withdrawal from the Joint Comprehensive Plan of Action with Iran,[10] abrogating the INF Treaty[11] and, most recently, announcing plans to withdraw from the 1992 Open Skies Treaty.[12] These issues have been well documented and thus will not be detailed here.

The last arms control agreement or limitation that still stands between the USA and Russia is New START. Both countries have brought down their numbers of deployed warheads and delivery vehicles pursuant to the treaty, but the inspection provisions will expire on 5 February 2021 if not extended. This is important because the inspections under New START provide important insight and predictability regarding the intentions of the two countries vis-à-vis the deployment of new nuclear weapons systems.

Russia has advocated for the treaty's extension, but the USA has stalled, signalling that its vision of the future of arms control is not bilateral, but multilateral. However, China, which has become a major player in the nuclear field over the past decades, has been frank in its reluctance to take part in arms reductions while the USA and Russia maintain such disproportionately higher arsenal numbers. The other nuclear weapon states under the NPT, France and the UK, have expressed similar hesitation.

This is the impasse we see today. Arms control is no longer treated as a priority for the two nuclear superpowers and is vulnerable as collateral damage of other political conflict.

Geopolitical challenges in the 21st century

A resurgent Russia

The phases of US–Russian arms control roughly correspond to three periods: (1) the bipolar world order that defined much of the 20th century, (2) the unipolar world order after the collapse of the Soviet Union and (3) the multipolar world order that has come with a resurgent Russia. But many arms controllers in Washington seem to cling to the unipolar conception, in which the USA is the sole leader. As Russia became again more assertive in the early 2000s, it was less willing to accept this as a fact of life.

An example of this is NATO expansion, which has resulted in a large number of countries in Russia's sphere of interest being absorbed into the alliance. As Moscow has grown increasingly uncomfortable with the approach of this alliance – the expressed purpose of which was to contain the influence of the Soviet Union – it has reminded the international community of the informal promises made to it by Western leaders that NATO would not expand eastward. This issue boiled over in 2014 when, after years of feeling that its complaints on NATO expansion were ignored, Russia blocked the European integration process of Ukraine and annexed Crimea. Conflict in Ukraine has made US–Russian co-operation not impossible, but still markedly more difficult than it was before.

In a broader sense, Russia sees that it is not taken as a serious partner, equal in status to the US.[13] It feels that much of the discourse on arms control is US-centric and comes with expectations for it to make choices that contravene its security interests. In order for a future paradigm of arms control and non-proliferation to enjoy the earnest participation of Russia, these perceptions must be taken into account and counteracted. Doing so might help to bring Russia to the table in future arms negotiations and ensure their sustainability. A refusal to do so will aggravate the current situation, in which Russia is increasingly isolated and unwilling to engage with the USA on arms control and other issues.

The rise of China

China defines its nuclear policy by possessing the minimum capabilities needed to deter a first strike from a potential aggressor. It was the first state to declare a no-first-use policy and has always argued that it would not engage in negotiations with the USA and Russian Federation until their numbers came down to China's level, estimated at 350 nuclear warheads in March 2021 (while the US and Russian stockpiles, including deployed and non-deployed but excluding retired warheads, are estimated at 3,800 and 4,497, respectively).[14]

So, what is China's role in arms control and strategic stability? China has always kept a low profile in arms control matters, yet concomitant with its rise as a major geopolitical actor has embarked on a military spending spree. Annual military spending rose from $32.6 billion in 1998 to $266 billion in 2019 (at 2019 prices and exchange rates).[15] It has enabled China to modernise and expand its nuclear delivery systems, as well as purchase military hardware and multiply its conventional missile inventory. This latter aspect was cited by the USA as contributing to the abrogation of the INF Treaty, in addition to the INF violations blamed on Russia.

President Trump has been outspoken in wanting China to take its seat at the arms control table. If it was expected that this would accelerate pressure on China to engage in trilateral arms control negotiations, that calculation proved profoundly wrong. China today is a powerful player, second only to the USA, and feels confident in stating its positions. The proposal by President Trump to transform New START into a trilateral agreement, for example, was firmly rejected by China[16] which accused the USA of "covering up the serious damage caused by the USA's breaching of and withdrawing from multilateral agreements, as well as their unilateral acts of bullying."[17]

Why would China agree to become more transparent and engage in arms control negotiations? Sitting at the table with the USA and Russia would confirm its status as a world power, but that is clearly not enough. No other inducements were offered and it is unclear at this point what is the US roadmap for including China in trilateral negotiations or even if there is one. The asymmetrical nature of the nuclear arsenal would require other weapons and capacities to be drawn into the process. Capping nuclear arsenals at different levels would not be acceptable, as this would be seen simply as containing China's capacities while keeping US – and Russian – superior nuclear arsenals. No wonder China is rejecting this proposal out of hand.

Challenges posed by new technology

In addition to geopolitical considerations, new technologies pose challenges to arms control and the global security landscape. The emergence of offensive cyber capabilities in statecraft has raised disturbing questions about what cyberwar could mean, including threats to nuclear command, control and communication (NC3) systems. Lethal autonomous weapon systems (LAWS) represent an entirely new class of weapons and the international community does not even share a definition of the term "autonomous." The USA and Russia are developing a range of new weapon systems, some of which do not fit under limits defined by New START. In order to be effective, new approaches to arms control will need to take into account the risks posed by these new technologies.

Cyber warfare, miscalculation and NC3 systems

At the beginning of the 2000s a number of major cyber incidents brought offensive cyber capabilities to the forefront of defence planners' minds. Notable among them was a series of cyberattacks against Estonia in 2007 that paralysed local and government infrastructure, which led to the development of the Tallinn Manual, meant to establish rules and practices in international law applicable to cyber warfare. Later, hacking against the US Democratic National Convention was meant to sabotage the candidacy of Hillary Clinton during the 2016 presidential elections. Russia has been implicated in both attacks, though it is not the only country that has engaged in offensive cyber activities. The use of the Stuxnet virus by the USA in 2010 to sabotage Iranian centrifuges is another example. China, Iran, the Democratic People's Republic of Korea (DPRK, or North Korea) and non-state actors have also allegedly used cyber-weapons.

BOX 31.1 CONTROVERSY ON CYBERSECURITY VS. INFORMATION SECURITY

The USA focuses on **cybersecurity,** defined in the US National Cyber Strategy as "effectively identifying, protecting, and ensuring resilience of their networks, systems, functions, and data as well as detecting, responding to, and recovering from incidents." The Russian Federation sees the issue more broadly as **information security**, defined in the Doctrine of Information Security of the Russian Federation as: "the state of protection of the individual, society and the State against internal and external information threats, allowing to ensure the constitutional human and civil rights and freedoms, the decent quality and standard of living for citizens, the sovereignty, the territorial integrity and sustainable socio-economic development of the Russian Federation, as well as defence and security of the State." This fundamental difference in perspective on cyber issues has been a major barrier to agreement on governance.

The National Cyber Strategy of the USA is available here: https://digital.library.unt.edu/ark:/67531/metadc1259394/m2/1/high_res_d/National-Cyber-Strategy.pdf

The Doctrine of Information Security of the Russian Federation is available here: www.mid.ru/en/foreign_policy/official_documents/-/asset_publisher/CptICkB6BZ29/content/id/2563163.

Attempts to establish regulation in the cyber field have thus far been unsuccessful. The impact of the Tallinn Manual, first published in 2013 and updated in 2017, has been relatively limited, chiefly because the USA and Russia cannot agree on how to define cyberwar or on what such a conversation even should encompass (see Box 31.1). Various initiatives in the United Nations (UN) context have attempted to establish guidelines for responsible behaviour in cyberspace, including a concurrently running Open Ended Working Group (OEWG) backed by Russia and a 25-member Group of Governmental Experts (GGE) backed by the USA. There is little reason to believe that either process will conclude with consensus recommendations that have a chance of being adopted by the major cyber actors, despite consensus in the GGE in 2013 that international law and the UN Charter are applicable to cyberspace.[18]

According to the UN, 23 countries have shown evidence of commanding offensive cyber capabilities, and a further 30 have shown indications that they are developing such capabilities.[19] Just as the number of countries in this field is growing, so are the ways in which these capabilities can be utilised. The 2007 attacks against Estonia were distributed denial of service (DDOS) attacks, which essentially overwhelm servers until they shut down. DDOS attacks are disruptive and represent the majority of cyberattacks today. However, there is evidence to suggest that the major cyber actors are considering uses for cyberattacks in the nuclear field.

The risks of cyber-weaponry in the nuclear field are primarily related to miscalculation and an absence of predictability and transparency. While the risk of a nuclear strike owing to the use of cyber-weapons remains seemingly out of reach today, state cyber capabilities are growing more robust by the day. On the one hand, because of the anonymity of the internet, a cyberattack on a nuclear installation might be perceived as a first strike by an opponent, or even masked to appear as such. On the other hand, the identity of perpetrators of a cyberattack – be they state or non-state actors – is difficult to find and more difficult to prove, which could make response a dangerous calculation in the nuclear domain.

Since at least 2015 US officials have expressed the need for increased capabilities in missile defence "left of launch," meaning non-kinetic defensive capabilities that would neutralise an enemy missile as soon as a launch was considered imminent. This includes "technological development efforts related to non-kinetic defensive capabilities, such as cyber warfare and directed energy."[20]

To interfere with another state's NC3 systems with cyber means would be to put the concept of credible deterrence at risk, which would be detrimental to strategic stability. In a situation where tensions are escalating, the perception that one's first-strike capability is compromised might itself precipitate a pre-emptive strike. Hence, cyberattacks on NC3 systems should be something that the nuclear powers work to regulate and ban, rather than develop.

Developments like this exemplify the importance of the UN processes to establish widely, if not universally agreed upon guidelines and best practices in cyber governance, including in the arms control field. Nuclear-armed nations, especially the five permanent members of the UN Security Council (P5), should be leaders in the establishment of cyber governance in the nuclear field, rather than to slow the process down, owing to disagreements in the geopolitical sphere. Moreover, while agreement about definitions is important, it might be time to explicitly address the effect that cyber will have on the nuclear weapons space now, rather than develop offensive capability that will require regulation to catch up.

Autonomous weapon systems and artificial intelligence

One area where technology, definition, ethics, law and society all come together is in the debate on LAWS. It is a debate that was kicked off in 2013 by the report of a UN Special Rapporteur on extrajudicial, summary or arbitrary execution, Christof Heyns.[21] It has brought out deep divisions between states. The deliberations on this issue are taking place in Geneva under the Convention on Certain Conventional Weapons (CCW). So far, no legally binding or political actions have been adopted. In fact, past years have increased the gulf between those who wish to engage in negotiations to achieve a ban on LAWS and those who fervently oppose it.

Twenty-nine countries have explicitly called for a prohibition of LAWS, as has the Non-Aligned Movement. Twelve countries are opposed to a prohibition or a treaty.[22] Prominent artificial intelligence scientists have signed declarations and letters to warn of LAWS; UN Secretary-General António Guterres has called these weapons morally repugnant, as has Pope Francis.

What has become clear is that the trend towards increasing autonomy in military systems will continue and is likely to affect all domains of warfare, perhaps even the nuclear domain. Technological superiority is likely to decide who wins on the battlefield and robots do not get tired or influenced by emotions or stress. It is an absolute must to consider the risks inherent in this development. Where lies the accountability for the actions of an autonomous weapon? With the innovator? The programmer? Who takes the responsibility for killing innocent civilians?

The debate about LAWS is not confined to the CCW meeting rooms in Geneva. The European Parliament, for example, adopted in 2018 a resolution that called on the European Union "to develop and adopt, as a matter of urgency … a common position on lethal autonomous weapon systems" and "to work towards the start of international negotiations on a legally binding instrument prohibiting lethal autonomous weapon systems."[23] The European Commission has indeed issued guidelines and standards for AI (most recently in February 2020), but none of these include any mention of LAWS, though ethics, excellence and trust feature prominently in the titles.[24]

LAWS will continue to be developed – and once ready to be deployed, they will find customers, not only governments, but probably also non-state actors. The decision over life and death has to be one where international humanitarian and human rights law have to prevail. Human life and dignity have to trump all other concerns and meaningful human control has to be maintained, though how "meaningful human control" is defined has not been agreed by all.

Updating arms control: The way forward

Working with the new geopolitical reality

Arms control and non-proliferation discussions seem stuck in the 20th century. What worked then, no longer does. The USA and the Soviet Union/Russian Federation are not alone on the world stage anymore. China is now a third dominant player, albeit one that is taking a more discreet role in arms control politics. A fourth player is new technology; it is unclear yet how dominance in technology will play out on the multilateral stage.

Discussions and negotiations on arms control have always been conducted in silos: nuclear here, conventional weapons there, other topics – such as LAWS or outer space, for example – equally separate. This division is no longer applicable, but that reality has not yet been reflected in the various disarmament fora. Another outdated concept is the focus on numbers: the yardstick of total number of nuclear weapons needs to be seen against deployment, against alert status, against size, against modernisation.

The NPT – still called the "gold standard of nuclear non-proliferation" – has lost its lustre. It enshrined the nuclear status of five countries and denied others party to the treaty from ever acquiring nuclear weapons, yet there are now four other countries outside the NPT possessing nuclear weapons. Except for the DPRK (which is subject to severe sanctions), none of the other three (India, Israel, Pakistan) were punished or ostracised for their nuclear weapons possession.

The recognition of this double standard has long dogged the NPT deliberations. Stalemate in implementing accords and agendas – agreed in NPT Review Conferences by consensus – led in 2017 to the adoption of a new instrument, the Treaty on the Prohibition of Nuclear Weapons (TPNW) that now has entered into force.

The dismissal of the TPNW by the five nuclear weapon states and those under their nuclear protection is unfortunate and short-sighted, as the treaty will not disappear if ignored. Instead, the chorus of those arguing against the arms spiral, against modernising nuclear and other arms, against the massive spending on military weapons, is increasing.

Pope Francis has long been a vocal opponent of nuclear weapons and is mobilising his followers all over the world to advocate for the abolition of nuclear weapons. UN Secretary-General Guterres has also been outspoken on this issue, as have other political leaders. Together with the tireless efforts of civil society, this chorus of voices is amplified by the younger generation, the millennials. In a poll conducted at the request of the International Committee of the Red Cross in 2019, 84 percent of the millennials believed that the use of nuclear weapons is never acceptable and 54 percent supported a nuclear weapons ban.[25] This shows that politicians arguing for continued – or even enhanced – possession of nuclear weapons are out of sync with the population. The question now remains when the effect of these developments will change policies.

Adapting arms control to new technology

New technologies are fundamentally changing the arms control landscape. Not only are lethal autonomous weapon systems on the horizon but the impact of developments in cyber weapons, new missile technology and other fields such as biotechnology are impacting arms control considerations.

There are currently no international rules in place for these new technologies. Many of these are developed, used and sold by private industry rather than government. A younger generation of government and military experts is needed to understand these challenges and to address them in negotiations which also has to include private actors. The challenge is compounded by accelerating at the same time as the US–Russian arms control architecture is breaking down.

An initiative to find solutions was launched in March 2019 by the Foreign Minister of Germany, Heiko Maas, who hosted a conference in Berlin that was also attended by the foreign ministers of the Netherlands and Sweden. "We must find solutions for the technological challenges of tomorrow. In a nutshell, we must re-think arms control," Maas said. "Our common systems of rules have almost always responded too late. They are not keeping pace with technological development and they therefore continue to be flawed," he stated.[26]

In this context, it is important not to demonise technology, most of which is beneficial. Many new and emerging technologies offer potential benefits to arms control, especially in monitoring and verification. Distributed ledger technology (a combination of technologies and computing concepts that allows a network of participants to share and validate data across a tamper-evident ledger) could, for example, offer an authoritative record that would improve continuity of knowledge during the implementation of an agreement.[27] Similarly, satellite imagery and remote sensing technology could serve as confidence-building measures rather than a source of suspicion.

The difficulty lies in finding the right response to technologies that are or could be harmful. These responses must be tailored to the individual technological challenges: One approach is not enough, yet it is also true that some of the technologies interact, which makes it more complex to address the challenges.

New and innovative approaches coupled with serious efforts to advance arms control negotiations are required. Lack of leadership by the USA and Russia make it difficult; it remains to be seen whether the German, Dutch and Swedish initiative can make meaningful progress, yet they are being cheered on by those of us who support enhanced engagement in arms control. A follow-on conference to this initiative is scheduled for November 2020, indicating that governments besides the USA and Russia are taking steps to fill the vacuum in arms control leadership.

Risk reduction in absence of political will

The last treaty limiting nuclear weapons was concluded ten years ago. No new negotiations are being conducted, nor are any envisaged. Instead, a new arms race is under way. In the absence of political will by the nuclear-armed states to curb the arms spiral further, what can be done to reduce the risk of a nuclear explosion?

The effects of the explosions in Hiroshima and Nagasaki are well documented, yet these were small nuclear bombs compared to the arsenals available today. What would be the effects of a nuclear detonation on the human population, most of whom are now living in dense urban areas? What would be the climatic and environmental consequences?

The debate of 40 years ago when "nuclear winter" was in the public consciousness has long faded. Most likely, the scenarios then foreseen were imprecise at best. Today, with technological advances in computing power, in availability of data and modelling, much more precise predictions are available. Scientists and AI specialists should be engaged to study the various possibilities of a nuclear explosion: the size and number of the nuclear weapon/s, the yield, directed at what target, with what consequences, for people and the environment.

Such fact sets would immeasurably enhance the quality of the discussion and force nuclear possessors to respond, not only to "Create an Environment for Nuclear Disarmament," as put forward by the USA, but also to address the consequences of – and responsibility for – a nuclear detonation and its inevitable catastrophic result on humans and the environment. This responsibility should be put on the global agenda, as there is no "planet B," a warning we often see on banners carried by young demonstrators.

Equally important are other measures to reduce risk: the US-initiated Nuclear Security Summits in 2010, 2012, 2014 and 2016 brought a focus on nuclear materials and led to a series of measures and commitments to strengthen nuclear security. Of the 53 countries participating, over 90 percent shared information and issued national progress reports explaining how they implemented their responsibilities in this field, a welcome step to increase transparency. A large quantity of highly enriched uranium was recovered or removed from civilian use, training centres were established and national laws on nuclear security were introduced or updated. Yet the Security Summits were seen as controversial by those countries that were not invited to participate in them and did not lead to increased co-operation in other fora, such as multilateral institutions like the UN or the International Atomic Energy Agency. Could a modified security summit be devised? With a larger group of countries, with gift baskets and voluntary commitments as the entrance ticket? Could such an initiative be spearheaded by the G-20?

NATO admitted its 30th member, North Macedonia, in March 2020. The bloc calls itself a nuclear alliance, but its strategic concept was agreed ten years ago. Would it not be time to discuss the changes in the global nuclear order and propose policy adjustments, especially on agreed best practices for emerging technology? Might policy adjustments prepare NATO for a return to a focus on crisis response, rather than collective defence? Could the working methods in the NPT conferences be changed to increase the accountability of nuclear weapon states, to explain their non-implementation of measures agreed upon in earlier meetings by consensus? To explain their adherence to the policy of nuclear deterrence and what, in their opinion, is enough? Perhaps by considering these questions seriously – rather than dismissing them – the nuclear weapon states, in particular the US and Russia, could help to reduce the growing tension in global order.

Conclusion

The past has shown that a calamity often changes the course of history. Not only through wars, but also through other events, such as a pandemic. After several years of a number of states increasingly turning inward and giving their national agenda priority over all other considerations, the Covid-19 pandemic reminds us that our world is interconnected, that problems do not stop at borders and that technology ties us even closer together than we ever imagined possible 50 years ago.

This could be a turning point in the assessment of nuclear weapons by those who possess them. Are these weapons a shield for security, for safeguarding populations? Or are they a status symbol of projecting power? And would the modernisation of strategic nuclear forces really be relevant to protect people and hence a priority at this time as suggested by US Secretary of Defense Mark Esper?[28] Would the huge amounts of money spent on armaments not be better used to help the economy, to mitigate the effects of the pandemic on the population, to return to intensifying international co-ordination and co-operation?

We are both internationalists and for us, the answer is obvious: a pandemic can shift the focus, make us painfully aware that there are threats to security and well-being that are not related to weapons and armaments. But will states share this view and adjust their priorities? States remain the world's most important players and they control the actions to be taken. Just as it takes time to adjust priorities, it also takes time to build up relationships of co-operation, maybe even of co-management; let's push for it – and for nuclear disarmament.

Notes

1 This article was first published as *Global Governance Spotlight* 1|2020 of the Development and Peace Foundation, www.sef-bonn.org.
2 Joint Soviet-United States Statement on the Summit Meeting in Geneva, 21 November 1985, www.reaganlibrary.gov/research/speeches/112185a.
3 Christopher A. Ford, "The Politics of Arms Control: Getting Beyond Post-Cold War Pathologies and Finding Security in a Competitive Environment," speech at the International Institute of Strategic Studies, London, 11 February 2020, www.iiss.org/events/2020/02/the-politics-of-arms-control.
4 Vladimir I. Yermakov, "Washington Should Return Home its Nuclear Weapons from Europe," Interfax (unofficial translation from Russian), Moscow, 11 February 2020, www.interfax.ru/interview/694859.
5 John F. Kennedy, "The Cuban Missile Crisis: President Kennedy's Address to the Nation, 22 October 1962," *Prologue Magazine*, 34:3 (2002), www.archives.gov/publications/prologue/2002/fall/cuban-missiles.html.
6 Robert S. Norris, and Hans M. Kristensen, 2010: "Global nuclear weapons inventories, 1945–2010," *Bulletin of the Atomic Scientists*, 66:3 (2010): 77–83.
7 "World Nuclear Weapon Stockpile," Ploughshares Fund, 1 February 2021, www.ploughshares.org/world-nuclear-stockpile-report.
8 Eli Corin, "Presidential Nuclear Initiatives: An Alternative Paradigm for Arms Control," Nuclear Threat Initiative, Washington, DC, 1 March 2004, www.nti.org/analysis/articles/presidential-nuclear-initiatives.
9 Wade Boese, "U.S. Withdraws From ABM Treaty; Global Response Muted," *Arms Control Today*, 32 (July/August 2002), www.armscontrol.org/act/2002-07/news/us-withdraws-abm-treaty-global-response-muted.
10 "Fact Sheets: President Trump is Ending United States Participation in an Unacceptable Iran Deal," https://kr.usembassy.gov/050818-fact-sheets-president-trump-is-ending-united-states-participation-in-an-unacceptable-iran-deal.

11 Michael R. Pompeo, "U.S. Withdrawal from the INF Treaty on 2 August, 2019," press statement, Washington, DC, 2 August 2019, https://ru.usembassy.gov/u-s-withdrawal-from-the-inf-treaty-on-august-2-2019.

12 "Remarks by President Trump Before Marine One Departure for Michigan," 21 May 2020, www.c-span.org/video/?472354-1/president-trump-departs-white-house-trip-michigan.

13 Jack Matlock, "US and Russia 1991–2017: Keynote Address with Ambassador Jack Matlock," Monterey Summer Symposium on Russia of Graduate Initiative in Russian Studies, 19 June 2017, www.youtube.com/watch?v=4TvqM0QMTd0.

14 Hans M. Kristensen, and Matt Korda, "Status of World Nuclear Forces," Federation of American Scientists, March 2021, https://fas.org/issues/nuclear-weapons/status-world-nuclear-forces.

15 "SIPRI Military Expenditure Database," Stockholm International Peace Research Institute, no date (accessed 13 April 2021), www.sipri.org/databases/milex.

16 "Foreign Ministry Spokesperson Zhao Lijian's Regular Press Conference on 6 March 2020," Beijing, www.fmprc.gov.cn/mfa_eng/xwfw_665399/s2510_665401/t1753086.shtml.

17 "Statement by Ambassador Fu Cong, Director-General of the Department of Arms Control of the Ministry of Foreign Affairs of China, at the General Debate of the First Committee of the 74th Session of the UNGA," 12 October 2019, www.fmprc.gov.cn/mfa_eng/wjdt_665385/zyjh_665391/t1707314.shtml.

18 *Report of the Group of Governmental Experts on Developments in the Field of Information and Telecommunications in the Context of International Security* (New York: United Nations General Assembly document A/68/98, 24 June 2013), www.unidir.org/files/medias/pdfs/developments-in-the-field-of-information-and-telecommunications-in-the-context-of-international-security-2012-2013-a-68-98-eng-0-578.pdf.; and Angela Kane, "The Rocky Road to Consensus: The Work of UN Groups of Governmental Experts in the Field of ICTs and in the Context of International Security, 1998–2013," *American Foreign Policy Interests*, 36:5 (2014): 314–21, www.tandfonline.com/doi/abs/10.1080/10803920.2014.969175

19 "UN GGE and OEWG," *digwatch*, Geneva Internet Platform Digital Watch (no date, accessed 13 April 2021), https://dig.watch/processes/un-gge.

20 Committee on Armed Services, House of Representatives, Washington DC, Hearing, 19 March 2015, www.govinfo.gov/content/pkg/CHRG-114hhrg94227/pdf/CHRG-114hhrg94227.pdf.

21 *Report of the Special Rapporteur on extrajudicial, summary or arbitrary executions, Christof Heyns* (New York: United Nations General Assembly document A/HRC/23/47, 9 April 2013), www.ohchr.org/Documents/HRBodies/HRCouncil/RegularSession/Session23/A-HRC-23-47_en.pdf.

22 Campaign to Stop Killer Robots, "Country Views on Killer Robots," 21 August 2019, www.stopkillerrobots.org/wp-content/uploads/2019/08/KRC_CountryViews21Aug2019.pdf.

23 "European Parliament resolution of 12 September 2018 on autonomous weapon systems" (2018/2752(RSP)), www.europarl.europa.eu/doceo/document/TA-8-2018-0341_EN.html.

24 *White Paper On Artificial Intelligence – A European approach to excellence and trust* ((Brussels: European Commission, COM(2020) 65 final, 19 February 2020), https://ec.europa.eu/info/sites/info/files/commission-white-paper-artificial-intelligence-feb2020_en.pdf.

25 *Millennials on War. Topline Report for the International Committee of the Red Cross* (Ipsos, 25 November 2019), www.ipsos.com/sites/default/files/ct/news/documents/2020-01/ipsos_millennials_on_war_full_report_0_1.pdf.

26 "Speech by Federal Foreign Minister Heiko Maas at the conference 2019 Capturing Technology. Rethinking Arms Control," Berlin, 15 March 2019, www.auswaertiges-amt.de/en/newsroom/news/maas-conference-2019-capturing-technology-rethinking-arms-control/2199902.

27 Sarah Frazar, Cindy Vestergaard, Benjamin Loehrke, and Luisa Kenausis, *Evaluating Member State Acceptance of Blockchain for Nuclear Safeguards* (Stanley Center for Peace and Security, Nuclear Weapons Readout & Recommendations December 2019), (Muscatine: Stanley Center for Peace and Security, December 2019), www.stimson.org/wp-content/files/file-attachments/NWRR-EvaluatingBlkChainAcceptance12-20-20-1.pdf.
28 Tweet of 4 April 2020, https://twitter.com/esperdod/status/1246469849590771712?s=11 (accessed 13 April 2021).

32

ARMS CONTROL AND WORLD ORDER[1]

Sverre Lodgaard

On the way to a new world order we do not yet know, disorder is the new normal. The world is in a state of flux. Six features are particularly noteworthy:

1. Sovereign states are re-emphasised and reconfirmed as the basic building blocks of international affairs.
2. Trade and technology wars and economic sanctions have moved to the top of the international agenda.
3. International norms, institutions and agreements are falling apart.
4. Geopolitically, the tense relationship between the USA and China is increasingly dominant.
5. New technologies nurture new forms of influence and capacities for violence.
6. Inherent in all of this, international affairs have become more unpredictable.

Such a world does not leave many options for co-operative action. In the military field, states have returned to unilateral security policies as primitive as those of the Cold War. There is one overriding common concern, however: to avoid nuclear war. To this end, stability measures – the primary objective of arms control – are of the essence. The need for a global framework for responsible nuclear conduct, arms control and disarmament, realistic enough to gain traction while capturing the aspiration of a world free of nuclear dangers, is at least as strong as 60 years ago, when arms control was first introduced.

The question

This commentary starts with the regression of security mind-sets and the unravelling of the arms control architecture. In a replay of the classical security dilemma, states engage in action-reaction cycles only to find that their security diminishes. It

DOI: 10.4324/9781003227502-36

goes on to review current world order changes. There is no longer consensus on the basic premises of global governance; international norms are increasingly questioned; multilateralism and the institutions upholding it are under pressure; arms control and disarmament agreements are unravelling; and big power relations are strained by arms modernisation and expansion. Zero sum thinking is gaining ground and negotiated solutions for the common benefit are a rare commodity. In such a turbulent world, where big powers compete for positions and influence in the face of an unpredictable future, what are the prospects, if any, for co-operative security policies, arms control and disarmament?

Common security, co-operative security and arms control

When the "International Commission on Security and Disarmament Issues" (also known as the Palme Commission after its chairman, Swedish Prime Minister Olof Palme), introduced the concept of common security in the beginning of the 1980s, the security establishments were intensely preoccupied with the dangers posed by nuclear weapons.[2] The commission took issue with prevailing policies: the major powers acquired new weapons in search of unilateral advantage, only to realise that the gains were short-lived and that the long-term effect was more tension and diminished security. Common security pointed to a way out of this security dilemma, emphasising that in the nuclear age, security cannot be obtained unilaterally, but has to be built together with one's adversaries. It has to be a win-win activity. During the 1980s the message gained ground in Europe and the Soviet Union, but in this century, the big powers have reverted to the old logic. And this time, it is more difficult to chart a way out of it because there are more powers involved and more conflicts of interest. Complex deterrence equations are the name of the game, and common endeavours are, at best, mere add-ons.

Common security is a generic concept. In the period of opportunity after the end of the Cold War, it inspired the concept of co-operative security, defined as a "strategic principle that seeks to accomplish its purposes through institutional consent rather than through threats of material or physical coercion."[3] Another definition says that the central purpose is:

> to prevent war and to do so primarily by preventing the means for successful aggression from being assembled, thus also obviating the need for states so threatened to make their own counter-preparations. Cooperative security thus displaces the centrepiece of security planning from preparing to counter threats to preventing such threats from arising – from deterring aggression to making preparations for it more difficult.[4]

Co-operative security became an important principle of European security policy enshrined in documents of the Conference on Security and Co-operation in Europe (later the Organization for Security and Co-operation in Europe).

The opposite of co-operative strategies is non-co-operative ones. The latter are typically zero-sum exercises; the former, positive sum. Non-co-operative strategies aim to deter premeditated attack; in order to be credible, the parties have to be prepared to go to war. Co-operative strategies aim to reduce the risk of inadvertent escalation and depend on the willingness of all to co-operate. They are essentially preventive in nature. Non-co-operative and co-operative strategies therefore address two fundamentally different scenarios. Similarly, they are relevant to different parts of an escalatory process: co-operative strategies can be effective at early stages of the process, to stop further escalation, but if this does not succeed and one of the parties is unwilling to co-operate, non-co-operative strategies of deterrence come into play. Seen this way they are not opposites, but complementary.[5]

The concept of arms control was introduced around 1960 as an enlargement of the scope of military strategy. It rests on the recognition that big power relations are not ones of pure conflict, but involve strong elements of mutual interest in the avoidance of war that none of them want; in minimising the costs and risks of arms competition; and in limiting the destructive effects of war in the event that it occurs.[6] Different from disarmament agreements, which aim at reduction and elimination of weapons, arms control agreements encourage countries to manage their weapons in limited co-operation with each other. The key objective is stability, which comes in different versions: strategic stability, crisis stability and arms race stability.[7]

The Cuban missile crisis of 1962 boosted practical applications of the concept. The twin negotiations of the Anti-Ballistic Missile (ABM) Treaty of 1972 and the Strategic Arms Limitation Treaty (SALT) of 1972 were conducted in the spirit of stability. Nationwide ballistic missile defences were considered destabilising. Three years later, military confidence-building measures were introduced in Europe. The first generation was largely symbolic – little more than expressions of good will – but the second-generation Stockholm conference confidence and security building measures (CSBM) were militarily significant. They built trust, became stepping stones to substantial disarmament agreements and helped to end the Cold War. In this increasingly benign security environment, the major disarmament treaties – the Intermediate-Range Nuclear Forces (INF) Treaty, the Conventional Armed Forces in Europe Treaty (CFE), the Strategic Arms Reduction Treaty (START) and the Presidential Nuclear Initiatives – became possible. Later, nuclear disarmament continued, half-heartedly with the Strategic Offensive Reductions Treaty (SORT) of 2002 and more substantially with the New START of 2010. The CFE Treaty, which eliminated tens of thousands of battle tanks, armoured combat vehicles, artillery, aircraft and combat helicopters, was shaken by the break-down of the Soviet Union and finally came to an end in 2007.

Since New START, there have been no negotiations between the two leading nuclear powers. Instead, 122 states negotiated the Treaty on the Prohibition of Nuclear Weapons (TPNW). Similar to nuclear-weapon-free zones, which ensure the absence of nuclear weapons in regions without a "nuclear shadow," the signers of the TPNW all were non-nuclear-weapon states. The treaty aims to stigmatise nuclear weapons, strengthen anti-nuclear sentiments around the world and hold the nuclear weapon states (NWS) accountable for their disregard of international obligations.

The relationship between co-operative measures and the political environment is a two-way street. On the one hand, the Stockholm Conference CSBMs (1986) were made possible by the thaw in East–West relations under Soviet leader Mikhail Gorbachev. On the other hand, agreements on these measures did much to further improve international relations. Disarmament became possible on their heels as the Cold War drew to an end and a period of opportunity opened up. The CSBMs were precursors of those momentous developments.

In recent years, international relations have been fast deteriorating. The new normality is characterised by big power competition and arms build-up. Another ingredient is economic warfare in the form of trade and technology disputes and prolific use of economic sanctions. In addition, cyber warfare and new military technologies have opened new threat horizons, poorly understood so far but potentially monstrous. In such an environment of unpredictability and disorder, existing agreements on arms control and disarmament have crumbled and co-operative solutions to security problems have yielded to non-co-operative strategies.

The crumbling arms control architecture

The unravelling of the arms control and disarmament architecture is a mixed story of geopolitical change, technological pressures and the recent deterioration of international relations. The first geopolitical victim was the CFE Treaty between the North Atlantic Treaty Organization (NATO) and the Warsaw Pact; the first victim of technological change was the ABM Treaty. The rationale of that treaty was admirably simple and easy to understand: if you have a shield, it is easier to use the sword. Nationwide ballistic missile defences are destabilising, for they stimulate competitive acquisitions of offensive and defensive capabilities and obstruct the search for arms control and disarmament. However, by the turn of the century, the US ballistic missile defence programme had come to a stage where testing – prohibited by the treaty – was needed and in 2002, President George W. Bush withdrew from it. Other agreements such as the Outer Space Treaty of 1967 and the Seabed Treaty of 1971 were of marginal importance from the beginning and have since been relegated to the archives of history. The Comprehensive Nuclear-Test-Ban Treaty, which was opened for signature in 1996, is still not in force and the negotiation of a fissile-material cut-off agreement never started. The INF Treaty is on its way to the graveyard and the Open Skies Treaty is likely to follow suit.

Had President Joe Biden not agreed to a five-year extension of New START when that Treaty expired in February 2021, we would almost have been back to the first years after World War II when no rules had been agreed for the new nuclear age. What remains are the Non-Proliferation Treaty (NPT) and the Treaty on the

Prohibition of Nuclear Weapons (TPNW, also known as the Ban Treaty). The NPT and the TPNW are mutually reinforcing, however annoyed the NWS are with the latter, which does not recognise them as legitimate nuclear powers.

The NPT has proven its resilience. The bandwagon effect of the so-called Swedish lesson from the 1960s accounts for much of it: regardless of what the NWS are doing, it is not in Sweden's interest to acquire nuclear weapons. However, this treaty also is under stronger pressure than ever before. In its advisory opinion of 1996, the International Court of Justice (ICJ) said that there is an obligation to negotiate and to bring the negotiations to an early conclusion.[8] Since 2010 the NWS have not even negotiated.

The CSBMs negotiated by the Stockholm Conference have unravelled too. These measures built confidence by enhancing transparency and predictability. In the static East–West setting of the time, that was possible. The CSBMs encouraged participants to negotiate disarmament agreements and wind down hostilities. Without them, we might have seen not the end of the Cold War, but an early end of Gorbachev.

In this century, new uncertainties have been created about the redlines of European security affairs. The Russian annexation of Crimea in 2014 and the war in eastern Ukraine made a long-lasting difference. Big power tensions grew at the cost of transparency and predictability, not only in Europe but worldwide. In a turbulent and rapidly changing world, confidence must be promoted in ways other than by Stockholm-type CSBMs.

Political order changes

The concept of "international order" refers to the fundamental rules, principles, and institutions that make up the governing arrangements among states.[9] It can be based on hegemonic coercion, on convergence of state interests or on more or less formalised norms, regimes and institutions.

Throughout modern history, new orders have typically been formed after major wars. After the Peace of Westphalia in 1648, relations between states were for the first time organised on the basis of state sovereignty. In the nineteenth century, after the Napoleonic Wars, the "Concert of Europe" shaped interstate relations on the basis of mutual respect and self-restraint, which kept the peace for many decades. Liberal internationalism can be traced back to the end of World War I and the League of Nations, which underperformed. It was reinvigorated after World War II with the United Nations (UN) and the Bretton Woods institutions – the World Bank, International Monetary Fund and General Agreement on Tariffs and Trade– as primary governing bodies. Over time, many more agreements and organisations were added to it. The liberal world order, with democratic countries at its core, became an increasingly institutionalised order. Distinctly Western from the beginning, the driving force and undisputed leader was the USA.

Global governance

In 1945 the UN Charter defined three basic principles of international relations: state sovereignty, non-interference in internal affairs and territorial integrity. The first two were increasingly challenged by key tenets of liberal internationalism such as global civil society, development aid tied to good governance and by the doctrine of Responsibility to Protect (R2P) adopted at the UN World Summit in 2005. However, the first application of it was in Libya in 2011, where it was misused for the purpose of regime change.

By this time, the liberal challenge to the Charter principles had begun to dissipate. In Asia, in particular, states tend to behave the way the authors of the UN Charter said they should behave back in 1945 – less so in the case of India, more so in China and Russia. US President Donald Trump has tipped the scales in the same direction. For the BRICS states (Brazil, Russia, India, China, South Africa) and others, sovereign states determine their own domestic order while dealing with each other on a market basis. Communal rather than individual traditions are strong. State stewardship of the economy is the dominant ideology. International institutions have no legitimate business other than to serve and facilitate these ends. For BRICS and many other countries, the Charter principles fit their interests hand in glove: non-interference facilitates co-operation with others while the principle of non-intervention can be invoked to keep Western rivals out.

International law

When Russia annexed Crimea, it violated all relevant international law: the UN Charter, the Helsinki Final Act and the Budapest Memorandum of 1994, in which Russia, the United Kingdom and the USA extended security guarantees to Ukraine. Foremost among the critics were states that usually violate international law when they go to war, which they frequently do. It is hard to escape the conclusion that on questions of war and peace, international law is increasingly ignored and used as matter of convenience, even in Europe.

Other examples are equally unnerving. When the ICJ ruled that China's claim to historic rights in the South China Sea was "extinguished" by the UN Convention on the Law of the Sea, which China had ratified, China reacted with contempt. The disputed area covers 90 percent of the South China Sea, an area of the size of Mexico. The Philippines, which had filed the case, won on virtually all points by unanimous decision. In the Chinese narrative, however, control of the South China Sea is an essential part of the restoration of the country to global greatness after the century of humiliation (1839–1949). International law, however unambiguous, was brushed aside.

When the USA withdrew from the nuclear deal with Iran (the Joint Comprehensive Plan of Action, JCPOA) and announced that it would reimpose the highest level of international sanctions, this was a blatant violation of international law. The agreement was negotiated by Iran and the big powers (the USA, the United

Kingdom, France, Russia, China, Germany and the European Union, EU) and unanimously endorsed in UN Security Council Resolution S/RES/2231, so it was binding on all member states. The withdrawal was made without any mention of international law or, for that matter, of the UN.[10]

The USA used to be the champion of liberal internationalism – in principle, that is. In practice, the values underpinning it were often put aside. With Trump having abandoned the principle, the remaining bulwark of liberal internationalism is the EU. The Europeans, too, are bound to make compromises. Hard economic and political interests sometimes take the front seat. However, being based on international rules, norms and standards, the EU is programmatically committed to them in its external affairs. Other countries join in, but there is no denying that in recent years, defence of international law has become a more demanding task.

Multilateralism

To help countries recover from the ruins of World War II, multilateralism grew out of a clear objective: to avoid another devastating war and raise living standards. Progress was measured in reference to wars not fought and lives not lost, and in terms of the wellbeing of people.

Seventy-five years later, multilateralism for the sake of peace does not have the same appeal. The war generations are gone, so first-hand memories are no longer available. Multilateralism for the sake of welfare is questioned as well. Significant population segments have lost faith in it for a variety of reasons, most notably the growing inequalities of income, wealth and opportunity. Globalisation has been a blessing for macroeconomic growth, but the distributional effects have not been addressed. Moreover, new technologies hitting the work force unevenly make people fear for their jobs and in many Western countries, immigration pressures and fear of "the other" have inspired nationalist and autocratic movements. The culture wars that make many feel disrespected nurture scepticism and negative attitudes of multilateralism.

Sparked by the Trump administration, economic protectionism and trade wars are taking a heavy toll on multilateralism. At the centre of it is the power struggle with China, and the essence of that struggle is not about unfair trade conditions and gross US deficits, but about technological leadership. The USA wants to limit technology transfers to China and on this the EU co-operates, for many Chinese practices are detrimental to European economic interests as well. In particular, the USA is taking aim at "Made in China 2025," which is a programme for a comprehensive innovation-driven upgrade of Chinese industry.[11]

Trump withdrew from the Trans-Pacific Partnership, the Paris climate accord and the Iran nuclear deal. He negotiated bilaterally with Mexico and Canada to adjust the North American Free Trade Agreement (NAFTA) and he put the World Trade Organisation (WTO) and other international institutions under pressure. These were low-hanging fruit, however. The economic costs to the USA were modest, remote or hard to calculate, and by picking them he delivered on his

"America First" election promises. Withdrawing from WTO, NATO or the UN would cost much more both economically and politically. None of them is "sacred," however. The EU can be counted on to protect multilateralism as best as it can.

The BRICS summits also promise to be vigilant in guarding against inward-looking policies and to oppose protectionism. Clearly, the EU, China and others have common interests in this regard. However, as long as the Europeans feel heavily dependent on the USA for their own security and economic well-being, the transatlantic bonds are major constraints on common action.

The USA is substituting bilateral deals for multilateral agreements. It is in bilateral settings that big powers can become the most effective and, in relation to much smaller partners, be overwhelming. Conversely, small states usually prefer to handle important matters in multilateral frameworks. In the presence of many others, it is easier to resist undue pressure and forge coalitions against the big states.

Geopolitics: Growing bipolarity in a multipolar setting

In his 2012 book *Strategic Vision*, Zbigniew Brzezinski describes the multipolar world of big powers, noting that small states in their neighbourhoods are "endangered species."[12] Two years later, it seemed prophetic: Russia's renewed claim to spheres of interest was exercised at Ukraine's expense. China is expanding into the South China Sea, disregarding the interests of its smaller neighbours. India's interventions in Bangladesh, Sri Lanka and the Maldives are manifestations of the same phenomenon. Today, Trump is following suit, abandoning the liberal internationalist world order and claiming instead a right to influence that is commensurate with US power. The USA has become more like other big powers, only the most powerful among them.

In the days of the British Empire, London had its eyes fixed on the "second country" – that is, on the one(s) next to it in the international hierarchy of power, which might be able to overtake it. For the USA, the "second country" is China. China is growing faster than its competitors, but will not be on a par with the USA for many years to come. The growth of its comprehensive national strength has slowed down and the rate of growth might continue to decrease, but the gap between China and those next to it in the hierarchy is also growing. The USA and China will make up an increasingly dominant bilateral dimension in the wider multipolar setting.

The contours of a revived Middle Kingdom emerge with heightened clarity, located midway between the mighty American competitor and the world's largest trading bloc on the European side of the landmass. Historically, China stayed in Asia while Western empires took control of other regions by military means. In classical geopolitical parlance, contemporary China is reaching out economically to the World Island[13] – the Eurasian landmass and Africa – by means of the gigantic Belt and Road Initiative. This effort, which is laying the groundwork for comprehensive co-operation, initially aroused enthusiasm along its routes. But conflict as well as co-operation is unavoidable on its heels, in a mix that cannot be foreseen.

The USA and China are facing a classical dilemma, last illustrated by the nuclear competition between the USA and the Soviet Union in the 1970s. The Soviets said they were aiming for no more than parity, but the USA saw a rising curve threatening to overtake its own – and in the beginning of the 1980s a formidable arms race followed. That time, the world escaped Armageddon. Historically, however, power shifts at the top of the pyramid often ended in war. Graham Allison identified 16 such shifts over the latest 500 years and found that 12 of them ended in war.[14] The outcome of the US–Chinese rivalry is not a given and, in the USA, the debate between those who believe it can be managed peacefully and those who believe it will end in war continues. Opponents meet in discussions of hedging, of what is enough and what is excessive – that is, provoking a war that should be avoided.

The worrisome state of the multipolar setting appears very clearly when juxtaposed with the Concert of Europe. Henry Kissinger, an authority on concert diplomacy, described it as a system in which:

> the great powers work together to enforce international norms … Power emerges from a sense of community and it is exercised by an allocation of responsibilities related to a country's resources. It is a kind of world order either without a dominating power or in which the potentially dominating power leads through self-restraint.[15]

Kissinger believed that the Obama administration favoured some kind of concert diplomacy.

Today, there is no common willingness to enforce international norms and no allocation of responsibilities in this respect. Mutual respect and self-restraint are rare commodities. The dominating power strives to maintain its dominance and other powers try to reduce it. The sense of community that characterised concert diplomacy is totally absent. In the big power dyads, conflict of interest is the rule and conflict manifestations flourish. Common interests are at best of a tactical nature.

Sanctions

Imposition and threats of sanctions are a much-favoured US foreign policy instrument. The president's authority to issue sanctions rests on the International Emergency Economic Powers Act (IEEPA) of 1977 and the main implementing body is the Treasury Department's Office of Foreign Assets Control. Since 2000 presidents have used IEEPA in more than 400 executive actions. Not all of them were new; some extended the timetable or expanded the scope of previous orders.[16]

The USA has imposed sanctions on Iran, the Democratic People's Republic of Korea (DPRK, North Korea), Russia, Syria, South Sudan, Venezuela, Cuba and many others. Among the stated reasons are threats of terrorism, proliferation of weapons of mass destruction, human rights violations, narcotics trafficking and money laundering. In some cases, the EU, other Western countries, Japan and others in East Asia have joined in and taken similar action. The selection of targets is guided by realpolitik and has become a foreign policy tool of choice.

Sanctions are a humiliating, top-down form of conflict manifestation and they seldom work as intended. Rather than giving in, states mobilise to stand up to the pressure. The topical cases of the day have proved it beyond doubt. In the case of the DPRK, the world witnessed the same sequence over and over again: North Korea tests, the world condemns, the UN Security Council meets, the USA proposes more sanctions, China negotiates to dilute them, and North Korea continues – until serious negotiations began. Similarly, with the case of Iran: from 2006 to 2013 more sanctions and more enrichment. The lesson is clear: for sanctions to work as intended and lead to conflict resolution, they must be combined with good-faith negotiations and realistic prospects of sanctions relief.

Generally, states that stick to the letter of the UN Charter of 1945 disapprove of unilateral sanctions because they violate core principles such as sovereign equality and non-interference. Only the Security Council has the right and obligation to take such measures to maintain international peace and security. Secondary sanctions are particularly objectionable. Strength decides, however, and the USA is quick to exploit its dominance of the international financial system.

The comprehensive imposition of sanctions, like those against Iran, is a burden on international affairs that poisons the atmosphere for co-operative ventures. However, to what extent this happens automatically or is neatly controlled by national governments is hard to say. In a sense, it is analogous to the debate about spillover in international integration theory, the one being about the spread of conflict and the other about the spread of co-operation.[17]

Hidden warfare: From covert operations to cyber

All powers of some size engage in covert operations, which represent a third category of foreign policy activity between ordinary diplomacy and the use of force. The definition differs among countries, but covert operations are all about efforts to influence the course of events in a foreign country without the identity of the sponsor being known, or else to permit the sponsors plausible denial of operations. The means are economic, political, informational and physical, ranging from provision of funds and advice to the use of paramilitary force. In the USA, which is best known for covert operations, such actions were left to the CIA to execute from the early years of the Cold War. Their scope and scale have been enormous, but their effectiveness has been mixed.[18]

President Dwight D. Eisenhower was attracted by the flexibility and versatility of these instruments. He was used to sending large numbers of soldiers into bloody wars: covert operations could achieve a lot in less brutal ways. As the world became more interconnected and the US global reach increased, the range of such actions increased as well, and new technologies offered new options.

One of the latest additions to the toolbox is cyber warfare. The Stuxnet attack, known by the code name Olympic Games, opened the floodgates. This was the first truly sophisticated state-on-state attack. The USA, in co-operation with Israel, smuggled malware into Iran's uranium enrichment facility in Natanz and affected the software so that hundreds of centrifuges spun out of control and collapsed. President Barack Obama reportedly gave the green light for the operation in order to stop Israel from going to war, which would very likely have drawn in the USA as well. Literally understood, a covert cyber operation substituted for regular warfare on a scale that had never been seen before.

In *The Perfect Weapon*, David Sanger outlines four categories of cyber warfare: espionage, which today means doing much more effectively what opening of letters, tapping of phones and observation by satellites had done in the past; data manipulation, such as tapping banks and rerouting money to one's own accounts; attacks for destructive purposes, such as Stuxnet; and information warfare – that is, disinformation campaigns for whatever purpose.[19]

Two predictions appear plausible. First, these covert actions are likely to grow in scope and intensity since cyber warfare can be conducted by both state and non-state actors and by small as well as large states; since the world is interconnected and modern societies, in particular, are very vulnerable; and as it could be hard to trace attacks back to their sources. Second, the growth of cyber warfare will make the world even more unpredictable and chaotic.

Mirror images: Changes in the world order and the fate of arms control

In the above analysis, six features are particularly noteworthy. First, *sovereign states* are reemphasised and reconfirmed as the basic building blocks of international affairs. Second, *trade and technology wars and economic sanctions* have moved to the top of the international agenda and become major sources and expressions of conflict. Third, *international norms, institutions and agreements, are falling apart.* The glue is wearing thinner and the world is fragmenting. Fourth, international affairs have become more *unpredictable.* Unpredictability has become a part of US strategy. Fifth, in the multipolar geopolitical setting, *the bilateral relationship between the USA and China is increasingly dominant.* The USA perceives China as an adversary and enemy, not as a partner. Sixth, *new technologies nurture new forms of influence and capacity for violence* – disinformation, cyber warfare, military applications of artificial intelligence and hybrid warfare – posing new threats.

These changes in the world order are mirrored in the unravelling of the arms control architecture. The relationship between the USA and China is particularly worrisome. Economic warfare, geopolitical rivalry, technological change and unpredictability coalesce into an atmosphere that militates against co-operative security ventures. The essence of common security – that security is something you have to promote in tandem with your adversary, not pursue unilaterally – is further away from big power politics than ever since the darkest days of the Cold War.

Will liberal internationalism strike back?

Hegelian dialectics says that in all social processes, there are contradictory elements. It is the tension between these elements that create the dynamics of developments. Taken to the extremes that the pendulum might swing, in due course leading to new syntheses.[20]

Some observers caution that another US administration might try to revive liberal internationalism and its own leadership role in it and that the EU – which stays committed to multilateralism, international law and liberal values – will not crumble, but carry the integration project forward and grow stronger. If so, transatlantic bonds and liberal internationalism could be revived.

The US after Trump

The experiences and beliefs that leaders bring to their high offices have a distinct tendency to stick and to shape their working mode, the recruitment of advisers and ultimately the decisions that they make.[21] This is the intellectual capital they will consume as long as they stay in office. One year before Trump's inauguration, Thomas Wright argued that Trump had three distinct beliefs – against trade (that is, free trade), against alliances and in favour of strongmen abroad. In a follow-up article, he argues that during the first two years of Trump's presidency, many of his closest collaborators tried to tone down his most extreme inclinations in order to make administration policies more broadly acceptable, but in the next two years his team was composed of people who tried to elaborate on his ideas and take them forward.[22] The president himself stayed true to his beliefs and promises.

New leaders will bring new ideas. But far from being a one-time exception to the rule of liberal governance, Trump might personify longer-lasting economic, cultural and political trends.

Technological change might be the most inexorable of them. Its speed, its uneven effects on the workforce, the inequalities it produces and the uncertainties it creates threaten key elements of the liberal order. Open economies are among the victims. Brakes on globalisation are deemed necessary to preserve national identities and enhanced border control is called for to protect against terrorism. For some time, nationalism and populism have been on the rise. Much of this is seen both in the USA and in other parts of the world. The liberal order is threatened both from within and without. It strains the imagination, therefore, to believe that the USA will go back to liberal internationalism just because Trump is out of office.

America First is a national platform for pursuit of national advantage – not on the basis of norms and institutions, but bilaterally, selectively and pragmatically as opportunities arise. For big powers to extricate themselves from international obligations in order to be free to use their assets at will is nothing new, but Trump took it further in his own peculiar way.

This is not to say that the USA is reverting to isolationism. More than ever before, national economies are interwoven with each other. Production chains have been internationalised. The privileges the USA enjoys in the international financial system and the foreign policy tools that they offer are precious assets. The unwavering commitment to military superiority and its global military reach leaves the same message: isolationism is not an option.

The European integration project: Under pressure, but resilient

The European Coal and Steel Community – the path-breaking initiative that developed into today's EU – was established in the belief that mutual dependence between old enemies, particularly Germany and France, could prevent future wars between them. From this starting point, an integration project took shape, co-ordinating national policies and ceding state sovereignty to common institutions. When the Cold War was over, the EU expanded to include Central and Eastern European states on the condition that they would settle their bilateral conflicts. Keen to place their civilisational anchor in the West, they largely succeeded in doing so. In retrospect, the EU has been a formidable peace project, for which it was awarded the Nobel Peace Prize in 2011.

Other regions have created institutional arrangements facilitating co-operation between sovereign states, but without aiming at political integration. The EU remains an exception. Growing interdependence has been a trend for decades, but this is no guarantee against armed conflict. In the beginning of the 20th century, trade between European states was comprehensive and growing – right up to World War I. A century later, trade between India and China has been sky-rocketing, but their security problems seem unaffected by it. It is as if there is a firewall between the economic sector and the security field. Much the same applies to the relationship between China and Japan.

In recent years, two classical questions in integration theory have come to the fore. First, is there a point at which the European integration process can stop and stay, or does standstill mean regression? The EU is the strongest and most ardent supporter of liberal values, but the combination of enlargement and anti-liberal winds from Poland, Hungary, Romania and significant minorities in other member states have put the integration project on the defensive. Will they destroy it? Second, will external pressure, notably from the USA, lead to deeper integration to stand up to the challenge, or will the pressure from Trump be so strong that more cracks open up?

The Europeans are increasingly torn between China and the USA. To the east, relations with China are growing more substantial as the Silk Road enters Europe, although closer contact means more conflict as well. To the west, the transatlantic bonds are getting weaker. US and European political cultures have become much different, but economic interdependence remains tight. Trump sees the EU as an economic foe, however, and is disposed to zero-sum thinking, while the EU and China are seeking co-operation for mutual benefit. Arms control discussions between the Europeans and the Chinese have barely started and so have an untested potential.[23]

Implications for arms control

What are the prospects of common security thinking and co-operative security policies in the world described above? What is the role, if any, of confidence building, arms control and disarmament?

The transitional nature of world affairs, where big powers compete for positions and influence in the face of an unpredictable future, leaves little space for such policies. For the time being, co-operative security policies are modest exceptions to the rule of unilateral, competitive arms build-ups. There is one overriding common concern, however: *to avoid nuclear war.* To this end, stability measures are needed, and stability is the number-one objective of arms control. The need for arms control is at least as strong as when it was introduced 60 years ago, but can it be revived?

The superpower rivals of the Cold War adopted a number of measures both bilaterally and domestically to reduce the risk of Armageddon. They were two countries, 5000km apart and they had no territorial conflict with each other. When the Cold War ended and the rivalry stopped, they no longer had any incentive to resort to nuclear weapons. The smaller NWS – the UK, France and China – had no such incentive either. Except for the residual risk of unintentional use, nuclear stability had been achieved.[24]

In today's world of nine nuclear-armed states, this is much different. In many dyads among these countries, stability concerns are not confined to nuclear forces. Conventional forces have assumed a larger role in nuclear calculations. Rather than accept defeat, the weaker state might feel compelled to resort to nuclear arms. Border skirmishes and clashes that do not raise the spectre of regime collapse or territorial disintegration might not lead that far, but even such cases can put the parties' capacity to exercise restraint to a severe test. The Asian triangle – China, India and Pakistan – is particularly complex and delicate in this respect, for these countries are not only bordering on each other, but also have unresolved territorial conflicts.

In a sense, we are back to the logic of the Russell-Einstein Manifesto of 1955,[25] which said that agreements reached in time of peace would no longer be considered binding in time of war. Both sides would set to work to manufacture H-bombs as soon as war broke out. In the starkest of terms, the manifesto therefore presented two alternatives: find a way to abolish war, or the human race will come to an end. Today, abolishing war between the nuclear-armed states is a long shot, but confidence-building measures and arms control can reduce the risk of conventional conflicts breaking out and escalating to nuclear warfare.

Confidence- and security-building measures

Transparency leads to predictability, which in turn inspires confidence. This was the rationale for military confidence-building measures, first introduced at the Helsinki Conference on Security and Cooperation in Europe in 1975 and further developed at the Stockholm Conference a decade later.

When the Cold War was over, Russia adopted a policy of *glasnost* (openness), but the window of opportunity was short-lived. By the middle of the decade it was closing and renewed tensions developed to the detriment of transparency. Still, disarmament agreements provided for comprehensive information exchanges and detailed verification procedures, but these gains are now getting lost as agreements unravel.

The second element of the confidence-building equation – predictability – has been undermined for other reasons as well. Big powers want to be free to apply their superior strength at will and are therefore leery of international constraints. Having abandoned leadership of the liberal world order, Trump was no exception, but took it a step farther. Having declared America first, he has recommended the same precept for others. For Trump, unpredictability is a favoured way of doing business and he applied the same approach to the conduct of foreign affairs. Under this approach, to be predictable is stupid; not to let the others know what to expect is advantageous. Unpredictability can deter others, small states in particular, from taking issue with US policies because it is hard to calculate the consequences.

All of this – the lack of transparency and the appreciation of unpredictability – undermines confidence. The equation is therefore failing in both respects – the predictability element because of the USA and the transparency part because of the Asian powers, Russia included.

In the social sciences, all laws are qualified in some way: x relates to y if (a) and (b) apply. The confidence-building equation rests on the premise that none of the parties harbours any intention to change the territorial status quo by military means. In Europe of the Cold War, that seemed to be the case. Crises were followed by normalisation of relations. The most recent example was the events in Georgia in 2008; a few months afterwards, the USA and Russia pushed the reset button. However, after the Russian territorial encroachment on Ukraine in 2014, suspicions and sanctions have substituted for good-faith co-operation, making Stockholm-type CSBMs unfeasible.

South Asia is well known to be in a similar state because of the territorial conflict in Kashmir. Confidence building has been tried by India and Pakistan, but it has turned out to be a frustrating activity, climbing up the mountain and sliding down again. In East Asia, the situation is similar: the territorial conflicts in the East and South China Seas are major obstacles to confidence-building measures in the region. None of this excludes initiatives to build confidence in other security-related fields: for instance, institutionalised political dialogue can do much to reduce uncertainties and alleviate tensions.

Arms control

In an unpredictable world of suspicions and distrust, states address their perceived security needs by enhancing their own relative strength. Co-operative arms control draws little attention, for such policies depend on a business-like atmosphere in which mutual understandings can be developed in good faith.

States therefore prepare for wars they do not want and that they usually do not wage. Wars are costly and war between the nuclear-armed states must by all means be avoided, so they look for less dramatic substitutes. The world's leading military power – the USA, which is by no means unfamiliar with the use of force – prefers covert action, economic sanctions and cyber warfare to make others accommodate, but keeps the military option "on the table." The role of diplomacy has shrunk dramatically.

The field of cyber-security is completely unregulated. The USA might be the technological front-runner and leading agent of offensive cyber operations, but US society is also among the most vulnerable to attack by others. It is not far-fetched, therefore, to imagine that broad common interests in international regulations could emerge, however complex the issues. Tentative suggestions have been made for some kind of Geneva Convention to regulate the field, as a starter.[26] Enforcement of rules is beyond the horizon, but an international initiative might help recognise the seriousness of the problem and put innovative minds on a constructive co-operative track.

During the Cold War, arms control to reduce the risk of inadvertent escalation became a much-emphasised and sorely needed addendum to nuclear arms racing, for the stakes were the highest: all-out nuclear war. Today, the probability of nuclear-weapon use might be higher than ever before, but recognition of the dangers has slipped. Not only have arms control agreements disappeared, but the lines of communication have also deteriorated. This should be remedied as a matter of priority. Technical arrangements to reduce the risk of an inadvertent slide to war are low-hanging fruit that would serve the common interest.

As the fate of the INF Treaty has amply illustrated, arms control has become more of a global proposition. The structural problems are formidable, however. In terms of military strength, the USA remains the undisputed leader and is determined to maintain that position. To be serious, presidential candidates have to commit to it. In 2018 the US military budget stood at $649 billion and was 2.5 times that of China; China's was more than four times that of Russia, the United Kingdom or France.[27] The US and Russian nuclear arsenals are an order of magnitude larger than China's. Still, Trump aired the idea of a three-way deal with Russia and China, raising some fundamentally important issues of sequencing. The best approach might be the extension of New START; US–Russian reductions of deployed nuclear warheads to three-digit figures with special limits on tactical weapons and missile defence systems and maybe on other assets as well; and, on that basis, an invitation to China to join a subsequent phase of negotiations.[28]

A code of nuclear responsibility

What might a global framework that is realistic enough to gain traction while capturing the aspirations for a world free of nuclear dangers look like?

Starting from the assumption that there is a common interest in avoiding nuclear war, John Gower has introduced the concept of nuclear strategic stability as a metric of international relations. Nuclear strategic stability is high where the risk of any conflict being initiated using nuclear weapons, or of a conventional conflict escalating to the nuclear level, is low. Every posture, capability, or declaratory change should be assessed against this metric with a view to reducing the risk of nuclear weapon use.[29]

Gower identifies six components of nuclear strategic stability that the nuclear-armed states should use to guide their current and future actions, amounting to a code of nuclear responsibility. It starts with restraint in rhetoric, posture, activity and readiness; unambiguous communication pathways at the level of national control authorities; and abstention from using nuclear weapons as levers of statecraft except as strategic deterrents. It ends with a plea for nuclear-armed states to sketch out reduction paths towards less complex, maximally stable strategic systems on the way to zero. The code therefore comprises the whole range of measures from declaratory policy to arms control and disarmament. Confidence-building measures, arms control and disarmament in the conventional field should be built into it as well, with a view to reducing the risk of conventional war between nuclear-armed states and to avoid escalation to the nuclear level should it nevertheless occur. Such measures must be tailored to regional specifics.

The idea rests on the assumption that enhanced stability to reduce the risk of nuclear war can be discussed without linkage to other areas of contention and that the recommended changes can stay clear of ongoing power struggles. If not, the idea would be dead on arrival. The NPT is an appropriate setting for elaboration and discussion of such a code. Article 6 of this treaty clarifies that nuclear disarmament is a shared responsibility of all member states. Action items from previous review conferences could be drawn upon. Proponents of the ban treaty can be expected to join in; measures to reduce the risk of nuclear war have always been high on their list of practical follow-up actions.

Common security thinking and co-operative security policies

The concept of common security was a reaction to the second wave of the Cold War. At the 1986 summit with President Ronald Reagan in Reykjavik, Gorbachev applied common security thinking throughout. The concept did not gain favour in the USA, but the policy-oriented derivative – co-operative security – originated there. Today, however, all the big powers prioritise deterrence and arms build-ups. Co-operative measures have been reduced to a mere footnote in their statements, if at all mentioned – except for China.

In a speech to the Conference on Interaction and Confidence Building Measures in Asia, Chinese President Xi Jinping took exception to the zero-sum thinking of the Cold War and emphasised that nobody should try to dominate at the expense of others.[30] He went farther: security should not be pursued through unilateral action, but should be built on a co-operative basis. He explicitly used the term "common security," very much the way the International Commission on Security and Disarmament Issues had presented it. Declaratory policies seldom tell the full story, however: big power actions might not be in conformity with the public statements of their leaders.

In a major departure from Deng Xiaoping's advice to lie low while concentrating on domestic growth, Xi has emphasised that it is not enough to earn money. Rejuvenation also means that China has to win friends and the preferred means of doing so is co-operative win-win projects. The formidable Belt and Road Initiative is promoted on this basis. China's rise makes the basic tenets of its security thinking and its actual behaviour all the more important to watch.

All members of the NPT are legally obliged to push for nuclear disarmament through negotiations, that is, through co-operative action. Governments and civil society can do much to turn current mind-sets away from unilateralism by using the full potential of modern media to debate, argue and urge a shift to common security thinking. For China and the Europeans, win-win is known ground. For Russia, where geopolitical thinking based on zero-sum assumptions is commonplace, there is a longer way to go. The bottom line is that unless there is a change of security thinking in the USA – the leading military power – nuclear arms control and disarmament has a bleak future.

Notes

1 This article was first published in the *Journal for Peace and Nuclear Disarmament*, 2:1 (2019): 1–18, www.tandfonline.com/doi/full/10.1080/25751654.2019.1631243 and reprinted as a Toda Institute of Peace Policy Brief with permission.
2 International Commission for Security and Disarmament Issues, *Common Security: A Blueprint for Survival* (New York: Simon and Schuster, 1982).
3 Janne Nolan, "The Concept of Cooperative Security," in *Global Engagement, Cooperation and Security in the 21st Century*, edited by Janne Nolan et al. (Washington, DC: Brookings Institution, 1994), 4–5.
4 Ashton B. Carter, William J. Perry and John D. Steinbruner, *A New Concept of Cooperative Security* (Washington, DC: Brookings Institution, 1992).
5 For a comprehensive, in-depth analysis of the concept of cooperative security, see Heinz Vetchera, "Cooperative Security – The Concept and its Application in South Eastern Europe," n.d. www.bundesheer.at/pdf_pool/publikationen/10_wg13_aacs_40.pdf
6 Thomas C. Schelling and Morton H. Halperin, *Strategy and Arms Control* (New York: Twentieth Century Fund, 1961).
7 Crisis stability and arms race stability can be seen as subcategories of the comprehensive concept of strategic stability.
8 International Court of Justice, "Legality of the Threat or Use of Nuclear Weapons," Request for Advisory Opinion of the General Assembly of the United Nations, 8 July 1996.
9 G. John Ikenberry, *After Victory: Institutions, Strategic Restraint, and the Rebuilding of Order after Major Wars* (Princeton, NJ: Princeton University Press, 2001).
10 The USA also left important international agreements under George W. Bush. Unilateralism and exceptionalism were in high gear. However, if the agreements had a withdrawal clause, the administration withdrew the way the clause prescribed. Trump's unilateralism and exceptionalism represent a more naked exercise of power.
11 Its guiding principles are to make manufacturing innovation driven, emphasise quality over quantity, achieve green development, optimise the structure of Chinese industry, and nurture human talent. Scott Kennedy, "Made in China 2025," Center for Strategic and International Studies, Washington DC, 1 June 2018, www.csis.org/analysis/made-china-2025
12 Zbigniew Brzezinski, *Strategic Vision: America and the Crisis of Global Power* (New York: Basic Books, 2012).

13 Halford John Mackinder, *Democratic Ideals and Reality* (New York: W.W. Norton, [1919] 1962). Mackinder's basic reasoning was as follows: Who rules Eastern Europe rules the Heartland (the Eurasian landmass); who rules the Heartland commands the World-Island; who commands the World-Island commands the World.
14 Graham Allison, *Destined for War: Can America and China Escape Thucydides's Trap?* (New York: Houghton Mifflin Harcourt, 2017),
15 Henry Kissinger, "Obama's Foreign Policy Challenge," *The Washington Post*, 22 April 2009, www.henryakissinger.com/articles/obamas-foreign-policy-challenge.
16 Aaron Arnold, "Where Does Trump Get the Power to Reimpose Sanctions?" *Bulletin of the Atomic Scientists*, 15 August 2018, https://thebulletin.org/2018/08/where-does-trump-get-the-power-to-reimpose-sanctions.
17 Neofunctionalism holds that integration within one sector will tend to generate its own impetus and spread to other sectors, while intergovernmentalism argues that national governments control the level and speed of integration.
18 Examples from the first postwar decades are efforts to influence the outcome of elections in Western Europe during the early Cold War years, the 1953 overthrow of Mohammad Mossadegh in Iran, the 1954 overthrow of Jacobo Árbenz in Guatemala, the 1963 attempt to kill Fidel Castro in Cuba, the 1963 overthrow of Juan Bosch in the Dominican Republic, the 1965 propaganda campaign to overthrow the Sukarno government in Indonesia and the 1967 provision of aid to install Colonel Georgios Papadopoulos in Greece by means of a military coup.
19 David Sanger, *The Perfect Weapon: War, Sabotage and Fear in the Cyber Age* (New York: Random House, 2018).
20 On Hegelian dialectics, see *Stanford Encyclopedia of Philosophy*, https://plato.stanford.edu/entries/hegel-dialectics.
21 Elizabeth N Saunders, "Is Trump a Normal Foreign-Policy President?" *Foreign Affairs*, 18 January 2018, www.foreignaffairs.com/articles/united-states/2018-01-18/trump-normal-foreign-policy-president.
22 Thomas Wright, "Trump's Foreign Policy is No Longer Unpredictable," *Foreign Affairs*, 18 January 2019, www.foreignaffairs.com/articles/world/2019-01-18/trumps-foreign-policy-no-longer-unpredictable.
23 Sputnik,"German Foreign Minister: Berlin to Press China on 'Space, Robotic Weapons' Rules," *Sputnik*, 7 November 2018. https://sputniknews.com/world/201811071069577639-heiko-maas-china-arms control.
24 Dmitri Trenin, "Strategic Stability in the Changing World." Moscow: Carnegie Moscow Center, 21 March 2019, https://carnegie.ru/2019/03/21/strategic-stability-in-changing-world-pub-78650.
25 Russell-Einstein Manifesto, issued in London on 9 July 1955, http://umich.edu/~pugwash/Manifesto.ht ml.
26 David Sanger, *The Perfect Weapon: War, Sabotage and Fear in the Cyber Age* (New York: Random House, 2018).
27 SIPRI, "Military Expenditure Database." Stockholm: Stockholm International Peace Research Institute, April 2019.
28 Richard Burt and John Wolfsthal, "How Trump Can Transform Nuclear Arms Control," *The National Interest*, 10 May 2019, https://nationalinterest.org/feature/how-trump-can-transform-nuclear-arms-control-56892.
29 John Gower, "Framing 21st Century Arms Control: Nuclear Strategic Stability& an Arms Control Pathway." Draft Working Paper for the Toda/NUPI conference on Exploring New Approaches to Arms Control in the 21st Century, Oslo, 21 October 2018.
30 Xi Jinping, "New Asian Security Concept for New Progress in Security Cooperation," in Remarks to the Fourth Summit of the Conference on Interaction and Confidence-Building Measures, 21 May 2014, www.fmprc.gov.cn/mfa_eng/zxxx_662805/t1159951.shtml.

THE NPT AND THE BAN TREATY

Non-proliferation, prohibition, disarmament

Ramesh Thakur

Biological, chemical and nuclear weapons are collectively referred to as weapons of mass destruction (WMD). The first two were outlawed by international conventions in the last century. The Biological Weapons Convention, adopted in 1972 and in force since 1975, prohibits the development, production, acquisition, transfer, stockpiling and use of biological and toxin weapons. It has 183 states parties and four signatory states. The Chemical Weapons Convention (CWC), adopted in 1993 and in force since 1997, has 193 states parties covering 98 percent of the world's population. In addition to banning chemical weapons, its goal is to eliminate them by prohibiting the development, production, acquisition, stockpiling, retention, transfer or use of chemical weapons. To this end, unlike its biological counterpart, the CWC has an implementing organisation called the Organisation for the Prohibition of Chemical Weapons (OPCW).[1] With a budget of €71 million (2020), the OPCW has overseen the destruction of 98.6 percent of global stockpiles of declared chemical agents, 74 of the 97 declared chemical weapons production facilities and conversion of the remaining 23 into peaceful purposes, and oversees a network of designated laboratories for ongoing verification purposes.[2] As this indicates and as confirmed by periodic reports of the use of chemical weapons in Syria over the last decade, the agenda of the complete elimination of the banned category of weapons is almost but not fully complete.

From January 2021 the one remaining category of WMD has two international treaties in existence as the legal frameworks for global stewardship. The Nuclear Non-Proliferation Treaty (NPT) was adopted in 1968 and entered into force in 1970. Mostly successful as a non-proliferation regime, it has proven to be stillborn as a nuclear disarmament treaty. To fill the legal gap and exert normative pressure towards elimination, 122 NPT states parties adopted a new United Nations (UN) instrument in July 2017 called the Treaty on the Prohibition of Nuclear Weapons (TPNW, simplified in common parlance to the Ban Treaty). As at June 2021, it

DOI: 10.4324/9781003227502-37

had 54 states parties and another 34 signatory states. The Ban Treaty is the subject of this book. All the chapters in the book were written after the treaty's adoption and some were written on the eve of or immediately following its entry into force.

Major themes

There are some key themes that run through the several chapters. The first is an acknowledgment of the historical and continuing importance of the NPT. Not one of the authors questions that the NPT has been a critical pillar of the international security architecture for half a century and that there would be seriously damaging consequences were it to collapse. However, doubts are increasing about whether the NPT might have reached the limits of its potential for advancing the cause of nuclear disarmament. This explains why despite its proven resilience, the NPT is facing unprecedented pressure, notes Sverre Lodgaard. If the possessor and umbrella states are not prepared to give up nuclear weapons, Tom Sauer asks, what have the non-nuclear weapon states got to lose by withdrawing from the NPT? Perhaps more pressingly, is the threat of withdrawal their one remaining effective leverage on the policies of the nuclear-armed states?

A second recurrent theme is that regardless of what one thinks of the NPT's historical record in underpinning strategic stability, in recent years nuclear risks have grown with heightened geopolitical tensions, additional roles for nuclear weapons, blurred boundaries between nuclear and precision conventional munitions, and expanding frontiers in space, cyber and artificial intelligence (AI) technologies. Moreover, the transformation of the Cold War-era nuclear dyad into interlinked nuclear chains, some of them in geographical theatres of contiguous nuclear-armed rivals, diminishes the relevance of the traditional approaches to managing strategic stability among nuclear-armed states, not to mention the added risks from non-state actors. As Lodgaard puts it: "The NPT is in miserable shape, betrayed on the disarmament dimension, stuck in the Middle East and mostly irrelevant to the Asian nuclear-armed states."

To this list, as Tanya Ogilvie-White reminds us with reference to the four erratic and volatile years of the Donald Trump presidency, must be added: "the unexpected does happen; political leaders do behave irrationally; and the reckless actions of unhinged leaders can and do go unchecked, including in democracies once held up as beacons to the world." Few will dispute today that the liberal international order is under threat from within and without. This gives us another reason to shed nuclear complacency and instead take concrete steps to act on "our shared responsibility to maintain strategic stability." As Ogilvie-White concludes, "if even the US leadership can't be relied upon to prevent a descent into chaos, surely it adds weight to the argument that the risks from the continued existence of nuclear weapons are just too great for us not to ban and eliminate them."

A third dominant theme in chapters supportive of the Ban Treaty is that an important motivation for it was the stubborn refusal of the five NPT nuclear weapon states (NWS) to act on their Article 6 commitment to nuclear disarmament. This background reality is indispensable for understanding the mounting frustrations among the NPT non-NWS that gradually turned into anger and a determination to seize control of the nuclear disarmament agenda. As Alexander Kmentt puts it: "It is the double-standard in the NPT and the lacklustre implementation of its Article 6 that weakens it, not the TPNW with its new normative standard to redress exactly those weaknesses and strengthen the NPT."

The fourth and related theme is the crucial importance of reframing the debate from disarmament as a security issue into a pressing humanitarian concern. The old paradigm had proven unable to break through what Kmentt calls "the wall of the nuclear deterrence dogma." This further facilitated "a democratic shift" in the nuclear debate with non-NWS using the UN General Assembly, the central democratic body of the UN system, as the site and forum of TPNW negotiations and adoption. Matching the universality of the General Assembly, the no exceptions prohibition is a "manifestation of the demand for a more egalitarian approach to nuclear weapons," Kmentt says. Sauer and Thakur note further that the 2020 coronavirus pandemic was a striking if unexpected validation of the core premises of the Humanitarian Initiative behind the Ban Treaty. They then note that, as the new normative benchmark, the world's intensive care units' bed capacity is grossly inadequate to cope with the humanitarian disaster that would be unleashed with a nuclear war. Because no after-the-fact response to a nuclear bomb explosion would work, they conclude, prevention in the form of the Ban Treaty vaccine must be universally administered.

The reframing of a traditional security debate into a humanitarian discourse had an important precedent in the Ottawa Treaty that banned anti-personnel landmines. In an article published towards the end of the last century, William Maley and Ramesh Thakur argued that the treaty was better understood as an international humanitarian treaty than as an arms control treaty.[3] An equally important feature of the Ottawa Treaty, replicated in the Responsibility to Protect principle in 2001, was the role of a state champion in the carriage of state–civil society partnership to successful conclusion at an international conference or summit. For civil society representatives might be permitted a voice in some intergovernmental processes but lack a vote. Thus the International Campaign to Abolish Nuclear Weapons (ICAN) was to the TPNW what the International Campaign to Ban Landmines was to the Ottawa Treaty in forging a global coalition of civil society groups and like-minded states – and both received deserved global recognition by being awarded the Nobel Peace Prize. It's hardly surprising that ICAN's Gem Romuld should underscore the positive obligations of the TPNW to compensate the victim and remediate the environmental damages of nuclear testing. However, Lodgaard reminds us that for North Atlantic Treaty Organization (NATO) allies, the security narrative in fact can be shown to converge with the humanitarian approach, not the least because of the credibility paradox at the heart of the alliance.

A fifth theme is the impact of the Ban Treaty on those non-NWS countries that have relied on what Kmentt calls the "nuclear deterrence-based security architecture" of the alliance leader's nuclear weapons. As Jorge Hersschens informs us, the position of Belgium is pivotal, because Brussels is the seat of NATO and the European Union and also because Belgium is one of the few non-NWS to host the nuclear weapons of allies on its territory. The last consideration is reinforced by Moritz Kütt, Jan Hoekama and Tom Sauer in their chapter on Belgium, Germany and the Netherlands. They also draw attention to a report from the German Parliament concluding there is no legal incompatibility between the Ban Treaty and the NPT. The NPT had camouflaged the underlying hypocrisy of many states in pretending to support nuclear disarmament – just not yet, like St Augustine's plea on chastity – while hosting nuclear weapons, relying on nuclear deterrence for national security and sheltering under the nuclear umbrella of allies. While the NPT had enabled them to fudge the tensions between membership of a nuclear alliance and commitment to nuclear disarmament, the TPNW has compelled them to confront the hypocrisy head on. This might well explain the ferocity of their objections to it: it shows the mirror of their disingenuousness to their own peoples and they do not like it.

Sauer notes that the NWS and their umbrella allies have in effect formed a mutual support group whereby possession of the bomb is justified by pointing to the demands for nuclear deterrence-based security from the allies. The Ban Treaty forces the issue: do the nuclear-dependent states intend to continue to shelter under the nuclear umbrella or start behaving like non-NWS? In other words the treaty has the potential to embarrass umbrella states by reopening fundamental domestic debates on the role of nuclear weapons and deterrence strategies. At the same time, as is the case with the nuclear-armed states, instead of sermonising or pointing fingers, Ban Treaty advocates will have to engage with the nuclear-dependent states to assuage their security concerns. Paul Meyer expresses this succinctly: "To fold the metaphorical 'nuclear umbrella' it will be necessary to convince those sheltering under it that it is safe to come out and to recognise that the umbrella might be more of a danger than a protection" – a nuclear lightning rod more than a repellent? His compatriot Douglas Roche detects a subtle softening of Canada's previously strident opposition to the Ban Treaty in a letter to him from the foreign ministry on 26 October 2020.

A sixth recurring theme is the legal implications of the Ban Treaty for non-parties. Several authors assert that the comprehensive prohibitions of the Ban Treaty are now part of international law. But what exactly does this mean? In particular, does it mean that the possession of nuclear weapons by nine nuclear-armed states suddenly became illegal on 22 January 2021? Given the identity of the nine, the fact that five of them are the five permanent members of the UN Security Council (P5), and the repeated opposition to the treaty by them and their substantial number of allies before and during the conference to negotiate the treaty followed by reiterating their opposition and objections after it was adopted, it seems highly unlikely that the legal obligations of the treaty apply to the non-signatories. Equally, however, since it is a UN-negotiated treaty following a UN-authorised process and conference, the claim that it has no implications for the legality and legitimacy of nuclear weapons possession and practices also seems implausible. Joelien Pretorius holds that non-signatory possessor states are placing themselves "outside the law" and the balance of incentives and disincentives for individuals and companies, as well as states, has been recalibrated by the TPNW's entry into force. Punitive consequences could follow in due course, she says, if patterns of practice and expectation evolve to give the prohibition the status of customary international law. Thakur also points to another unwelcome danger from the successful delegitimisation of the P5 as possessor states. What, he asks, does this mean for their enforcement role as custodians of the global nuclear order and peace?

American, British and French opposition to the Ban Treaty, backed by Western allies in Europe and the Indo-Pacific, are familiar to most of us who follow this debate in the English language. Vladimir Baranovsky presents an analysis of the lesser known Russian calculus of decision-making behind Moscow's objections in four clusters: on principle, in particular the importance of due regard to the undiminished security of all states; as a challenge to Russia's self-identity as an international actor and ensuing role in world affairs, including credibility as a UN Security Council permanent member as a nuclear-armed state despite its "numerous and significant" weaknesses; the prevailing trends in nuclear weapons thinking and planning in the possessor states that highlight the centrality of nuclear weapons in national security doctrines; and objections to numerous concrete setbacks for the project, including the US habit of unilateral terminations of existing nuclear arms control treaties in light of which the lack of verification and compliance mechanisms in the TPNW reduces it to "an explanatory note" more than "an international treaty on arms control." One of his more interesting observations is how the Cold War logic has been reversed: now it is Russia that justifies nuclear weapons as compensation for weakness vis-à-vis NATO in conventional armaments. But he does note that Russia could yet choose to support the TPNW and abide by some of its provisions without signing it, avoid criticising it and promote constructive engagement between treaty parties and non-signatories.

The last would be welcomed by most TPNW supporters. Kmentt, Angela Kane and Tariq Rauf in particular address most of the criticisms levelled at the TPNW for undermining the NPT and its own flaws. For example, on safeguards the TPNW is said to weaken the existing standards. This is curious, say Kane and Rauf. Each TPNW state party is required to maintain its existing safeguards arrangements "at a minimum" and may adopt "additional relevant instruments" in the future. Similarly, Rauf wonders why the various regional nuclear-weapon-free zones have been hailed as complementary to the NPT but the Ban Treaty is suddenly a competitor and a threat. Regardless, the detailed discussion of safeguards by John Carlson and Thomas Shea alert us to the immense technical, political, organisational and procedural challenges and complexities involved in constructing a verification system to monitor compliance with TPNW obligations by states parties.

Kmentt also responds to the charge that advocates of the Ban Treaty acted recklessly and irresponsibly to undermine the NPT, damage its integrity and put its very survivability at risk. On the contrary, he says, the non-NWS NPT states parties were discharging their individual and collective responsibility to pursue nuclear disarmament under Article 6 of the NPT. Thakur develops this argument by referencing the reconceptualisation of sovereignty as responsibility in 2001/2005 by the International Commission on Intervention and State Sovereignty and the UN world summit. And Cesar Jaramillo reminds us that it is in implementation of this shared responsibility that Latin American states have demonstrated the most enthusiastic, regionally universal and earliest series of measures to ban and forestall nuclear armament in their region and now internationally. Noting that the Latin American nuclear-weapon-free zone predates the NPT, he highlights the region's contributions to the process as well as the outcome of the TPNW.

Harmonisation and reconciliation between the "NPT only" and "NPT plus TPNW" groups

The hostility between the Ban Treaty states parties and advocates, on the one hand, and the nuclear-armed states and allies on the other, which reject the Ban Treaty as a threat to the integrity and health of the NPT-centric regime, is entirely one-sided. Many of the authors note that the TPNW critics are often the ones using intemperate language against treaty parties. Their approach to finding common ground resembles the negotiating tactic of "What's mine is mine, what's your is open to discussion." They run the very real risk of converting relentless criticisms into a self-implementing analysis. The logic of their analysis is hard to fathom. Why exactly, asks Kane as a former UN Under-Secretary-General for Disarmament, will nuclear disarmament be made more difficult by the treaty's effort to delegitimise the bomb and reduce dependence on it in national security policies? The reason it does not outline concrete pathways to disarmament is precisely the simple reality that only possessor states can take such steps and they chose to boycott the negotiations.

By contrast, another theme addressed in several chapters by strong supporters and TPNW-friendly-in-principle authors is the need for and possible pathways to harmonising the two complementary-cum-competitive treaties. Thus Meyer says that the possessor states could more usefully begin to act on the commitments of successive NPT review conferences to nuclear disarmament and risk reduction measures. Rakesh Sood too posits that nuclear risk reduction measures might make it possible to finesse the NPT-TPNW divide. Similarly, Manpreet Sethi argues for a nuclear restraint regime encompassing many dimensions of nuclear weapons: types and numbers, role, targets, force postures and so on. Each individual restraint, she suggests, would add another layer of protection and as "the circle of their utility becomes smaller," eventual elimination of nuclear weapons will become feasible. With Russia and the USA locked in a spiral of escalation in rhetoric, upgrades and deployments, she hopes that China and India perhaps could formalise their no-first-use postures and lead the way.

Kane in particular draws on her insight, that the Ban Treaty has converted a long-standing *aspiration* into a *legal framework*, to suggest some very practical steps as the way forward. She asks the nuclear-armed states to clarify the floor of nuclear weapon numbers for credible nuclear deterrence, the level of stability as the prerequisite to begin disarmament negotiations and to issue negative security assurances. On the other side, she asks TPNW supporters to reflect on why the stigma that attaches to chemical and biological weapons has not applied to nuclear weapons, to address the security concerns not just of individual countries, but also of NATO as an alliance that relies on nuclear deterrence, and to propose a monitoring and inspection system for a post-nuclear world in which all states can have confidence. Finally, she asks us all to identify "bridge-builders" who could help both sides arrive at a discussion that is free of hostility and emotion.

Few would disagree with Lodgaard's caution that "There is a long way from mutual recriminations to passive co-existence to bridge-building to exploitation of synergies." But several of the contributors add the further consideration that engagement with the TPNW parties and process, starting with attending the inaugural meeting of states parties as observers, would enable the Ban Treaty sceptics to influence its future evolution while also assuaging their own domestic public worries. Thus Kane concludes that possessor states should accept the Ban Treaty as the new reality and focus on the way forward through dialogue and co-operation with the non-NWS.

Gaps in the book

This book was not conceived as a comprehensive handbook on the nuclear Ban Treaty. Rather, it was designed to offer a range of commentary in anticipation of and to mark the entry into force of the treaty in January 2021, three-and-a-half years after its adoption. Moreover, in order to retain the flavour of freshness, we decided to republish the articles more or less as is, just occasionally changing the tense of events that had been foreshadowed, such as entry into force. This is why also we did not go back to the authors to ask them to revise and update, as that would have delayed the project by several months and lost the vital freshness. As a result there are some obvious but major gaps in the scope of the book and it is our hope that others will rise to the task to fill these gaps.

To start with, for a handbook that aimed to be comprehensive, it would be necessary to have a chapter on every one of the nine nuclear-armed states, discussing the strength of their opposition, reasons for their hesitancy and the circumstances in which, and the manner in which, they might consider joining the treaty. Similarly, given Japan's unique position as the only victim of atomic bombing, a powerful and emotionally resonant advocate for nuclear disarmament, but a US ally huddled for security under the American nuclear umbrella, a chapter on Japan's competing pulls and pressures would have been interesting and important.[4] So would a chapter analysing the role of ICAN, even though two of the authors are from ICAN – Romuld and Tilman Ruff – and several others mention its critical role. Fortunately, thanks to the well-deserved award of the Nobel Peace Prize, no one who follows this issue is unaware of ICAN's crucial role in the state–

civil society partnership that resulted in the adoption of the treaty. Two other significant gaps in coverage that deserve rectification are feminist perspectives and indigenous peoples' perspectives, both of which are important new features of the TPNW. For the same reason, finally, a thorough consideration, not just passing reference, needs to be paid to the treaty's positive obligations on victim assistance and environmental remediation.

Next steps

In a broad historical sweep of the world since 1945, first David Holloway and then Kane and Noah Mayhew recapitulate some salient points about the relationship between transformations in world affairs, the global order (defined by Lodgaard as "the fundamental rules, principles, and institutions that make up the governing arrangements among states") and nuclear orders. Lodgaard complements their analysis firstly by going still farther back in history to the Peace of Westphalia (1648) and secondly by embedding the nuclear arms control discussion in the conceptual vocabulary of common and co-operative security. The rules-based order that emerged after the Second World War was largely the creation of US leadership and its contours were shaped by the bipolar Cold War. Scanning the trans-Atlantic horizon, leaders drawn from the world war generation are long gone and internalised memories of the horrors of war no longer inform policymakers' decisions. We currently seem to be on a historical pivot without fully comprehending the world into which we are transitioning, other than that bipolarity has given way to a multipolar or polycentric order.

In the Cold War nuclear dyad, strategic stability between the two leading antagonists was enhanced by a series of arms control agreements that, driven by the realisation that the alternative was unimaginable, sought to lessen the risks of the nuclear rivalry by providing predictability and reassurance. This was done through limits and then reductions in numbers of weapons and delivery platforms backed by verification protocols. As the cornerstone of the global nuclear order, the bilateral accords supplemented the NPT in managing both the military and civil engagement with nuclear technology. In the still inchoate emerging world order, the pillars of the old nuclear order are crumbling, there is recognition that arms control structures must be updated to the current geopolitical realities and rapidly developing technologies, but possible replacements are unclear. The dwindling trust in the US–Russia–China strategic triangle – Kane and Mayhew even add new technologies as a fourth player – and the reluctance of all three power contestants to accept losses as part of the shifting global order does not augur well for the new order. Kane and Mayhew also remind us that too much of the arms control discourse remains US- and Atlantic-centric, still seemingly stuck in the last century. Only shared understandings of the catastrophic consequences of any use of nuclear weapons, the risks of the full array of crises that could quickly escalate through the nuclear threshold and the synergy between offensive and defensive nuclear weapons and systems can provide order, stability, predictability and reassurance regarding the future of nuclear peace.

The divisions, between the NPT NWS and their allies on the one side, and the TPNW states parties and advocates on the other, suggest that we are still some distance from such common understandings. Hence Joseph Camilleri's caution that the "long night's journey into day" "has only just begun." Most authors have alluded to four factors behind the push for the adoption of a new and comprehensive prohibition treaty. As the movement gathered force, it gained enhanced legitimacy by being repackaged as the Humanitarian Initiative. First, anxieties were heightened about the risk of nuclear weapon use, whether by design or accident, and the catastrophic consequences of any such use. Part of this was growing recognition that the strategic assumptions, bilateral agreements and understandings, force postures, weapons deployments and institutionalised practices that underpinned the strategic stability of the Cold War dyad cannot easily be transposed to the Indo-Pacific nuclear chains. A second factor was the growing normalisation of nuclear weapons possession and threats of use in the heated rhetorical exchange between the USA and the Democratic People's Republic of Korea (North Korea), NATO and Russia, and India and Pakistan. But within the overall nuclear context, Herbert Wulf reminds us, there is also a militarisation of aspects of European international civilian assistance. Lodgaard ruminates about the continuing willingness and ability of the Europeans to protect the principles and institutions underpinning the global multilateral order. A third was the failure by the five NPT-recognised NWS to implement their nuclear disarmament obligation under Article 6 of the treaty. And a fourth was the crumbling normative architecture of nuclear arms control as existing agreements were weaponised as part of intensifying geopolitical rivalries instead of being quarantined from wider tensions and used to lessen them. Similarly, Lodgaard notes, trade and technology wars and economic and financial sanctions too have become sources of tension as well as instruments of conflict.

Arms control simultaneously contributes to and benefits from a stable multilateral order. The future policy agenda is how to move from prohibition to elimination and recreate a new normative architecture that addresses all the dimensions of nuclear weapons policy far more comprehensively and universally than the NPT ever did. To start with, Ruff notes, it is crucial to recognise and to restate at every opportunity that now it is not the NPT, but the TPNW as the one and only "internationally agreed and treaty-codified framework for the elimination" of the bomb, that will function as the international standard for judging action and inaction in relation to nuclear weapons. The TPNW, he says eloquently, "is the best tool we now have against our worst weapons" and it is incumbent on us "to use it well."

Kmentt and Thakur directed their comments to the responsibility of the non-NWS states parties of the NPT to act in relation to Article 6 of the NPT. Building on their arguments on the relationship between state sovereignty and the TPNW, Hugh Miall notes the suggestion that the nuclear-armed states could themselves adopt a Code of Nuclear Responsibility, an idea taken up also by Lodgaard in the last chapter. George Perkovich offers an interesting idea in a related vein. He says that while attention has focussed on the disarmament and prohibition clauses of the TPNW, there is also an element of accountability by nuclear-armed states which hitherto has been neglected. Specifically, are the possessor states prepared to give undertakings in advance to accept responsibility for – and to redress – the damage resulting from any use of nuclear weapons? Posing this question would certainly help to move the conversation away from the sterile and stalemated debate in which the TPNW and NWS are presently mired. Kane and Mayhew too say that the nuclear-armed states must "address the consequences of – and responsibility for – a nuclear detonation and its inevitable catastrophic result on humans and the environment."

In part the stalemate reflects the changed global strategic landscape from the halcyon days of the nuclear arms control architecture that served as the governance framework during the Cold War. As Miall points out, the world has transitioned to a multipolar nuclear order and technological developments, such as conventional munitions of greater precision and nuclear explosive yield-equivalent lethality, cyber-warfare capabilities and AI advances have blurred the old distinctions between conventional and nuclear weapons. Numerical limits on warheads and missiles in categories defined by range and purpose are no longer all that helpful. Instead fresh approaches are needed to eliminate nuclear-armed cruise missiles, reduce stocks of strategic nuclear weapons and adopt nuclear risk-reduction and confidence-building measures in a multilateralised and universal arms control framework expanded to accommodate additional actors and more types of weapons and systems. China especially must be brought into nuclear arms control discussions as, even though its numbers are comparable to the nuclear-armed states other than Russia and the USA, unlike the other six China is a systemically significant actor in world affairs and, alongside US primacy, the second reality is the growing capability gap between China and the others.

One of the most critical requirements for getting to a nuclear-weapon-free world will be a credible and effective verification system with requirements for inspection and monitoring. All states must have confidence that any cheating on disarmament obligations and attempts to break out will be detected in time and compliance is enforceable. Shea and Carlson outline various ideas to build such a verification system, including definitions of key terms and common understandings and agreements on modalities, capabilities and procedures that will together make up "a web of confidence." In creating this complex but vital machinery, the states can draw on the considerable body of experience that already exists in the International Atomic Energy Agency system, bilateral and multilateral arrangements and collaboration, and national technical intelligence capabilities. Carlson also offers a helpful if indicative list of possible steps to take in a graduated move from minimisation to complete elimination of nuclear weapons.

And so we end with a challenge that is common to both the NPT and the Ban Treaty: How do we recreate a global normative framework for responsible nuclear conduct that is at once sufficiently steeped in realism to gain purchase with the nine nuclear-armed states and their allies, yet so infused with vision as to capture the aspiration of a world free of the existence and threat of nuclear weapons?

Notes

1 See Ramesh Thakur and Ere Haru, eds, *The Chemical Weapons Convention: Implementation, Challenges and Opportunities* (Tokyo: United Nations University Press, 2006).
2 OPCW, "OPCW by the Numbers," www.opcw.org/media-centre/opcw-numbers.
3 Ramesh Thakur and William Maley, "The Ottawa Convention on Landmines: A Landmark Humanitarian Treaty in Arms Control?" *Global Governance*, 5:3: (1999): 273–302.
4 See: Yasuyoshi Komizo, "Japan and the Nuclear Ban Treaty," Toda *Policy Brief*, 110 (June 2021), https://toda.org/policy-briefs-and-resources/policy-briefs/japan-and-the-nuclear-ban-treaty.html; and Ramesh Thakur, "Japan and the Nuclear Weapons Prohibition Treaty: The Wrong side of History, Geography, Legality, Morality and Humanity," *Journal for Peace and Nuclear Disarmament*, 1:1 (2018): 11–31.

Annex

Treaty on the Prohibition of Nuclear Weapons

The States Parties to this Treaty,

Determined to contribute to the realization of the purposes and principles of the Charter of the United Nations,

Deeply concerned about the catastrophic humanitarian consequences that would result from any use of nuclear weapons, and recognizing the consequent need to completely eliminate such weapons, which remains the only way to guarantee that nuclear weapons are never used again under any circumstances,

Mindful of the risks posed by the continued existence of nuclear weapons, including from any nuclear-weapon detonation by accident, miscalculation or design, and emphasizing that these risks concern the security of all humanity, and that all States share the responsibility to prevent any use of nuclear weapons,

Cognizant that the catastrophic consequences of nuclear weapons cannot be adequately addressed, transcend national borders, pose grave implications for human survival, the environment, socioeconomic development, the global economy, food security and the health of current and future generations, and have a disproportionate impact on women and girls, including as a result of ionizing radiation,

Acknowledging the ethical imperatives for nuclear disarmament and the urgency of achieving and maintaining a nuclear-weapon-free world, which is a global public good of the highest order, serving both national and collective security interests,

Mindful of the unacceptable suffering of and harm caused to the victims of the use of nuclear weapons (*hibakusha*), as well as of those affected by the testing of nuclear weapons,

Recognizing the disproportionate impact of nuclear-weapon activities on indigenous peoples,

Reaffirming the need for all States at all times to comply with applicable international law, including international humanitarian law and international human rights law,

Basing themselves on the principles and rules of international humanitarian law, in particular the principle that the right of parties to an armed conflict to choose methods or means of warfare is not unlimited, the rule of distinction, the prohibition against indiscriminate attacks, the rules on proportionality and precautions in attack, the prohibition on the use of weapons of a nature to cause superfluous injury or unnecessary suffering, and the rules for the protection of the natural environment,

Considering that any use of nuclear weapons would be contrary to the rules of international law applicable in armed conflict, in particular the principles and rules of international humanitarian law,

Reaffirming that any use of nuclear weapons would also be abhorrent to the principles of humanity and the dictates of public conscience,

Recalling that, in accordance with the Charter of the United Nations, States must refrain in their international relations from the threat or use of force against the territorial integrity or political independence of any State, or in any other manner inconsistent with the Purposes of the United Nations, and that the establishment and maintenance of international peace and security are to be promoted with the least diversion for armaments of the world's human and economic resources,

Recalling also the first resolution of the General Assembly of the United Nations, adopted on 24 January 1946, and subsequent resolutions which call for the elimination of nuclear weapons,

Concerned by the slow pace of nuclear disarmament, the continued reliance on nuclear weapons in military and security concepts, doctrines and policies, and the waste of economic and human resources on programmes for the production, maintenance and modernization of nuclear weapons,

Recognizing that a legally binding prohibition of nuclear weapons constitutes an important contribution towards the achievement and maintenance of a world free of nuclear weapons, including the irreversible, verifiable and transparent elimination of nuclear weapons, and determined to act towards that end,

Determined to act with a view to achieving effective progress towards general and complete disarmament under strict and effective international control,

Reaffirming that there exists an obligation to pursue in good faith and bring to a conclusion negotiations leading to nuclear disarmament in all its aspects under strict and effective international control,

Reaffirming also that the full and effective implementation of the Treaty on the Non-Proliferation of Nuclear Weapons, which serves as the cornerstone of the nuclear disarmament and non-proliferation regime, has a vital role to play in promoting international peace and security,

Recognizing the vital importance of the Comprehensive Nuclear-Test-Ban Treaty and its verification regime as a core element of the nuclear disarmament and non-proliferation regime,

Reaffirming the conviction that the establishment of the internationally recognized nuclear-weapon-free zones on the basis of arrangements freely arrived at among the States of the region concerned enhances global and regional peace and security, strengthens the nuclear non-proliferation regime and contributes towards realizing the objective of nuclear disarmament,

Emphasizing that nothing in this Treaty shall be interpreted as affecting the inalienable right of its States Parties to develop research, production and use of nuclear energy for peaceful purposes without discrimination,

Recognizing that the equal, full and effective participation of both women and men is an essential factor for the promotion and attainment of sustainable peace and security, and committed to supporting and strengthening the effective participation of women in nuclear disarmament,

Recognizing also the importance of peace and disarmament education in all its aspects and of raising awareness of the risks and consequences of nuclear weapons for current and future generations, and committed to the dissemination of the principles and norms of this Treaty,

Stressing the role of public conscience in the furthering of the principles of humanity as evidenced by the call for the total elimination of nuclear weapons, and recognizing the efforts to that end undertaken by the United Nations, the International Red Cross and Red Crescent Movement, other international and regional organizations, non-governmental organizations, religious leaders, parliamentarians, academics and the *hibakusha*, Have agreed as follows:

Article 1

Prohibitions

1. Each State Party undertakes never under any circumstances to:

   a Develop, test, produce, manufacture, otherwise acquire, possess or stockpile nuclear weapons or other nuclear explosive devices;
   b Transfer to any recipient whatsoever nuclear weapons or other nuclear explosive devices or control over such weapons or explosive devices directly or indirectly;
   c Receive the transfer of or control over nuclear weapons or other nuclear explosive devices directly or indirectly;
   d Use or threaten to use nuclear weapons or other nuclear explosive devices;
   e Assist, encourage or induce, in any way, anyone to engage in any activity prohibited to a State Party under this Treaty;
   f Seek or receive any assistance, in any way, from anyone to engage in any activity prohibited to a State Party under this Treaty;
   g Allow any stationing, installation or deployment of any nuclear weapons or other nuclear explosive devices in its territory or at any place under its jurisdiction or control.

Article 2

Declarations

1. Each State Party shall submit to the Secretary-General of the United Nations, not later than 30 days after this Treaty enters into force for that State Party, a declaration in which it shall:

a Declare whether it owned, possessed or controlled nuclear weapons or nuclear explosive devices and eliminated its nuclear-weapon programme, including the elimination or irreversible conversion of all nuclear-weapons-related facilities, prior to the entry into force of this Treaty for that State Party;
b Notwithstanding Article 1 (a), declare whether it owns, possesses or controls any nuclear weapons or other nuclear explosive devices;
c Notwithstanding Article 1 (g), declare whether there are any nuclear weapons or other nuclear explosive devices in its territory or in any place under its jurisdiction or control that are owned, possessed or controlled by another State.

2. The Secretary-General of the United Nations shall transmit all such declarations received to the States Parties.

Article 3

Safeguards

1. Each State Party to which Article 4, paragraph 1 or 2, does not apply shall, at a minimum, maintain its International Atomic Energy Agency safeguards obligations in force at the time of entry into force of this Treaty, without prejudice to any additional relevant instruments that it may adopt in the future.
2. Each State Party to which Article 4, paragraph 1 or 2, does not apply that has not yet done so shall conclude with the International Atomic Energy Agency and bring into force a comprehensive safeguards agreement (INFCIRC/153 (Corrected)). Negotiation of such agreement shall commence within 180 days from the entry into force of this Treaty for that State Party. The agreement shall enter into force no later than 18 months from the entry into force of this Treaty for that State Party. Each State Party shall thereafter maintain such obligations, without prejudice to any additional relevant instruments that it may adopt in the future.

Article 4

Towards the total elimination of nuclear weapons

1. Each State Party that after 7 July 2017 owned, possessed or controlled nuclear weapons or other nuclear explosive devices and eliminated its nuclear-weapon programme, including the elimination or irreversible conversion of all nuclear- weapons-related facilities, prior to the entry into force of this Treaty for it, shall cooperate with the competent international authority designated pursuant to paragraph 6 of this Article for the purpose of verifying the irreversible elimination of its nuclear-weapon programme. The competent international

authority shall report to the States Parties. Such a State Party shall conclude a safeguards agreement with the International Atomic Energy Agency sufficient to provide credible assurance of the non-diversion of declared nuclear material from peaceful nuclear activities and of the absence of undeclared nuclear material or activities in that State Party as a whole. Negotiation of such agreement shall commence within 180 days from the entry into force of this Treaty for that State Party. The agreement shall enter into force no later than 18 months from the entry into force of this Treaty for that State Party. That State Party shall thereafter, at a minimum, maintain these safeguards obligations, without prejudice to any additional relevant instruments that it may adopt in the future.

2. Notwithstanding Article 1 (a), each State Party that owns, possesses or controls nuclear weapons or other nuclear explosive devices shall immediately remove them from operational status, and destroy them as soon as possible but not later than a deadline to be determined by the first meeting of States Parties, in accordance with a legally binding, time-bound plan for the verified and irreversible elimination of that State Party's nuclear-weapon programme, including the elimination or irreversible conversion of all nuclear-weapons-related facilities. The State Party, no later than 60 days after the entry into force of this Treaty for that State Party, shall submit this plan to the States Parties or to a competent international authority designated by the States Parties. The plan shall then be negotiated with the competent international authority, which shall submit it to the subsequent meeting of States Parties or review conference, whichever comes first, for approval in accordance with its rules of procedure.
3. A State Party to which paragraph 2 above applies shall conclude a safeguards agreement with the International Atomic Energy Agency sufficient to provide credible assurance of the non-diversion of declared nuclear material from peaceful nuclear activities and of the absence of undeclared nuclear material or activities in the State as a whole. Negotiation of such agreement shall commence no later than the date upon which implementation of the plan referred to in paragraph 2 is completed. The agreement shall enter into force no later than 18 months after the date of initiation of negotiations. That State Party shall thereafter, at a minimum, maintain these safeguards obligations, without prejudice to any additional relevant instruments that it may adopt in the future. Following the entry into force of the agreement referred to in this paragraph, the State Party shall submit to the Secretary-General of the United Nations a final declaration that it has fulfilled its obligations under this Article.
4. Notwithstanding Article 1 (b) and (g), each State Party that has any nuclear weapons or other nuclear explosive devices in its territory or in any place under its jurisdiction or control that are owned, possessed or controlled by another State shall ensure the prompt removal of such weapons, as soon as possible but not later than a deadline to be determined by the first meeting of States Parties. Upon the removal of such weapons or other explosive devices,

that State Party shall submit to the Secretary-General of the United Nations a declaration that it has fulfilled its obligations under this Article.

5. Each State Party to which this Article applies shall submit a report to each meeting of States Parties and each review conference on the progress made towards the implementation of its obligations under this Article, until such time as they are fulfilled.
6. The States Parties shall designate a competent international authority or authorities to negotiate and verify the irreversible elimination of nuclear-weapons programmes, including the elimination or irreversible conversion of all nuclear- weapons-related facilities in accordance with paragraphs 1, 2 and 3 of this Article. In the event that such a designation has not been made prior to the entry into force of this Treaty for a State Party to which paragraph 1 or 2 of this Article applies, the Secretary-General of the United Nations shall convene an extraordinary meeting of States Parties to take any decisions that may be required.

Article 5

National implementation

1. Each State Party shall adopt the necessary measures to implement its obligations under this Treaty.
2. Each State Party shall take all appropriate legal, administrative and other measures, including the imposition of penal sanctions, to prevent and suppress any activity prohibited to a State Party under this Treaty undertaken by persons or on territory under its jurisdiction or control.

Article 6

Victim assistance and environmental remediation

1. Each State Party shall, with respect to individuals under its jurisdiction who are affected by the use or testing of nuclear weapons, in accordance with applicable international humanitarian and human rights law, adequately provide age- and gender-sensitive assistance, without discrimination, including medical care, rehabilitation and psychological support, as well as provide for their social and economic inclusion.
2. Each State Party, with respect to areas under its jurisdiction or control contaminated as a result of activities related to the testing or use of nuclear weapons or other nuclear explosive devices, shall take necessary and appropriate measures towards the environmental remediation of areas so contaminated.
3. The obligations under paragraphs 1 and 2 above shall be without prejudice to the duties and obligations of any other States under international law or bilateral agreements.

Article 7

International cooperation and assistance

1. Each State Party shall cooperate with other States Parties to facilitate the implementation of this Treaty.
2. In fulfilling its obligations under this Treaty, each State Party shall have the right to seek and receive assistance, where feasible, from other States Parties.
3. Each State Party in a position to do so shall provide technical, material and financial assistance to States Parties affected by nuclear-weapons use or testing, to further the implementation of this Treaty.
4. Each State Party in a position to do so shall provide assistance for the victims of the use or testing of nuclear weapons or other nuclear explosive devices.
5. Assistance under this Article may be provided, inter alia, through the United Nations system, international, regional or national organizations or institutions, non-governmental organizations or institutions, the International Committee of the Red Cross, the International Federation of Red Cross and Red Crescent Societies, or national Red Cross and Red Crescent Societies, or on a bilateral basis.
6. Without prejudice to any other duty or obligation that it may have under international law, a State Party that has used or tested nuclear weapons or any other nuclear explosive devices shall have a responsibility to provide adequate assistance to affected States Parties, for the purpose of victim assistance and environmental remediation.

Article 8

Meeting of States Parties

1. The States Parties shall meet regularly in order to consider and, where necessary, take decisions in respect of any matter with regard to the application or implementation of this Treaty, in accordance with its relevant provisions, and on further measures for nuclear disarmament, including:

   a The implementation and status of this Treaty;
   b Measures for the verified, time-bound and irreversible elimination of nuclear-weapon programmes, including additional protocols to this Treaty;
   c Any other matters pursuant to and consistent with the provisions of this Treaty.

2. The first meeting of States Parties shall be convened by the Secretary-General of the United Nations within one year of the entry into force of this Treaty. Further meetings of States Parties shall be convened by the Secretary-General of the United Nations on a biennial basis, unless otherwise agreed by the States Parties. The meeting of States Parties shall adopt its rules of procedure at its first session. Pending their adoption, the rules of procedure of the

United Nations conference to negotiate a legally binding instrument to prohibit nuclear weapons, leading towards their total elimination, shall apply.

3. Extraordinary meetings of States Parties shall be convened, as may be deemed necessary, by the Secretary-General of the United Nations, at the written request of any State Party provided that this request is supported by at least one third of the States Parties.
4. After a period of five years following the entry into force of this Treaty, the Secretary-General of the United Nations shall convene a conference to review the operation of the Treaty and the progress in achieving the purposes of the Treaty. The Secretary-General of the United Nations shall convene further review conferences at intervals of six years with the same objective, unless otherwise agreed by the States Parties.
5. States not party to this Treaty, as well as the relevant entities of the United Nations system, other relevant international organizations or institutions, regional organizations, the International Committee of the Red Cross, the International Federation of Red Cross and Red Crescent Societies and relevant non-governmental organizations, shall be invited to attend the meetings of States Parties and the review conferences as observers.

Article 9

Costs

1. The costs of the meetings of States Parties, the review conferences and the extraordinary meetings of States Parties shall be borne by the States Parties and States not party to this Treaty participating therein as observers, in accordance with the United Nations scale of assessment adjusted appropriately.
2. The costs incurred by the Secretary-General of the United Nations in the circulation of declarations under Article 2, reports under Article 4 and proposed amendments under Article 10 of this Treaty shall be borne by the States Parties in accordance with the United Nations scale of assessment adjusted appropriately.
3. The cost related to the implementation of verification measures required under Article 4 as well as the costs related to the destruction of nuclear weapons or other nuclear explosive devices, and the elimination of nuclear-weapon programmes, including the elimination or conversion of all nuclear-weapons-related facilities, should be borne by the States Parties to which they apply.

Article 10

Amendments

1. At any time after the entry into force of this Treaty, any State Party may propose amendments to the Treaty. The text of a proposed amendment shall be communicated to the Secretary-General of the United Nations, who shall

circulate it to all States Parties and shall seek their views on whether to consider the proposal. If a majority of the States Parties notify the Secretary-General of the United Nations no later than 90 days after its circulation that they support further consideration of the proposal, the proposal shall be considered at the next meeting of States Parties or review conference, whichever comes first.

2. A meeting of States Parties or a review conference may agree upon amendments which shall be adopted by a positive vote of a majority of two thirds of the States Parties. The Depositary shall communicate any adopted amendment to all States Parties.
3. The amendment shall enter into force for each State Party that deposits its instrument of ratification or acceptance of the amendment 90 days following the deposit of such instruments of ratification or acceptance by a majority of the States Parties at the time of adoption. Thereafter, it shall enter into force for any other State Party 90 days following the deposit of its instrument of ratification or acceptance of the amendment.

Article 11

Settlement of disputes

1. When a dispute arises between two or more States Parties relating to the interpretation or application of this Treaty, the parties concerned shall consult together with a view to the settlement of the dispute by negotiation or by other peaceful means of the parties' choice in accordance with Article 33 of the Charter of the United Nations.
2. The meeting of States Parties may contribute to the settlement of the dispute, including by offering its good offices, calling upon the States Parties concerned to start the settlement procedure of their choice and recommending a time limit for any agreed procedure, in accordance with the relevant provisions of this Treaty and the Charter of the United Nations.

Article 12

Universality

Each State Party shall encourage States not party to this Treaty to sign, ratify, accept, approve or accede to the Treaty, with the goal of universal adherence of all States to the Treaty.

Article 13

Signature

This Treaty shall be open for signature to all States at United Nations Headquarters in New York as from 20 September 2017.

Article 14

Ratification, acceptance, approval or accession

This Treaty shall be subject to ratification, acceptance or approval by signatory States. The Treaty shall be open for accession.

Article 15

Entry into force

1. This Treaty shall enter into force 90 days after the fiftieth instrument of ratification, acceptance, approval or accession has been deposited.
2. For any State that deposits its instrument of ratification, acceptance, approval or accession after the date of the deposit of the fiftieth instrument of ratification, acceptance, approval or accession, this Treaty shall enter into force 90 days after the date on which that State has deposited its instrument of ratification, acceptance, approval or accession.

Article 16

Reservations

The Articles of this Treaty shall not be subject to reservations.

Article 17

Duration and withdrawal

1. This Treaty shall be of unlimited duration.
2. Each State Party shall, in exercising its national sovereignty, have the right to withdraw from this Treaty if it decides that extraordinary events related to the subject matter of the Treaty have jeopardized the supreme interests of its country. It shall give notice of such withdrawal to the Depositary. Such notice shall include a statement of the extraordinary events that it regards as having jeopardized its supreme interests.
3. Such withdrawal shall only take effect 12 months after the date of the receipt of the notification of withdrawal by the Depositary. If, however, on the expiry of that 12-month period, the withdrawing State Party is a party to an armed conflict, the State Party shall continue to be bound by the obligations of this Treaty and of any additional protocols until it is no longer party to an armed conflict.

Article 18

Relationship with other agreements

The implementation of this Treaty shall not prejudice obligations undertaken by States Parties with regard to existing international agreements, to which they are party, where those obligations are consistent with the Treaty.

Article 19

Depositary

The Secretary-General of the United Nations is hereby designated as the Depositary of this Treaty.

Article 20

Authentic texts

The Arabic, Chinese, English, French, Russian and Spanish texts of this Treaty shall be equally authentic.

DONE at New York, this seventh day of July, two thousand and seventeen.

Status as at 1 July 2021:

Adopted in New York: 7 July 2017

Opened for signature in New York: 20 September 2017

Entry into force: 22 January 2021

Number of Signatory States: 86

Number of States Parties: 54

Source: United Nations Office for Disarmament Affairs, https://treaties.unoda.org/t/tpnw.

INDEX

Note: Locators in *italic* and **bold** refer figures and tables respectively, and locators followed by "n" refer end notes.

For Product Safety Concerns and Information please contact our EU representative GPSR@taylorandfrancis.com
Taylor & Francis Verlag GmbH, Kaufingerstraße 24, 80331 München, Germany

www.ingramcontent.com/pod-product-compliance
Ingram Content Group UK Ltd.
Pitfield, Milton Keynes, MK11 3LW, UK
UKHW020150200926
475702UK00016B/2638
9781032130705